NETWORK DEMOCRACY

MCGILL-QUEEN'S STUDIES IN THE HISTORY OF IDEAS
Series Editor: Philip J. Cercone

NETWORK DEMOCRACY

Conservative Politics and the Violence of the Liberal Age

Jared Giesbrecht

McGill-Queen's University Press
Montreal & Kingston • London • Chicago

ISBN 978-0-7735-4821-3 (cloth)
ISBN 978-0-7735-4853-4 (ePDF)
ISBN 978-0-7735-4854-1 (ePUB)

Legal deposit first quarter 2017
Bibliothèque nationale du Québec

Printed in Canada on acid-free paper that is 100% ancient forest free
(100% post-consumer recycled), processed chlorine free

This book has been published with the help of a grant from the Canadian
Federation for the Humanities and Social Sciences, through the Awards to
Scholarly Publications Program, using funds provided by the Social Sciences
and Humanities Research Council of Canada.

McGill-Queen's University Press acknowledges the support of the Canada
Council for the Arts for our publishing program. We also acknowledge the
financial support of the Government of Canada through the Canada Book
Fund for our publishing activities.

Library and Archives Canada Cataloguing in Publication

Giesbrecht, Jared, 1979–, author
    Network democracy: conservative politics and the violence of the liberal age /
Jared Giesbrecht.

    (McGill-Queen's studies in the history of ideas; 68)
    Includes bibliographical references and index.
    Issued in print and electronic formats.
    ISBN 978-0-7735-4821-3 (cloth). – ISBN 978-0-7735-4853-4 (ePDF). –
ISBN 978-0-7735-4854-1 (ePUB)

    1. Democracy. 2. Conservatism. 3. Liberalism. 4. Violence. 5. Time pressure.
I. Title. II. Series: McGill-Queen's studies in the history of ideas; 68

JC423.G53 2017   321.8   C2016-905647-3
                                                             C2016-905648-1

This book was typeset by Marquis Interscript in 10/12 New Baskerville.

Contents

NETWORK DEMOCRACY

Introduction

"We have got on to slippery ice where there is no friction and so in a certain sense the conditions are ideal, but also, just because of that, we are unable to walk. We want to walk: so we need friction. Back to the rough ground!"

Ludwig Wittgenstein, *Philosophical Investigations*

A. THE VIOLENCE OF THE LIBERAL AGE

Understanding the violence of the liberal age in which we live begins with an acknowledgement that our world is speeding up. In stating this, I do mean to be as broad and sweeping as I sound. Everything in our modern world is accelerating. Our high-tech economies are driving us forward with breakneck speed as we struggle to keep afloat in the fast-paced world of the twenty-first century. Computation, communication, transportation, resource extraction, manufacturing, and consumption are all speeding up. Not to be outdone, our social relations are also speeding up. Increasing rates of change in familial relations, religious practices, sexual practices, vocations, and social obligations mean that many of our acceptable norms and values have become almost unrecognizable since a mere two generations ago.

The speeding up of socio-economic changes is taking place in tandem with developments in moral and political philosophy. And this should not surprise us. The causal interplay between thought and behaviour goes two ways. Patterns of thought lead us to behave in certain ways but patterns of behaviour also lead us to think in certain ways. Acceleration is a distinct feature of modern industrial society that takes place through a causal interplay between technological, natural, and social changes as well as certain shifts in moral and political philosophy that have taken place in the last few hundred years. This two-way causation that fuels acceleration is, admittedly, a relatively recent development in world history. But, it has nevertheless become a globally pervasive phenomenon. Nothing in our world today remains untouched by this acceleration.

Why should we be concerned by acceleration? Is acceleration enough of a concern to cause us to re-evaluate the Anglo-American tradition of liberal democratic theory and its particular approach to justice in law and politics?

In the following chapters, I will suggest that acceleration should be a central concern to us because the speeding-up of everything is not simply pervasive – it is transformative. The forward thrust of acceleration has very real material, social, and spiritual consequences. It means not simply a quantitative speeding-up, but a qualitative change that takes place within the relations that make up our lives and the world. So, it is not simply *more* movement in less time. It is *different* movement all the time. Changes in our temporal structures transform our cultures, economies, our relations with the natural world, and more. Although we are prone to forget it, our being is fundamentally historical and changes in the patterns of our lives means qualitative changes in who and what we are. In other words, these transformations therefore have significant moral and political implications. They deserve our attention.

I should note that there are some political theorists who problematize acceleration because they view liberal democracy as a political system that requires sufficient time for representation, deliberation, etc. They feel that acceleration, if intense enough, will hinder or even dismantle liberal democratic models of political decision-making.[1] Although these scholars are tuned in to an interesting problem regarding acceleration and are certainly correct that processes of representation, deliberation, etc. depend upon a certain pace of life, this is not the kind of concern that is most needed. Instead of protecting our liberal democratic model of governance from the pressures of acceleration, we should problematize liberal democracy itself and begin to understand how acceleration, and the dramatic transformations that accompany it, are fuelled by liberalism's underlying logic. Indeed, the goal of this book is precisely that: to show how liberalism itself is fuelling acceleration and to suggest some reasons why we might seek to re-discover a conservative moral and political philosophy that has developed over the last few hundred years in opposition to the dominant liberal tradition.

---

1 For example, William Scheuerman argues that traditional institutions of liberal democracy (e.g. a separation of power) are grounded in temporal assumptions and, more importantly, that the legitimacy of democratic power is dependent upon adequate time being taken for deliberation and debate. See Scheuerman, *Liberal Democracy*.

In order to account for recent changes in social and institutional behaviour, some critical theorists such as Hartmut Rosa have sought to develop a systematic socio-scientific concept of time that would ensure the
temporal structures in society become a central consideration in social
theory.[2] By systematically connecting the sociology of time with empirical research programs, Rosa seeks to open the eyes of social theory to
some previously shadowed principles and tendencies underlying the
modern world. His work is founded on the idea that effective diagnoses
of "the times" should actually be diagnoses of the temporal structures of
society. Or, put differently, he argues that our understanding of the distinct characteristics of the modern world will lack cohesion and precision unless we also simultaneously examine the structures of time in the
modern world. Rosa presents a thorough and insightful analysis of acceleration and critical theory's diagnosis of modernity, but I take a different approach in this book.

Instead of arguing for a greater understanding of the phenomenon of
acceleration or even the problematization of acceleration, I am seeking
to reveal a certain way of approaching acceleration and coming to understand the problem that it represents. I take it as a given that our understanding of acceleration itself, and hence the way we conceive of the
problem of acceleration, is politically charged. There are deep-down
things within the ways our mind work that shape and colour how we are
able to perceive changing temporal structures and, even more, problematize acceleration by perceiving the moral and political implications
of changing temporal structures. In referring to "deep-down things" I
am not seeking to conjure up images of hard-wiring or bio-structural patterns of thought. Rather, I mean the penetrating and pervading patterns
of thought and behaviour that are with us everyday and corral us into
a certain range of thinking, a certain range of behaving. I am inviting
us, therefore, to re-imagine the theoretical landscape before us and to
view moral and political theory anew from the perspective of a counter-
tradition that is in stark contrast to the tradition that has come to so
completely govern our world. As such, what follows is not a systematic
analysis that diagnoses a problem and then prescribes remedies. It is as
much a work of imagination as of analysis. So, instead of arguing for a
systematic approach to the temporal structures of the modern world, I
ask how we might begin to practice a way of diagnosing the hidden assumptions behind moral and political theory in the Anglo-American
world that have fuelled acceleration in the first place? Or even, how

2 For an excellent example of this kind of scholarship see Rosa, *Social Acceleration*.

might we begin to diagnose the kind of thinking that stimulates the kind of behaviour that contributes to acceleration? What are the theoretical foundations of acceleration that have lain hidden due to the fact that our moral and political tradition of liberalism guides and governs the range of thought open before us?

It should be noted that, although it will serve as little more than an entry point, this process of excavating our theoretical foundations and re-imagining the framework of liberal thought that has given rise to our moral and political assumptions will also include some discussion that is meant to stimulate a redefinition and reproblematization of accelera-tion. So, before discussing liberalism and examining its theoretical foun-dations, we might question a little further why acceleration is a problem worthy of our consideration. And, as a way of beginning to edge outside the liberal tradition, I will be arguing that acceleration should be a cen-tral concern when theorizing regarding justice in law and politics – be-cause not only is our world speeding up, this acceleration is also causing significant structural violence through disruption and displacement. We are now moving so fast forward that we are losing our connectivity to our past, and this disconnection hinders our ability to live in keeping with the patternings of our nature and our traditions. Acceleration is a prob-lem because rapid change fragments and dislocates; it does violence to the material, social, and spiritual networks that make up our world and defines us. Transformative change violates the relations of our lives and enacts violence through processes of destabilization, disruption, and dis-placement. This kind of disconnection produces a radical disorientation and disintegrates society. And, I will suggest in what follows that, al-though indigenous peoples and traditional communities are perhaps feeling this disintegration of society most acutely, no one remains un-harmed by the isolation and disorientation that has become pervasive in the modern world. We are all losing touch with those things that have made us who we are.

I mentioned the material, social, and spiritual patternings that make up our nature and the world around us but this is almost certainly a strange way of thinking for many readers. What do I mean when I talk about these "patternings"? In a general sense, patternings are the kinds of networked relations that are being made and re-made throughout his-tory. They are not simply habits of behaviour – they are ways of being in the world. And they are not simply human ways of being in the world – the world itself is made up of network patternings that persist through time. Although we will discuss patternings in greater detail in chapter 1, it is important to note at this point that the patternings of the world are characterized by both stability and flux. They are always changing to some degree, but the patternings of the world possess a kind of inherent stability at work within their structures. In more technical terms, network patternings maintain their integrity through structural causation – i.e. the self-structuring processes characteristic of complex distributive network systems that produce a persistence of form beyond constituent parts based upon a power flow internal to the system as a whole. Put simply, this stability is what allows us to understand things as coherent wholes and to see persons, for example, as moral and political agents rather than simply as a set of interactions. The flux makes up the change and growth that take place in the various metabolic rates of living and non-living things in the world. There are relatively persistent orderings that make up the world – i.e. what is sometimes called a "natural" ordering in the world. Although these patternings are ever-changing and subject to reconfigurations through time, they nevertheless possess stability and resilience in the face of change. So there is always change and flux in network patternings, but dramatic change is violent: it violates the patternings of relations existing and persisting through time.

Acceleration is transforming patternings and, as such, it is a certain kind of domination that is active within the modern world. What do I mean by "domination"? We will examine this concept in greater detail but for now it may be enough to consider how it is that patternings not only persist through time with some degree of structural integrity but also change and adapt as patternings around them change and adapt. The change active that reconfigures patternings is always met with a degree of resistance that provides stability and resilience. We might best understand this reconfiguring change that pushes against resistance as power. In other words, power is never entirely non-coercive; it is always acting to alter a process already underway. When power is strong enough, we begin to describe it as violent because it is violating patternings to such a degree that we begin to be attentive. We begin to be concerned. This violation of patternings is happening all the time throughout the world so there is no reason to understand violence itself as morally wrong. Instead, whether we deem this violation of patternings to be either acceptable or inappropriate depends upon whether we believe the violation to be excessive or not. And, I suggest that it is the excessive violations of patternings that we should describe as domination. Put another way, violence is dramatic power (such that it violates the structural integrity of social, material, and spiritual patternings) and domination is excessive violence (such that it is deemed to be unacceptable or immoral). The qualitative distinction between power, violence, and domination may therefore be seen to be stemming from our negative normative judgment regarding whether or not the degree of power is "excessive."

In the discussions that follow, I will go through this argument in more detail and provide support for coming to see acceleration as rooted in a kind of domination I call "protocolic domination." Because in order to understand acceleration and the nature of change in the modern world, as well as its significance for moral and political philosophy, we must give some thought to its underlying cause – standardization through the advancement of protocol. By "standardization" and "protocol" I refer to a homogenization of the structures and processes taking place in the development of patternings. This is a homogenization that takes place through an abstraction away from the diverse temporal experiences of various locales in an overcoming of the particular or the specific. Protocol governs the way patterns change and adapt by overlaying actions and orderings with second-order coordinations through standardized interactions. If it is to be effective in overcoming the resistance of patternings and governing through coordinating action, protocol must homogenize through standardization. Protocol cannot transcend the variations and deep diversity within the patternings of the world without universalizing. It must develop a kind of homogeneity or standardization if it is to open up connectivity and ensure effective coordination. In this manner, standardization through the advancement of protocol collapses space and time through coordinations and synchronizations that are only possible in abstractions away from the differences and diversity of real-world patternings.

Protocol in the modern world does not govern simply by standardizing interactions within patternings, but through increasingly rapid shifts in the standardization – i.e. through modulations of protocolic control. Patternings are being transformed through violent protocolic modulations that fuel acceleration by continually disrupting the internal pattern-developing or pattern-re-enforcing changes of network patternings. In other words, protocolic modulations are undermining or subverting the stability and resilience of patternings in the world that are produced through structural causation. I find it appropriate, therefore, to describe these increasingly rapid protocolic modulations as "protocolic domination" – the excess, or illegitimate, violation of patternings.

A couple questions still remain: how does this general discussion of patternings, violence, and protocolic domination relate to moral and political philosophy? And, more specifically, in what ways might this concern regarding the acceleration that is caused by standardization lead us toward a conservative approach to democracy?

Not only is the violence of increasingly rapid protocolic modulations being facilitated and caused by standardizations that are abstractions away from the deep differences of the world, but there is also another

level of causation underlying acceleration. The standardizations of protocolic control are fuelled by the logic at work in the core normative
commitments of liberalism. As we briefly discussed above, when standardization takes place, the local and particular in patterned relations
must be transcended through a process of abstraction. For, it is only in
the abstract that the broad coordination and symmetrical synchronization of standardization can take place. This process of abstraction involves a depersonalization, deterritorialization, and atomization as it
moves away from the lifeworlds of persons to minimize the specificity
and maximize universality. I will be arguing that liberalism, although it is
a diverse and multifaceted tradition, contains – within its most fundamental orientation – a dualistic logic of abstraction that manifests itself
in a totalizing impulse that fuels acceleration.

The dualistic logic of liberalism, put simply, is a simultaneous individuation and universalization. By "liberalism" I mean that school of thought
driven by a normative commitment to building a society in which all
persons are self-determining and equal individuals. The central mechanism for accomplishing this vision is a substitution of "the right" for "the
good." The search for the good is subsumed under a primarily proceduralist account of normative obligations. Liberals are, therefore, also committed to the idea that an overarching progressive social movement will
arise from multiple interactions between individuals (e.g. in the market,
in science, in cosmopolitan politics, etc.). The drive to progress toward a
society in which all individuals are free and equal involves a disavowal of
provincial "goods" and elevates the right procedures, which – through
their universal application – will standardize relations between individuals. It means we isolate political actors by viewing them as inherently
valuable and self-determining atomistic actors while at the same time
placing them within a universal framework of possible moral action that
determines what is acceptable for anyone anywhere. This logic of isolation and universal orientation not only causes us to flip-flop between
emphasizing the importance of individuals on one hand and insisting
upon the sacrifice individuals must make for the whole of society on the
other, it also gives rise to a dangerous totalizing impulse that problematizes difference.

This problematization of difference arises from a logic of power legitimization built around singularity (through a totalization of a dualistic
relation). The dualistic logic of liberalism eclipses multiplicity and denies history by totalizing the relationality between an isolated unit and a
whole whether this is a subject-object, self-other, citizen-state, or other
single-whole relation. That is, the difference and diversity of real-world
patterns of relation that persist through time as asymmetrical, and hence

localized, nestings of power relations are transcended and superseded by a singular oscillation between the isolated, individuated unit and the universal. The totalization of dualistic logic causes us to fixate upon the oscillation and all in-between worlds of asymmetrical and localized relationality become supplanted.

These real-world patterns of power relations are multifaceted and inherently messy. We can catch a glimpse of them in the overlapping commitments families face in both good times and bad. How much power and authority should an individual member of the family have in making decisions about his future? Does the family come before the individual? Who is included within the family? How much should the traditions of the family change with the times? What is a woman's role within the family? In what situations should the interests of the child come before the interests of the parent? Does the law of the state supersede the decision of the family? How much authority do the traditions of the church have over the family? These kinds of questions are not only complex, they are inherently messy because they are inherently localized and situational, indeed, existential. How one might respond to these kinds of questions stems from who one is (and who one's family, church, and state is). The asymmetrical, localized power relations of life form the messy background for what we know of today as identity politics.

The frequency and urgency with which these questions arise are being eroded by the dualistic logic of liberalism that is spreading around the globe. And this erosion – the problematization of difference – can be seen in our increasing two-part response to the kind of questions raised above. The first part of the response is to view these questions as antiquated and the things of times past. It is to not just deny their depth and their urgency, but to simply fail to see the depth and urgency of these questions on a day-to-day basis because the messiness of asymmetry and multiplicity of power relations within one's life have already been dramatically eroded. The other part of the response is to seek out the root of what makes these questions difficult for a family and to discover that the answer is very distasteful. It is to realize that the inequality and asymmetry of the power relations underlying these questions makes one uneasy and uncomfortable. The problematization of difference can be witnessed in the fact that inequality and asymmetry often appear as problems to be overcome. Deep pluralism is a challenge for liberal theorists and, at one point or another, becomes dangerous and threatening to the whole liberal enterprise and necessitates a return to the basic ideals of freedom and equality.

The problematization of difference reveals a dangerous homogenizing impulse that runs through the centre of our liberal notions of justice. It has been grafted onto liberal democratic theory at the root and prevents liberals from committing wholeheartedly to deep pluralism. For example, within mainstream liberal legal and political theory, discussions regarding the nature of justice consistently problematize, albeit most often unwittingly, difference and specificity. The question motivating each new scholarly work is nearly always the same: how can we manage the tension between freedom and equality to ensure our interaction as individuals and communities produces a more just world? In my search for a conservative approach to democracy below, I take a step back. I question the assumptions underlying this mainstream project and consider the role these assumptions play in preventing us from pluralizing our societies. Specifically, I argue that the problematization of difference stems from the fact that liberal political theory has developed a dominant language of normative theorizing built upon a dualistic logic that simultaneously individuates and universalizes. This logic undermines the localized normative and political relations of communities and therefore prevents pluralism from deepening beyond a relatively superficial interactionalism. This logic fuels acceleration by standardizing within the abstractionism of an atomism that simultaneously individuates and totalizes.

Big picture, this book is meant to help us (a) identify an underlying logic at work in the twenty-first century's accelerating pace, (b) characterize and re-evaluate the normative theory animating this logic, (c) point toward an alternative normative theory, and (d) suggest some of the implications this alternative (conservative) normative theory might have for legal and political theory. But, why turn to normative philosophy? Really, it is all about normative philosophy. The transformations taking place in and through modern acceleration have important normative implications. It is my contention that the core normative commitments of liberalism are fuelling standardizations that, in turn, fuel acceleration. For example, liberalism is motivated by a normative commitment to ensuring all persons are treated as free, equal, and rational individuals. In contrast, this project represents an attempt to re-discover and re-vitalize political relations built upon conservative principles of peace, order, and good governance. As such, I am motivated by a different understanding of human nature and the being-in-the-world of humans than is liberalism: this book represents a commitment to fostering the normative orderings needed for stability and resilience in society.

B. THE REVIVAL OF CONSERVATISM

It should be acknowledged up front that the language I will be using may appear strange and even confusing. Indeed, the story I have just told with its emphasis upon the underlying normative logic behind the liberal tradition is itself quite likely foreign to many readers. There are a number of places where my concerns regarding a diffuse violence and institutions built upon liberal principles stem from a recognition of ordering in the universe (and therefore normativity) that is genuinely transcendent.[3] My comfort with talk of transcendent orderings in the universe leads me into ways of doing moral and political theory that are at odds with the dominant liberal tradition. The Anglo-American tradition of legal and political philosophy (in the last few centuries) has been dominated by debates among liberal constructivists and liberal positivists, who share a fundamental skepticism of any appeal to transcendent norms manifest in and through tradition. Reformist liberalism has so fundamentally shaped the last few centuries of Western philosophy that reverence for tradition and a concern for stability in systems of legal, economic, and political relations appears somewhat ridiculous to the modern reader. To be sure, talk of tradition is often accepted, but only if it is stripped of its authority and relativized within a larger project of constructing a new, forward-looking political and economic project – i.e. tradition is no longer the carrier of transcendent authority. There is a radical divide, therefore, between the progressive idealism that inspires a spirit of irreverence within liberalism and the devotion to the past that inspires a spirit of lamenting within conservatism. For quite some time we have been captured by an iconoclastic methodology of throwing off what has become seen as the shackles of tradition. An approach to theorizing regarding legal and political norms that seeks genuine devotion to tradition and submission to its expression of transcendent authority is shocking and dramatically out-of-step with contemporary debates within legal and political theory. So, because my arguments represent an attempt to revive in some small way a counter-tradition to the dominant liberal paradigm of modern thought, we should expect some degree of strangeness or awkwardness in the discussion that follows.

Although I am appealing to more traditional conceptions of authority and normativity, I am motivated by a relatively new problem (what I have referred to as the modulations of protocolic control) as well as a sense that modern liberal thought not only lacks the means of addressing this problem but actually exacerbates the problem. The modulations of protocolic control have arisen as a result of both: liberalism's idealistic

---

3 By "genuinely transcendent" I mean experience of that which comes from beyond ourselves (ontologically and epistemologically). This basic conception of transcendence in the ordering of the universe has provided the foundation for premodern understandings of natural law.

disdain for the authority of tradition, as well as our corresponding drive to control our future through technique and technological advancements. This forsaking of the past involves an attempt to minimize risk by means of simultaneously isolating actors and re-uniting them under universalizing procedural mechanisms of governance. But this transformation of patterns of interaction threatens humanity and our dependence upon our natural environment in a relatively new way. This new interactionalism at work within the world destabilizes and delocalizes in order to facilitate globalization and our domination over the natural world. Ironically, our attempts to minimize the risks posed by the darkness, the wilderness, and the stranger have given rise to extremely risky ways of life that are increasingly fragile and unable to withstand the diffuse violence of a globalized world. Within this radical instability and insecurity, the decaying of the modern nation state provides us with a tangible focal point for beginning to reconsider what it means to live lives characterized by just relations and democratic patterns of governance.[4] What does it mean to cultivate security and resilience in legal and political institutional arrangements when we live in a liberalized, globalized world? What kinds of violence are acceptable in a world beset by threats of disruption and displacement on every side?

Modern industrial society and its corresponding systems of governance – e.g. the market state's rule of law and the global economy it fosters – have been inspired by the liberal ideals of rationality, freedom, and equality. Conversely, however, these liberal ideals are themselves only made possible by the re-patterning of behaviour brought about by the industrial revolution. In this way, the liberal tradition both provides us with the conceptual tools for legitimizing the violence enacted by our systems of governance and, at the same time, is a tradition whose development and promulgation was only made possible by these same systems. Historically, liberalism made sense of a new industrial society and legitimized the violence of its systems of governance by attempting to

---

4 Numerous books have been published on the end of the nation state. Most relevant, though, is Philip Bobbitt's work showing how the state is changing in the twenty-first century. Bobbitt convincingly argues that the nation state is disintegrating in a rapidly changing globalized world, and that the battle over what the new model of the state will be – a struggle over what kind of governance is legitimate – has begun in earnest. In light of the travails of last century, the new state structure – the market state – is based upon the new promise of maximizing the opportunities of its peoples. See Bobbitt, *The Shield of Achilles*. Forsaking direct orderings of social and material life, the market state therefore increasingly governs through modulations in protocol-shifts in the way patterns of interactions develop. And of course the state itself is also very much altered and shaped through modulations of protocol because these modulations go far beyond the power structures of state institutions.

restrict and restrain excess violence. The communication revolution begun in the late twentieth century, much like the industrial revolution, is altering our patterns of living in coordination with each other and changing our relation to our natural environment. New patterns of thought are arising from these new patterns of living as we endeavour to understand and legitimize our way of being in the world. At this time, it remains to be seen what patterns of thought will dominate the twenty-first century. My contention in what follows is that liberalism does not hold the theoretical and practical tools needed for legitimizing the violence of protocolic modulation that besets us on all sides. The tradition of liberalism has, despite its own self-understanding of emancipation and progress, made substantial contributions to the violence that is now at work in the world. The normative ideals of liberalism are therefore unable to provide us with inspiration for an undermining of protocolic domination in the twenty-first century. Instead, we will only be able to do this to the degree that we undermine liberalism itself. And, in order to begin this process, I will be inviting readers to not only begin problematizing liberal norms, but to consider anew the importance of the underlying normative logic of traditions pre-dating both industrialism and liberalism.

There is a problematization of difference within our modern liberal approach to normative thought and judgment, I will argue, that stems from the fact that our thinking about politics, law, and the economy has developed a dominant language of normative theorizing built upon the abstractionism of standardization. As a result of a widespread dualistic logic, there is a dangerous homogenizing impulse that runs through the very centre of our liberal notions of justice and has been grafted onto our normative theory at the root. This grafting has led to dramatic tensions within theoretical traditions and, importantly, has also led to some significant blind spots in our concern for building a just society. For example, those peoples who are outside the mainstream systems of power find themselves desperately struggling to legitimize their ways of life in the midst of a flood of standardized procedures of interaction. That is, conservatives of all kinds seek to protect their particularities against disruption and displacement and search for areas of belief and practice where they can stabilize their lives and develop a greater attentiveness and devotion to their unique traditions.

By positing a universal normative metric (i.e. all persons should be considered to be free and afforded equal concern and respect), we have abstracted from the lives of real peoples and begun a violent process of simultaneous assimilation and exclusion perhaps most easily seen in the push for a universal citizenry or a universal marketplace. The homogenizing impulse, within this universalism, is dangerous because it has become such a fundamental part of our conception of justice that it can be very difficult to recognize the violence it does to the diversities of life and thought present within the world. There is a hidden violence – a pervasive violation – that is enacted upon many of those who are drawn into the influence of modern liberal society through the disruptive and unsettling power of abstract standardization. This violence, unfortunately, has been largely hidden by the normative logic that undergirds both egalitarian conceptions of justice as well as ideals of freedom rooted in a striving for self-determination or self-expression.

However, if our patterns of life in the modern world are built upon normative standardizations as I am suggesting, how might we begin conceiving of just relations that are not simply recognizing and reiterating these same standardizations? We can, for example, easily discuss the rights and freedom of individuals and the role of the state in fostering a growing economy. But, how can we avoid the pervasive oscillation between the individual and the global that is active within the dualistic logic of liberalism? We can really only conceive of just relations in a place and time where we have the capacity to become attentive to, and contemplate, not only the nature of the relations themselves, but also the ways in which those relations might be otherwise. For this to happen, we must possess intimations of our deprival. We must have an inkling of that which is no longer present or active within our world if we are to be struck by the injustice of a situation. However, the systems of meaning that used to guide and shape the way we related to each other and the natural world have grown dangerously close to extinct. So, when we turn out minds to consider the violence of the dualistic logic of liberalism, we feel like we are groping about in the darkness to find that which we have lost. We run into roadblocks at every turn as we struggle to remember that which we have forgotten. The severity of this problematic is perhaps best articulated by George Grant in his writing on technique and the technological society. In "A Platitude" he writes: "We can hold in our minds the enormous benefits of technological society, but we cannot so easily hold the ways it may have deprived us, because technique is ourselves ... All coherent languages beyond those which serve the drive to unlimited freedom through technique have been broken up in the coming to be of what we are ... We have been left with no words which cleave together and summon out of uncertainty the good of which we may sense the dispossession."[5] The just relations of communities seeking the

5 Grant, "A Platitude," 448–50.

good in relation to each other and the natural world, in other words, hide from us because the violent injustices perpetuated by standardized systems of governance are deep within us and shape our lives – our technology, our socio-economic systems, and our normative reasoning. We have a vague sense that our lives are different than they used to be before industrialism and liberalism's globalization, but we struggle to understand what we have lost and how this deprivation has changed our moral and political reasoning. How, then, might we begin to understand the depth of the injustices that are enacted in and through our new ways of living in mass society?

In order to better understand our new ways of living and their significance for developing our conceptions of just relations, we need to reflect upon the philosophical, political, and economic thought that has given rise to these contemporary ways of living. If we are interested in exploring the potentials of a radical critique of our contemporary ways of living, we must not only have an understanding of liberalism, but also a sense of the traditions in response to which liberalism arose. For, as I will be arguing below, a radical critique of liberalism – a critique that avoids replicating the violence of the dualistic logic of the liberal tradition – requires a revival of pre-liberal traditions and a restoration of their place in governing our lives today. It involves meditating upon those hints and allusions to discomfort and dissatisfaction with the liberal tradition. It means not only fostering those imaginative thoughts that afford us glimpses of a different world, but practicing ways of thinking and being that are discomforting in today's liberal world because they harken back to those ways of thinking and being that pre-existed liberalism.

Over the past few hundred years, liberal theory arose in response to the domineering totalizations of premodern authoritarian regimes. Building upon the Christian tradition's concern for the well-being of individuals, liberals engaged in a philosophical, political, and economic revolution that overturned previous assumptions regarding natural ordering and its origin in a divine creator. Liberals have engaged in furthering this revolution with varying degrees of concern for ontological, epistemological, legal, economic, or political matters as well as differing degrees of emphasis upon philosophical or practical policy questions. Nonetheless, although there are many different strains of thought within the liberal tradition and many different approaches to pursuing the ideal of a better society, there is a common thread that may be summarized in a twofold conviction:

1.   a rejection of the belief in a transcendent ordering and, therefore, a rejection of the belief in a transcendent normative authority governing the universe, and

2. the belief that just socio-economic relations can be developed through an appropriate process of interaction between a multiplicity of actor-units.

Put simply, liberalism has spread across the globe to undermine authoritarian regimes built upon the notion that the universe is governed by a transcendent authority. The hierarchical ordering of our social, political, and economic lives was therefore replaced with a belief that progress toward an ideal society can be made by constructing the procedural framework for ensuring that all persons interact as self-determining actors. Liberalism's interactionalism offered a way to undermine the violence of authoritarian regimes by forsaking the direct pursuit of the good society. Instead, the good society was to be achieved indirectly by ensuring the freedom of each individual to pursue his or her own understanding of the good life. Not surprisingly, then, the central mechanism for achieving the appropriate process of interaction is an elevation of the search for the right procedures above the search for the good life.[6]

Liberalism represents a truly innovative philosophical and political approach to understanding humanity, its place in the world, and, consequently, the nature of just relations between humans. Importantly, though, we should remember that the traditions against which liberalism distinguished itself did not simply come to an end but, as liberalism developed to become the dominant tradition, these traditions continued to develop as counter-traditions to liberalism. We might even say that modern conservatism has developed as a counter-tradition to revolutionary republican liberalism. Its beginning is often traced back to the publication of Edmund Burke's *Reflections on the Revolution in France* in 1790,[7] for it is in Burke's concern for the good endangered by liberalism's revolution – pursuing an ideal society indirectly through the interactions of individuals – that we see the predominant concern that has

6 As I will be arguing below, however, giving primacy to the right inevitably leads to an eclipse of the good. This unfortunate reification of proceduralism comes about through an erasure of the relations within which normative judgment and action can be made – i.e. the complex interrelated associations of dependence that make up society. As Philip Blond explains, "the most extreme form of liberal autonomy requires the repudiation of society – for human community influences and shapes the individual before any sovereign capacity to choose has taken shape. The liberal idea of man is then, first of all, an idea of nothing: not family, not ethnicity, not society or nation. But real people are formed by the society of others. For liberals, autonomy must precede everything else, but such a 'self' is a fiction. A society so constituted would be one that required a powerful central authority to manage the perpetual conflict between self-interested individuals. So the unanticipated bequest of an unlimited liberalism is that most illiberal of entities: the controlling state" ("Rise of the Red Tories," n.p.).

7 Burke, *Reflections.*

inspired and shaped modern conservative thought. Burke articulated
the character of this counter-tradition most clearly, and it may be further
explained as a disposition and a set of guiding principles. This disposition and set of guiding values offers us a helpful starting point for beginning to understand the violence of liberalism.

What, then, is the character of conservatism? In "On Being Conservative'" Michael Oakeshott has offered an explanation of conservatism in
terms of a disposition to prefer certain kinds of actions. Here, he suggests
that the characteristics of this disposition "centre upon a propensity to
use and to enjoy what is available rather than to wish for or to look for
something else; to delight in what is present rather than what was or what
may be."[8] The reason for this affection towards that which is present in
space and time is quite simple. He writes, "changes are without effect only
upon those who notice nothing, who are ignorant of what they possess
and apathetic to their circumstances; and they can be welcomed indis-
criminately only by those who esteem nothing, whose attachments are
fleeting and who are strangers to love and affection."[9] Conservatives are
deeply interested in the here and now and attached to that which they
understand to make us who we are. Of course, though, "to be conservative is not merely to be averse from change (which may be an idiosyncra-
sy); it is also a manner of accommodating ourselves to changes and activity
imposed upon all men. For, change is a threat to identity, and every
change is an emblem of extinction."[10] Conservatives believe that innovation means certain loss and only possible gain. However, this inevitable
loss can be mitigated to some degree if the innovation represents a kind
of organic growth from what has already gone before, and is in response
to a specific problem in need of correction rather than a general search
for the betterment of humanity. It also needs to be slow enough to allow
for corrections and adjustments as it proceeds.[11]

What this disposition means in terms of legal, political, and economic
theory is expressed by Anthony Quinton, who outlines three basic principles that characterize conservative thought: (a) a respect for traditional institutions and customs, (b) belief in the organic nature of society,
and (c) skepticism regarding abstract political theories.[12] Or, as Russell
Kirk suggests, conservatism in the last few hundred years has had the following six general characteristics:

8   Oakeshott, "On Being Conservative," 168.
9   Ibid., 170.
10 Ibid.
11 See ibid., 172.
12 See Quinton, *The Politics of Imperfection.* Also see Burke who wrote: "I reprobate no
form of government merely upon abstract principles." Burke, *Reflections,* 185.

1. belief in a transcendent order or natural law such that political problems are, at root, moral and religious problems;
2. appreciation for the variety and multiplicity in the mystery of humanity and nature;
3. conviction that a healthy society requires orders and classes rooted in the natural distinctions of persons;
4. an understanding that freedom requires access to capital – i.e. without the private ownership of property, the state will dominate;
5. distrust of those who would seek to re-design society based upon abstract principles; and
6. recognition that society must change in a piecemeal fashion in order to avoid the destructive implications of radical change.[13]

Although modern conservative tradition involves a diverse set of philosophical and political orientations, at root this disposition and set of principles typically arises from a belief that there is a natural ordering that governs the universe. This belief means that, as Kirk notes, "economics and politics are not independent sciences: they are no more than manifestations of a general order, and that order is moral."[14]

Therefore, conservatives typically resist the inclination to view the rule of law as a distinct, disembedded, and self-regulating system of norms to be constructed.[15] Normative orderings are instead understood to be complex and multilogical expressions of the good and therefore characterized by "order, difference, and interdependence" as dialogical and diachronic patternings of behaviour. Disdain is shown, therefore, for proceduralism or formalisms that reflect "sameness, equality, and independence."[16] Due to their belief in an underlying ordering to the universe, conservatives view the revolutions caused by liberalism's underlying procedural constructivism not simply as bad politics but as immoral and rebellious actions.[17] Systems of governance that provide the structures for engaging in political and economic life, in other words, are run through with normativity and must constantly be evaluated in relation to the transcendent orderings of the universe as expressed in tradition.

13 See Kirk, *The Conservative Mind*, 8–9.
14 Ibid., 65.
15 For example, note the actions and attitudes of the Tory loyalists in Upper Canada in the early nineteenth century. See Baker, "So Elegant a Web," 184.
16 Ibid., 194.
17 So, for example, François-René Chateaubriand suggests that "revolutions commit ravages in their course, like the poisonous streams, which cause the flowers to wither as they flow along. The eye of the law is closed during the convulsions of a state, and no longer watches over the citizen, who yields to his passions, and plunges into immorality." Chateaubriand, *Revolutions*, 386.

If this is the case, however, how can we expect to develop a conservative theory of democracy in what follows? Isn't the struggle to have society and its governing institutions accord with a transcendent ordering of the universe precisely what it means to *not* be democratic? Are we not dangerously close to seeking a return to the authoritarian and domineering regimes that liberals have fought to hard to overcome?

I would like to argue quite the opposite – we cannot be truly democratic without being conservative. But a conservative approach to democracy begins with a consideration of what we mean by conservative political theory itself and what it means to engage in recovering the conservative tradition. And the first step in recovering and restoring a genuinely conservative tradition begins by recognizing that liberalism has become the dominant normative tradition that pervades modern legal, political, and economic thought and practice. If we are to have any success in searching for ways of breathing new life into a tradition that has been marginalized as a counter-tradition, we need to get some sense of the depth of the challenge before us. Additionally, part of the first step along the path to conservatism involves spending some time trying to understand the darker side of liberalism and its tendency towards domineering, universalized legal, political, and economic structures. That is, we need to recognize that liberalism's revolution overturning the domineering authoritarian regimes of the past has not taken place without collateral damage and without giving rise to new forms of violent domination. We must become attentive to the kinds of violence and injustice that have been, and are currently being, committed in the name of peace and justice within liberalism.

An essential part of developing a conservative orientation also involves resisting the urge to search for an ideal society or even a grand vision of legal, political, and economic systems that include all peoples. Conservatives believe that, as Jacques Ellul has suggested in his 1969 work *The Theological Foundation of Law*, justice in this world cannot be defined; moreover it cannot be conceived of as invariable or eternal, and therefore cannot be universal. All we have are practical criteria that can be determined in various ways depending upon the persons, events, and environments involved.[18] A conservative impulse, therefore, will shun all attempts to build universal systems based upon abstract principles and will instead reorient us toward the piecemeal actions that are localized within our most immediate environments. It represents a more thoroughgoing restraint in normative theorizing as well as the

---

18 See Ellul, *The Theological Foundation of Law*, 86, 93.

application of this theory to the societies within which we live. So, as Keith Feiling writes, "every Tory is a realist, he knows that there are great forces in heaven and earth that man's philosophy cannot plumb or fathom."[19]

Not only does conservatism depend upon a degree of epistemological humility, however, but also an ethic of submission to authority that is beyond us. For example, as Burke taught, our "temporal order is only part of a transcendent order; and the foundation of social tranquility is reverence. Veneration lacking, life becomes no more than an interminable battle between usurpation and rebellion."[20] Importantly, therefore, conservatives take a different approach to politics because they understand that legal and political problems are, at root, moral and religious problems that demand submission to the authority of tradition.[21] Because of conservatives' belief in the transcendent ordering of the universe, in *The Conservative Mind*, Russell Kirk states that "reverence for the wisdom of our ancestors, through which works the design of Providence, is the first principle of all consistent conservative thought."[22] Conservatives reject utilitarianism, positivism, and pragmatism in a struggle to align ourselves with orderings that are above and beyond us. We cannot hope to begin this process of alignment, however, without an ethic of submission to that from which we come – physically, culturally, and spiritually. Indeed, the refusal to acknowledge and submit to transcendent authority is what fuels innovation and the revolutionary spirit of liberalism. As Burke writes: "a spirit of innovation is generally the result of a selfish temper and confined views. People will not look forward to posterity, who never look backward to their ancestors."[23] A spirit of conservation, in contrast, will seek protection from the disruption and displacement of innovation. A conservative strives for deeper roots, not stronger wings.

Part of growing deeper roots means coming to understand that liberalism has captured not only our hearts and our minds but it has also captured our bodies. The dualistic logic of liberalism has eclipsed former systems of meaning and conceptions of justice, but it has also transformed the legal, political, and economic systems that govern our daily lives. The political institutions of the market state, the rule of law, modern science and its technological revolutions, our globalized, and free-market economy are all operating within the framework of liberal ideology. So not only

19 Feiling, *Toryism*, 37–8.
20 Kirk, *The Conservative Mind*, 66–7.
21 Ibid., 8.
22 Ibid., 65.
23 Burke, *Reflections*, 31.

are our theoretical traditions dominated by liberalism, but our ways of life have been liberalized. How are we to gain perspective on this tradition when it is so pervasive? How can we possibly work, in a positive fashion, to revive a tradition so different from the one that has done so much to make us who we are today?

Importantly, a conservative approach to legal and political theory does not involve merely a theoretical or philosophical submission to abstract notions of transcendent orderings within the universe. Rather, if submission is a subversion of the liberal tradition it requires embodied actions and a way of being in the world that is active in resisting the standardizing abstractions of liberalism's legal, political, and economic systems. Effective resistance means fostering sacred places and times. It means devotion to, and a lived embodiment of, specificity or traditional patterns of behaviour that cannot be universalized because they are particular to a unique people, culture, and/or geography. For example, the traditional relationship many indigenous peoples have to the land cannot be replicated or inclusive of all peoples because it necessarily involves a *particular* people in relation to a *particular* place as distinct from all other peoples and all other places. To put it simply, it is this kind of specificity that represents the rallying point for the restoration of a conservative tradition in the face of sweeping liberal standardizations. We can begin to sense in some small way the violence of the oscillation between the singular and the universal within the dualistic logic of liberalism to the degree that we are able to begin submitting to the authority of a tradition that demands the protection of parochial interest. In a globalized and networked world, others have also noted the importance of the asymmetrical resistance posed by this kind of specificity. For example, in *The Exploit*, Alexander Galloway and Eugene Thacker write that "to be effective, future political movements must discover a new exploit. A wholly new topology of resistance must be invented that is as asymmetrical in relationship to networks as the network was in relationship to power centres. Resistance is asymmetry. The new exploit will be an 'antiweb.'"[24] Instead of being concerned with the smooth functioning of the whole, attentiveness must be given to particular parts in particular places. Instead of being fascinated with a smooth interface between the local and the global, resistance to standardization is engaged in through devotion to the localization of heritage

24 Galloway and Thacker, *The Exploit*, 22, emphasis removed.

and place.[25] A restoration of conservatism, therefore, will take place through the practiced veneration of our traditions and a practical recognition of the authority these traditions hold within our lives.

If we are set upon tracing back and exploring our own traditions rather than seeking to develop an ideal society to include all peoples, then we still have not answered the question posed above: why talk about democracy at all? Is democracy not a fundamentally liberal project? In the discussion below, I will define democracy as an ordering of society that possesses sufficiently resilient normative orderings to provide the foundation for legitimizing law. This resilience in normative orderings is manifest in a multiplicity of interacting localizations of power that make multiple, and most often competing, claims of authority upon persons and things.[26] And, in fact, democracy depends upon the distinctions and differentiations that arise between multiple claims of authority. Democratic governance is a check upon forces that push for the universality of consensus and the monopolization of violence because democracy is found in the disagreement arising from the difference of dependency upon various traditions rather than the standardization of such ideals as freedom and equality. In other words, democracy is best understood as a conservative method of governance and is, I will argue, supplanted by the ideals of liberalism and the institutions to which these ideals give rise.

Admittedly, we might still be temped to think that because liberalism involves a prioritization of the right over the good, it best represents modern democracy. However, it should become clear in the following chapters that this prioritization leads inevitably to not simply a substitution of the right for the good, but also an undermining of the searches for the good that are needed to animate democratic processes and prevent a monopolization of power. Liberalism's push to substitute the right for the good, in other words, entails a hidden universalization of the right because a substitution of the right for the good actually means a substitution of a singular right for multiple goods. Although we will discuss it in more detail below, the reason for this is quite simple: a search for the good life is, by definition, a localized endeavour – i.e. it depends

---

25 See Lasch, *The Revolt of the Elites*, 35. This kind of circuit-breaking resistance through parochialism and localism may be understood as being in direct contrast with the lives of today's elites who, as Lasch points out, go through life as if they were tourists rather than citizens at home in their own country.

26 For a helpful discussion of normative orderings and law as well as the competing claims of authority that are endemic to normative orderings, see Webber, "Naturalism and Agency in the Living Law," 201–21.

upon a rootedness in a certain life – but a substitution of the right over the good means a search for procedures that transcend the specificity and locality of embodied living. It should come as no surprise, therefore, when the liberal tradition and its most influential theorists of the day (e.g. John Rawls and Jürgen Habermas) consistently appeal to consensus and the normative singularity of egalitarianism in order to develop idealizations of democratic procedures. In contrast, a conservative-minded thinker understands that we may theorize in order to identify a question (for example "is this certain kind of violence excessive?") but the answers to this question must always persist as multiple, competing claims. Searches for the right procedures, therefore, can be democratic but only if they remain restrained by specific searches for the good life by people beholden to physical, socio-economic, and spiritual traditions.

C. METHOD AND OUTLINE

This book is an attempt to help recover the critical spirit of conservatism and reemphasize the importance of stability and resilience in society. And, in keeping with conservatives' hesitancy to promulgate an ideal conception of society, my conclusions are primarily diagnostic rather than prescriptive. I do not compare liberal and conservative visions of democracy and then decide that the conservative approach is the better way to go. Although I believe there are some helpful comparisons and contrasts to be made between liberalism and conservatism, you will not find a systematic comparative analysis that outlines the full range of liberal forms of resistance to acceleration and how they stack up against conservative forms of resistance. There should be no doubt that there are numerous liberal forms of resistance to acceleration – some more effective than others. The discussion that follows, however, is not designed to discover the solutions that will cure the modern world of its ills. In the last chapter, I point toward some possible values and ways of life that could flow from a conservative worldview. However, the analysis throughout ultimately centres upon understanding the underlying logic that has propelled liberalism into the dominant worldview in Anglo-American societies and, indeed, in the world. Liberalism has taken many different forms in the last few hundred years. What is the pattern of thought that unites liberals throughout the ages and around the world? Additionally, what has inspired a persistent, albeit increasingly subordinate, counter-tradition to liberalism throughout the past few centuries?

As I explore these two questions in the chapters that follow, I am torn between two different ways of engaging in moral and political theory. Attempting to both dissect a liberal approach to moral and political thought on the one hand and also explore a conservative way of thinking on the other causes some degree of methodological schizophrenia and results in a less conventional structure to this book. Readers looking for a systematic critical analysis of liberalism followed by an argument for the superiority of conservatism will be disappointed. I frequently jump back and forth between critiques of liberalism and arguments for conservatism because I seek to communicate with liberal readers and I myself struggle to be other than liberal. My goal in writing this book, therefore, is simultaneously very ambitious and very modest: it is to begin conceiving of democracy from a perspective outside the liberal tradition. And, in pursuing this goal, I seek to avoid falling into gross oversimplifications and generalizations that distort the liberal tradition, and to refrain from reverting to methods of theorizing that liberals have developed to describe themselves and their liberal interlocutors.

In the first chapter, I will begin to explore the notion that we can view ourselves as deeply dependent and persistently vulnerable beings rather than as free, equal, and rational individuals. I suggest that an understanding of ourselves as embodied and interconnected patternings-in-the-world – *res ecologia* – will allow us to better recognize a diffuse violence at work in the modern world. In chapter 2, I turn to the nature of causation and argue that a disruption of the internal stability of res ecologia should be the primary concern when considering the nature of violence and domination. In chapter 3, I invite us to understand the violence and domination arising in modern liberal societies – proto-colic modulations – as abstract standardization that ensures efficient synchronization between individuated or atomized actors. Further, I suggest that the rapid modulations of this kind of protocolic domination disrupt the structural causation within and between res ecologia. In chapter 4, I begin to show how the kind of violence and domination I have outlined is manifest in and through the tradition of liberalism by tracing out a shared, underlying dualistic logic that simultaneously individuates and totalizes. In chapter 5, I turn to the role of reason in creating freedom and legitimizing violence. Reason is seen to be contributing to both freedom and domination depending upon whether or not it creates resilience within society that resists standardizations. In chapter 6, I argue that the only way to effectively counter the excessive violence within the dualistic logic of liberalism is to cultivate an ethic of mutual support and restraint that invests society with stability and resilience. Finally, I conclude by contending that a resilient society requires intermediate structures and civil enterprises to instil tradition and reciprocal responsibilities in interdependent familial, socio-economic, and religious life.

1

Network Patternings

A. NETWORK ECOLOGY
The world is made up of nested patterns of material and immaterial network patternings that possess both stability and flux.

B. THE SELF AS *RES ECOLOGIA*
Humans, as networks-in-the-world, exist as deeply dependent and persistently vulnerable beings.

C. ACCELERATION
The flux of the network patternings of the world are speeding up and this acceleration, by threatening the stability of the networks, is changing the nature of these patternings.

INTRODUCTION

There is a growing sense that something has gone very wrong with liberal capitalism and its modern market state. It is becoming increasingly obvious that the collusion between the liberal state and market (the "market state") is disintegrating civil society, decapitalizing the poor, and destroying natural ecosystems at a tremendous rate. It is becoming increasingly difficult, therefore, to legitimize the degree of violence that is produced in and through this collusion. This violence is destroying the in-between worlds of mutual support between families and communities as well as distorting our interdependence with the natural world.

Despite a growing anxiety, however, proposed responses to contain and cope with the systemic violence of liberalism's market and state systems are disturbingly few. Even more disturbing is the fact that these systems of violence are so often reproduced in and through our critical responses themselves. We look for solutions to the problems of ecological destruction, poverty, social isolation, and antisocial behaviour without an understanding of either the depth of the challenges before us or the developmental history of these challenges. We struggle to understand the disruption and displacement that is taking place. What is it that is being disrupted and displaced? All too often we reproduce the underlying systems of violence in and through our well-meaning piecemeal solutions. The violence of the market state is reiterated and reinforced when we retain and continue to promulgate, albeit unwittingly, the core values that undergird and inspire the modern liberal institutions that make up the current market state. Despite our best intentions, we are swept up into the systems of violence at work in the world today when we fail to anchor ourselves down to values and principles of ordering that are at odds with the values and principles of ordering that make up our contemporary world.

A radically different approach to understanding political normativity is needed if we are to foster the development of social and economic institutions that do not suffer the same ills as our beleaguered liberal state. We cannot begin to shake the devils off our backs until we begin to experience the infilling of a different spirit, principles of ordering that are part of a different story – a story that is not contiguous with the rise of the market state. Indeed, a genuine transformation of our institutions fundamentally depends upon a transformation of the normative logic that undergirds these institutions. But, however uncomfortable it may be for us moderns, we also cannot hope to achieve our political goals without doing our ontological homework. The institutions of the market state are rooted in a normative logic that is itself inescapably entangled with an ontological narrative. And, if we seek to conceive of political relations and institutions that are not a part of the story that has given rise to modern liberalism and the violence of its market state, we must be inspired and molded by pre-liberal ideals rooted in pre-liberal ontologies. For example, if we are to develop the ability to recognize and make visible the breadth and the depth of violence enacted through the liberal pursuit of freedom and equality, we must begin to embrace a narrative of normativity that reaches back before the rise of modern liberalism. If we are to tell a story of just relations that is not centred upon a notion of freedom as self-determination and self-expression or the standardizations of egalitarianism, we need to begin conceiving of ourselves and our world as deeply interconnected and interdependent. Likewise, if we are to speak of a structural violence taking place within the increased rates of change in the world and within ourselves, we need to begin seeing the integrity of ecological, social, and spiritual patternings therein.

In this chapter, therefore, I will begin laying the groundwork needed to recognize and articulate the structural violence hidden within the

normative ideals of liberalism. I outline some of the basic elements needed to begin achieving the perspective that will allow us to recognize the
disruption and displacement that is at work within liberalism. After suggesting that we begin understanding the world as made up of nested
patterns of material and immaterial networks that possess both stability
and flux, I will suggest that we reflect upon ourselves as embodied networks-in-the-world. In striving to view ourselves as deeply dependent and
persistently vulnerable rather than as free, equal, and rational individuals, we are challenged to begin seeing ourselves as beings that come from
beyond ourselves. And, consequently, we are challenged to understand
ourselves as having the capacity for normative judgment precisely because we are embodied beings who are able to project into the future
along the trajectory of patternings that transcend ourselves. Further, if
we are attentive to the persistence of patternings that come from beyond
ourselves, we are able to gain some perspective on the damage that is
done when these patterns are distorted through acceleration. In this
manner, I am encouraging us to conceive of structural violence in
terms of the disruption of patterning processes and, consequently, hop-
ing that we will be able to effectively problematize the standardization of
relations that leads to acceleration.

A. NETWORK ECOLOGY

Before turning our minds to the problem of acceleration arising through
standardization and what that might mean for our understanding of justice and democracy, let us consider the potentials of a political ecology
rooted in a political ontology of networks. Why begin with talk of a new
political ecology and ontology? Further, what *prima facie* reasons might
we have for using networks as the central focal point in our analysis?[1]

I begin with a reconsideration of our political ecology because, as outlined in the introduction above, the current attempts to legitimize power
use within the traditional ontological framework of liberal democratic theory are beginning to ring hollow. The politics of difference, eco-
politics, and the rise of agonistic democratic theory have revealed the
dramatic harms done by liberal rationalism as a result of its push toward

---

1 The significance of network thinking can only be expected to become transparent
in and through the actual exercise of this approach in working out an understanding of
violence, the legitimation of violence, and the impossibility of legitimizing some kinds of
violence. Consequently, at this point, all that we need are some prima facie reasons why
we might consider the potential benefits of a network approach to reworking our political ontology.

political unity. The agonists, ecologists, and the theorists of the politics of difference, however, have themselves been unable to deproblematize difference as a result of their philosophical liberalism that prevents them from taking deep pluralism seriously. The fundamental ontological framework of liberal democratic theory – whether rationalist or agonist – continues to do significant violence through its inherent homogenizing impulse. For example, rationalist theorists like John Rawls and Jürgen Habermas and their followers are committed to a liberal ontology that, in order to posit a universal proceduralism, must simply exclude important ontological commitments regarding the self and its relation to the world from the realm of politics.[2] These ontological commitments of those outside the mainstream that lead to very real political and economic ways of life are excluded as not being legitimately "public" in their orientation. For an agonist like Chantal Mouffe, the social (and, hence, the political) are conceived of quite differently and in a much more pluralistic manner such that her notion of legitimation is not as explicitly homogenizing.[3] However, although Mouffe argues against the notion of a "universal consensus" (as liberal rationalists are prone to do), she nonetheless essentializes antagonism and thereby falls into the individuated/totalized dualistic trap of liberalism that we will discuss below.[4] Both the rationalist and the agonist, in their own ways, obscure systemic power flows that are shaping relational patternings in the space between the singular (subject) and absolute (object). Both, therefore, fail to develop what Val Plumwood calls "a common, integrated framework for the critique of both human domination and the domination of nature."[5] Some theorists have developed important critiques of the underlying atomistic ontology of liberalism in order to avoid the dualism of liberalism

2 See Rawls, *A Theory of Justice*, Rawls, *Political Liberalism*, Habermas, *Communicative Action*, Vol. I, and Habermas, *On the Pragmatics of Communication*.

3 Political questions, for her, "always involve decisions which require us to make a choice between conflicting alternatives" and, therefore, the political should be understood as "the dimension of antagonism which [is] constitutive of human societies." Mouffe, *On the Political*, 9–10. Therefore, the social is developed within a we-they dualism; it is constituted by the interplay between these two extremes.

4 As Crowder has pointed out, "all political positions rely on essentialist claims, because all propose norms that imply conceptions of human nature and the human good. Mouffe's own position is no exception"; her antagonistic dimension of the political is (as it is for Schmitt) an essential element of human nature. See Crowder, "Chantal Mouffe's Agonistic Democracy," 15.

5 Plumwood, *Feminism*, 1–2.

we see in rationalists and agonists.[6] However, they have sought to do this while continuing to posit the proceduralistic politics of liberalism as a means to legitimize power use – and have, therefore, continued to replicate some of the harmful dualisms of liberalism. Further, there is a sense in which such critical approaches have not yet been brought together into a positive theory of democracy that sees past the liberal paradigm to focus on the systemic violence fuelled by the political economy of liberalism. It is hoped that a turn to a network ontology will help us begin to theorize regarding the issues that have been so skilfully problematized by these thinkers and more effectively undermine the violence that continues to be hidden within the liberal political tradition.

Not only are the current theoretical approaches to legitimizing power use within the liberal tradition beginning to ring hollow, but there are some key practical reasons for seeking a new political ontology. First, our current political ontology is out of sync with our twenty-first century science. Second, our current political ontology is fostering an unjust and unsustainable economic system. Third, contemporary liberal theorists suffer from some significant blind spots in their attempts to reduce violence in the world and a network approach holds the promise of allowing us to identify these problem areas with renewed vigour.

First, then, in what way are the ontological categories that make up our scientific understanding of ourselves and our world – our physics, biology, and cosmology – as well as our understanding of causation out of sync with the political ontology of liberal democratic theory? Our patterns of political organization and, more importantly, our methods of legitimizing power use have developed in loose coordination with our scientific conceptions of the universe and humanity's place within it. Charles Taylor has rightly noted that there is often a dynamic relationship between one's ontology and policy commitments such that taking a position in one area (either ontology or policy) does not necessarily commit you to a certain position in the other area. And yet, as he rightly notes, the two areas are also not independent. So, although one's ontological commitments do not directly determine one's political priorities, they do form a kind of background language that determines the means of articulating political priorities. Likewise, the interpretive language we use to describe the workings of the physical world provides us with the language of politics that we use to describe our social realities (and, indeed, vice versa). The interpretive circle of political theory is tied into the interpretive circle of

6 For example, see Taylor, *Philosophy and the Human Sciences*; Taylor, *Philosophical Arguments*; Tully, *Democracy and Civic Freedom*; Webber, "A Nationalism that is Neither Chauvinistic nor Closed"; and Webber, "The Hobbesian Premise."

the sciences and, when looking back on the historical development of scientific and political thought, it is not surprising to see parallel paradigm shifts. Occasionally, however, our scientific and political ontologies become disconnected as one of the interpretive circles undergoes a paradigm shift before the other. And, if this takes place, a lack of resonance between our scientific and political understanding creates dissonance in our worldview and, what we are facing today, a crisis of legitimation.

The current crisis of legitimation has arisen, to some degree, because our scientific understanding of the world – especially in physics and biology – has shifted from the atomistic models of the modern era into the network models of the postmodern era. The "modern era" began in earnest in the seventeenth century and itself signaled a dramatic shift in conceptions of place and order in the universe. No longer was there a centre of the universe as an absolute point from which to develop a hierarchy of place as there was in an Aristotelian universe. Instead, the world was composed of atoms and all atoms were understood as equal and possessive of their properties independent of their relations with other atoms (i.e. they were interchangeable prior to their interactions). These atoms became defined in relation to a fixed framework of space and time under the Newtonian science. This kind of atomism was further advanced and re-enforced when Darwin's concept of natural selection not only undermined the idea of trans-temporally fixed species but, more importantly, also undermined the impetus to search for an understanding of ahistorical laws of organic form (i.e. the logic behind the apparent diversity of life).

This atomistic conception of the universe meant significant changes in politics – changes tied into notions of the person as an individual or self-contained being. As Taylor explains, from the moderns' perspective, "man is a free being in the sense that he is meant by God to find his paradigm purposes within himself, and not out of the order in which he is set. Hence, in the political realm, human freedom is prior to legitimate order, in that legitimate authority can arise only as the creation of human agents through consent."[7] This autonomy of the person became the primary conceptual foundation for liberal political theory and fostered commitments to objective normative metrics such as equality. As Charles Taylor (and George Grant before him) has explained, this kind of radical distinction between subjective and objective (i.e. an eclipse of the middle ground between self and world) lies at the root of both

7 Taylor, "Kant's Theory of Freedom," 319.

modern individualism and the rise of instrumental reason.[8] Importantly, this subjectification of the self in contrast to the objectification of the world also meant that, politically, human freedom (i.e. independence) was understood to be prior to legitimate order such that legitimate political authority can arise only through consent or egalitarianism or some combination of both.[9] So, along with changes in science, the standard for legitimizing power use changed. If each person was essentially self-contained (physically and spiritually), then law had to be written on each person's heart. No longer could one appeal to an understanding of the ordering of the world as the touchstone for legitimate power use. Instead, legitimacy itself was understood to be constructed in and through humanity's ability to transcend nature in a certain kind of interactional procedure between humans. One did not strive to attain access to a transcendent other/otherness, but one continually reinforced the integrity of one's own self by bumping up against the other in political community. Indeed, this "bumping up against in political community" was legitimate only insofar as it reinforced the boundaries of the self. It is this kind of fundamentally atomistic ontology underlying liberal democratic theory that is dramatically out of step with our current understanding of the world and its complexities.

In the twentieth century what might be called the "network era" began with a shift from the fixed frame reference of Newtonian physics to an Einsteinian theory of general relativity. Now, the universe becomes an ever-changing, pluralistic network of relations with no centre and no fixed frame of reference. There is no longer any "outside" from which to view and organize the universe – rather, the universe itself is understood to be at least somewhat self-organizing, with all properties definedthrough the interconnected relations. In this way the universe becomes understood not in atomistic or mechanistic terms, but in much more ecological and network terms. Causation, therefore, becomes less about self-contained bodies acting upon one another and more about resonance between networks as the whole of the network draws the parts into new relational patterns. An example of this kind of science can be seen in non-equilibrium (open system) thermodynamics, which studies systems in which the "centers of flow, growth, and change, are not static, still, or dead; they are not in equilibrium."[10] This includes energy flow systems that bring about complex structures that maintain

---

8 See Taylor, *The Malaise of Modernity*; Taylor, *Sources of the Self*, 33–4. Also Grant, *English-Speaking Justice*.

9 Taylor, "Kant's Theory of Freedom," 319.

10 Schneider and Sagan, *Into the Cool*, xii.

themselves as distinct from the environment but also grow and adapt in response to changes around them. This approach, therefore, understands biological processes as autocatalytic systems that "delay the instantaneous dissipation of energy and give rise to energy and material storage, cycling, and structure."[11] Agency and causation, in short, becomes understood as distributed through asymmetrical patterns of interconnectivity. Although we will not dive into it now, current understandings of causation and the legitimation of action – especially through the immanentism of postmodern thinkers – has been affected by this shift to the "network era." But, as we will see in the discussion that follows, the connection between current science and postmodern immanentists has not been thorough or unproblematic.[12]

Second, to what degree is our current political ontology fostering an unjust and unsustainable economic system? The political ontology of liberalism, I think undeniably, operates hand in hand with the economic liberalism of the free market and a relentlessly expansionist capitalism. Our systems of global markets, mass consumerism, and ecological exploitation are demonstrative of an atomistic and immanentist ontology and its corresponding logic of seeking the right above the good that has been entrenched within both the modern state and the free market.[13] Economic liberalism means a market system ostensibly operating independently of the interconnected ecological, social, and spiritual relations that make up our lives. It means a methodology of contractual relations that is divorced from our everyday co-operative economic relations that are embedded within familial and communal relations that are deeply charged with normativity. The liberal economy (the market economy) is a self-regulating system of markets that operates as a transcendent, amoral layering riding above ecological, social, and spiritual relations. The market economy is an elevation of material gain, in other words, above all other concerns; it is an economy that is understood to

11 Ibid., 330.

12 At a very basic level, by "immanentist" I refer to the dominant tradition of modern (and postmodern) philosophy, which is founded upon a natural philosophy that has lost faith in "that which is beyond." This denial of that which is beyond has significant implications for ontology, epistemology, phenomenology, and of course politics. See Blond, "Introduction," 43.

13 By economic liberalism of the free market I mean the three classical tenets outlined by Karl Polanyi in *The Great Transformation*: "that labor should find its price on the market; that the creation of money should be subject to an automatic mechanism; that goods should be free to flow from country to country without hindrance or preference; in short, for a labor market, the gold standard, and free trade." Polanyi, *The Great Transformation*, 135.

be divorced from its norms of reciprocity and redistribution. Of course, though, this elevation of material gain is rooted in a political ontology committed to viewing actors as individuals who are not only self-interested, but interested in nothing more than material gain. As Polanyi has suggested, modern (market) economics is actually liberal economics in the sense that it is focused upon material wealth as a separate field of study to be explored as a universe operating according to its own internal logic (e.g. see Adam Smith's *Wealth of the Nations*). Further, just as political liberalism depends upon the muscle of the modern welfare state, so too does the *laissez-faire* of economic liberalism depend upon the enforcements of the state. Importantly, however, the state does not dominate or control the market as a foreign power but actually develops in accordance with the logic of the market such that the state naturally fosters the laissez-faire of economic liberalism. The connection between liberal political ontology and liberal economics, therefore, can be seen in the submission of the liberal state to the market economy already in the late eighteenth century.[14] Economic liberalism's isolation and elevation of material gain inevitably results in the liberal state-sanctioned appropriation of non-profitmaking spheres of life by the market.[15]

As C.B. Macpherson and Philip Blond have noted, the liberal market state has become understood as a supplier of political goods and, in order to maintain its supply chain, supports a market that actually destroys society and operates out of sync with democracy. For, if you understand democracy as a search for a moral ideal pertaining to the flourishing of all peoples, economic and political liberalism offer little to no support. Liberalism's system of power is designed (with self-determination as the highest goal) to facilitate and promote the process of making of contracts for individual material gain.[16] This system of power at work in the liberal economy/polity, however, hides its own normative activity by elevating a search for the right procedures of political and economic interaction above a search for the good in political and economic relations. This formalism hides the morality (the inherent normativity) of the liberal system of power that operates as a simultaneous individuation and totalization of the self. (More on this in chapters 3 and 4 below.) In its dedication to the unhindered self-determination of the individual, the liberal system of power obscures the normativity promoted in and through this use of power. That is, the exercise of power is denied even as it is active in promoting an ethic of material gain for the individual

14   Ibid., 111ff, 139.
15   Blond, *Red Tory*, 186, and Perelman, *The Invention of Capitalism*.
16   See Macpherson, *The Real World of Democracy*.

through self-determination. And, although we will consider liberalism's eclipse of normative relations below in a discussion of its proceduralist turn, we should note that liberalism is relatively successful in this denial insofar as its underlying ontology (and the substitutionalist logic that accompanies it) remains unquestioned. Therefore, we have a prima facie reason to seek out a new political ontology of network interconnection and patterning to the degree that we are dissatisfied with the market state system of liberalism. If we are interested in remoralizing the market, we need to develop a political ontology that will allow us to simultaneously remoralize the state by focusing on our ecological, social, and spiritual interconnectedness rather than our ability to abstract into the realm of contractual procedures.

Third, what do we hope to highlight that previous ontologies – and, therefore, political ecologies – failed to bring to light? Or, alternately, how might a network ecology allow us to substantially rework our conception of legitimate power use?

A refocus on our interconnectedness through the development of a network ontology, holds the promise of shedding light on some of the blind spots that have developed within a dominant tradition of liberalism. Specifically, the language of networks allow us to focus in a little more clearly on a couple things:

(a) patterns of being that fundamentally transcend the individual (and, indeed, transcend humanity itself),
(b) the structural persistence of these relational patterns – i.e. what might be called natural ordering within the world, and
(c) opportunities for creating resistance to the structural violence that comes about through homogenizing impulses.

There is much to be said regarding these three points but, given the fact that this work is about the potentials of a network ontology, exploration of these three themes will best be taken up one step at a time in the chapters that follow rather than simply summarized here. But before we get ahead of ourselves let us consider what we might mean by networks, network ecology, the nature of things, and natural ordering in the world.

In our turning away from the atomistic conception of political ontology, let us begin considering what we might mean by "network ecology." By "network ecology" I mean understanding the world as being made up of (a) nested distributive patterns that are (b) both material and immaterial and (c) retain stability in their patternings while being perpetually in flux. As should become clearer in the discussion that follows, I refer to network "ecology" rather than simply "ontology" because I believe it is important to understand and direct our attention to (a) the world as made up of patterns of activity and (b) our participation in this activity (i.e. the inevitable connection between ontology and epistemology).

But, first, networks as nested distributive patterns: networks are typically understood as three basic kinds: centralized, decentralized, and distributive.[17] A centralized network is a simple, twofold hierarchy with a single node at the centre and all other nodes linked at the periphery. A decentralized network is a multi-layered hierarchy with a single node at the centre, intermediary-level nodes linking the centre node to the nodes at the periphery. A distributive network is without a centre and without an obvious hierarchy. In structural terms, it may be defined as an internally inconsistent or asymmetrical pattern of interrelationality that contains tensions within its own form and is capable of heterogeneous transformations and reconfigurations. Not only are these patterns fundamentally asymmetrical in their architecture, they are also highly complex in that they are also patternings nested within patternings. To put it another way, each nodal point should be understood as being itself a distributive network; each actor/node is at the same time a network. Instead of focusing on the distinction between agent and structure as if these were two distinct realities, the nesting of the networks means that all "beings" are beings-in-the-network or, more precisely, network-beings. The agent/actor and structure/network are not simply reversible, as Bruno Latour suggests, but because they are nested patternings, the agent/actor actually *is* a structure/network.[18] The question of agency (and hence of violence) is, therefore, a question of scoping. The patternings of networks can be seen and understood as active and internally stimulated at various levels depending upon one's level of analysis. In this sense there is, therefore, a scaling of networks that goes both lower and higher than our political understanding allows. This nested distributive network ontology provides us with a model beyond the fixed-frame reference of Newtonian physics that has drawn us into using a universal metric to understand what it means to be part of a larger structure.

Second, networks as nested patterns of both material (*res extensa*) and immaterial (*res spiritus*) relations. Networks should be understood as material and immaterial patterns or systems of, for example, biological, semiotic, organic, inorganic, natural, technological interrelationality; they are bio-material, techno-mechanistic, social, and spiritual. Therefore, a

17 See Galloway and Thacker, *The Exploit*. Simply put, a "network is a set of interconnected nodes. A node is the point at which a curve intersects itself." Castells, *The Rise of the Network Society*, 470.

18 See Latour, "Networks, Societies, Spheres."

network approach is a mode of inquiry that is neither materialist nor reductionist and, indeed, blurs over the lines that could be drawn between, for example, the biological and the semiotic in order to draw attention to a broad, diffuse agency that is part of each entity patterning within the world. As such, networks should be understood much more as ecosystems than as computer networks – i.e. messy and dynamic in their interrelations rather than mechanistic and precise. Their boundaries are always resisting clear and definite definition – they are always negotiated and indeed change depending on the negotiation process itself.

Third, networks as stable yet always in flux: complex distributive networks are best conceived of as dynamic and open-ended systems that are constantly changing through reconfiguration and the addition of further nodes and links.[19] Networks *are* patternings of interconnection – i.e. processes of forming and reforming patterns – that move matter, energy, information, etc. between network nodal points. These ever-changing process-flows of network formation simultaneously possess contingency and stability as network patterns develop over time; networks have both roots and wings. Roots because the patterning develops a kind of stability in its structure that resists change. Wings because networks are always active and in flux.

What, then, is the significance of network patternings? What political implications might we expect to arise from this turn to a network ecology?

As we have already noted, engaging in the development of a network ecology as a mode of inquiry into politics and, especially, the legitimization of power use, will (hopefully) allow us to move beyond some of the perpetually problematic conundrums of liberal democratic theory. And it will allow us to do this primarily because this network approach enables us to perceive the diffusion of agency or broaden our typical examination of how action is located and relocated. By reimagining agency as network pattern flux, we are able to bring into focus a kind of power at work in the world that operates within the very architecture of our world. And, further, with this understanding of a pervasive or structural power active within the world, a whole new realm of opportunities for identifying and creating resistance to structural violence opens up for us.

As Bruno Latour stated in a 2010 lecture to the Annenberg School for Communication and Journalism, "in its simplest but also in its deepest sense, the notion of network is of use *whenever action is to be redistributed*."[20]

---

19 Barabási, *Linked*, 106.
20 Latour, "Networks, Societies, Spheres," 2, emphasis in original.

That is, the network approach to understanding ecological, social, and spiritual relations allows us to more fully perceive and account for – to recognize – the agency of attributes that was previously concealed within conceptions of the world as made up of self-contained entities. Or, again as Latour suggests, a network is "what takes any *substance* that had seemed at first self contained (that's what the word means after all) and transforms it into what it needs to *subsist* through a complex ecology of tributaries, allies, accomplices, and helpers" – i.e. to transform an object "from a matter of fact to a matter of concerns."[21] The network, therefore, represents both a focal point for a new political ecology as well as a mode of inquiry for understanding ourselves and the objects of our world. The network represents a new kind of politics. This new kind of politics rooted in a network ecology means a reimagining of the individual/society and citizen/state relations within traditional political theory. Fundamentally, it is a reconsideration of the *res publica* – the public thing – and a turn to res ecologia – the ecological thing.

By "ecology" I mean the study of the household (i.e. from *oikos* "household" and *logos* "principle of order and knowledge"). An ecosystem is a number of living and non-living organisms and elements interacting as a complex pattern of relations. Ecosystems are the systems of relations within which we as humans find ourselves dwelling: they are our households. However, this network ecology approach means that not only is our *environment* best understood in terms of an integrated system or a number of integrated systems, but the *things* that make up these larger systems are themselves best understood ecologically – i.e. as res ecologia or as things-within-which-we-dwell. In other words, we must re-evaluate our understanding of things themselves if we are to take the network approach seriously.

Understanding things as res ecologia means at least three things:

(a) a thing is a relational set of attributes that constitutes a whole,
(b) a thing is a matter of contestation (i.e. a matter of concerns rather than a matter of fact), and
(c) a thing is a whole that is greater than the sum of its parts.

Despite his often-confusing ways of discussing things, German philosopher Martin Heidegger is surprisingly helpful when considering these three ways of understanding things as res ecologia. Simply put, Heidegger suggests that a thing presences to us as a gathering and this presencing

21 Ibid., 5.

can be thought of as the thing's essential nature.[22] Let us therefore briefly consider these three elements – presencing, gathering, and essential nature – for it is in considering these three elements that our understanding of res ecologia becomes more clear. It should be noted that I am playing off Heidegger's terms and themes rather than simply discussing his considerations of things. So, we might say that although my approach is phenomenological, I seek to walk a middle path between the transcendentalist phenomenology of Edmund Husserl and the immanentist phenomenology of Heidegger without falling into the humanist trap to which they have fallen prey.[23]

First, the thing as presencing: a thing does not exist as a thing-in-itself that is lifeless and inactive – i.e. as nature (res extensa) has been for the modern mind (*res cogitans*). Immanuel Kant's Copernican Revolution was the denial of the power of reason in the realm of the supersensible and a turn to considering the manner in which phenomena becomes cognizable by humans. Kant denied access to cognition by that thing (*noumena*) which transcends empirical experience (*phenomena*) and, therefore, to ensure we remain fixed upon the structures of our own conscious experience – i.e. remain focused upon the ability of res cogitans to take up and animate a lifeless res extensa. For Heidegger, and for us in this discussion, this denial of life to the thing-in-itself is unacceptable and we must embark upon a kind of counter-revolution to Kant's revolution. So, importantly, we must focus upon the active disclosure or revelation that makes things manifest or presents things to humans as space-time gatherings.[24] For example, in contrast to Husserl's reliance upon a transcendental subjectivity, Heidegger argues that the manifest givenness of phenomenon occurred regardless of any transcendental constitution within the subjectivity of humans.[25] Or, in other words, things presence themselves to us as space-time gatherings.

Second, then, the thing as gathering: to use Heidegger's verbiage, a thing things in its gathering. It presences to us in its gathering.[26] But, if we might add to Heidegger's language somewhat, we would do well to say also that the thing wholes in its gathering. Indeed, it presences as a whole. But, importantly, the presencing of the whole is not an activity accomplished in isolation. Rather, a thing presences as a whole in a twofold

---

22 Heidegger, "The Thing," quoted in Latour, "From Realpolitik to Dingpolitik," 272.
23 Cf. Blond, "Emmanuel Levinas," 195ff.
24 Harman, "Heidegger on Objects and Things," 270. Also see Harman, *Tool-Being.*
25 Blond, "Emmanuel Levinas," 195ff. Also see Heidegger, *Die Frage nach dem Ding,* 246, quoted in Harman, "Heidegger on Objects and Things," 269.
26 Heidegger, "The Thing," 174, from *Making Things Public,* 272.

relationality that is both "internal" and "external" to the whole. A thing is relational in its *gathering of the whole* (i.e. "internally") but it is also relational in its presencing to humans *as a whole* (i.e. "externally"). Therefore, things do not simply presence themselves to humans as singular, definite, or finalized beings-in-themselves, but as a gathering, as a contested matter of pertinence. Therefore, a "thing" used to denote "anything that in any way bears upon men, concerns them, and that accordingly is a matter for discourse."[27] Thing means a gathering, "and specifically a gathering to deliberate on a matter under discussion, a contested matter ... an affair or matter of pertinence."[28] If we understand things as res ecologia, then we understand that a thing presences as an ecology – a logos (ordering principle) of an oikos (dwelling place). It makes itself known as an ordering of a dwelling place that is, due to its relationality, at the same time both stable in its presencing as well as in flux. So, importantly, a thing does not presence simply as an ecosystem. It does not first whole and then move on to presence. Rather, it is wholing in and through its presencing. Again, it is relational both "internally" and "externally"; it is relational in its essence.

Third, the thing's essential nature: Heidegger suggests that we might think of a thing's presencing to humans as its essential nature. This presencing is a thing's essential nature, but a thing gathers as a whole that goes beyond its direct relations or encounter with humans. Like Heidegger, Latour is intent upon bringing to light the thing as a gathering and he seeks to understand this gathering as a democratic assembly in which the thing is both the assembled as well as that for which the assembled are assembled. For Latour, however, things do not presence themselves to humans as wholing things, but they do so as a data-set of disclosed and undisclosed attributes – i.e. as a whole realm of widely distributed action. Because things have no essence that remains regardless of their relational environments, an object is fully transformable in and through human considerations of it. This transformation is possible – at least in theory – all the way through the thing. Things are fundamentally contestable or, as he suggests, "we are not trying to go back to the old materialism of *Realpolitik*, because *matter itself* is up for grabs as well. To be materialist now implies that one enters a labyrinth more intricate than that built by Daedalus."[29] It is problematic, therefore, for Latour to speak of a thing's essential nature

27 Ibid., 272.
28 Ibid.
29 Latour, "From Realpolitik to Dingpolitik," 24.

because a thing is nothing but a set of attributes. Wholes are no greater than their parts. In fact, a whole is always less than its parts.[30]

Latour is certainly correct to speak of the widely distributed action of things. As we just discussed, things are best understood as gatherings. And, indeed, they are best understood this way because it brings to light the activity of their being-in-the-world – i.e. their being as relational activity. He is mistaken, however, to suggest that the whole is never greater than its parts. For, indeed, a thing wholes as much as it gathers and, therefore, it presences as a whole that has its being in its action as a whole. A thing should be understood as thoroughly relational, but its relationality is not flatly immanent. We do not, for example, encounter things as data-sets.[31] Rather, a thing presences on multiple levels and, as such, not only comes to us as parts *and* wholes (depending upon the nature of our encounter with the thing) but also transcends the encounter with humans. A thing is somewhat withdrawn from humans as something outside a space-time gathering-for-humans. Thus, things are not fundamentally contestable because they appear to us from beyond our perception as already engaged in a process of constituting and reconstituting. This process of constituting (or gathering together/wholing) therefore comes to us as something outside ourselves, as something that orders us and our world.

It is this wholing of things that allows them to exist and persist through time and, to a degree, persist despite changes in their relational environments. The integrity of wholes lies in their wholing, a process of which humans are a part but not the whole. A thing should be understood as a network that has integrity within its patterning. Admittedly, though, this integrity is not as an Aristotelian substance that persists regardless of its relations but an integrity that presences in and through relations that are relatively stable in and through time. We would do best to speak, therefore, of res ecologia rather than simply of res publica. Res publica has no integrity and is fully contestable in its immanence. It does not come from beyond but arises in the midst of the *demos*. Likewise, it will decompose or deconstruct as soon as the public disbands or is itself deconstructed.

Latour is quite correct to focus in on the fundamental interrelationality of existence and, therefore, the corresponding interrelationality between the inquirer and the entity. I share his emphasis upon using the

30 See, for example, Latour et al., "The Whole is Always Smaller than Its Parts." Also see Latour, *Reassembling the Social.*

31 Latour writes that "there is no world of beyond. It is all about *immanence.*" Latour, "An Attempt at a Compositionist Manifesto," 475.

network as a mode of inquiry with the goal of learning how to be attentive to a diffuse agency. For example, to help us recognize structural violence that has been hidden by liberalism or to make visible that which was previously invisible in an atomistic/organistic approach that can only contemplate entities as self-contained beings. However, it is not clear that, in turning to a network ontology, we need to be as dismissive of the notion of the whole as Latour is. For example, there is no such thing as society within Latour's radical relationalism; it is a mere phantom that has persisted as a leftover from the substantialism of Aristotle. Laying a good deal of blame at the feet of Durkheim, Latour argues that "to believe in the existence either of individual or of society is simply a way to say that we have been deprived of information on the individuals we started with; that we have little knowledge about their interactions; that we have lost the *precise conduits* through which what we call 'the whole' actually circulates. In effect, we have jettisoned the goal of understanding what the collective existence is all about."[32] In other words, the idea of the whole persisting through time, for Latour, is nothing more than an epistemic problem. Or, rather, it is a problem that is best understood as an error rooted in epistemological failings. The whole is something we turn to when giving up on understanding the vast array of connections that make up the world.

Importantly, although I will argue precisely the opposite, Latour also suggests that this kind of neo-nominalism is necessary if there is to be politics. For example, he writes that "if you accept the notion of organism as something different or superior or even emerging, you lose what an organization is (and I would add you ruin the possibility of doing politics). A phenomenon may be collective without being social."[33] However, Latour fails to recognize that the whole is fundamentally and simultaneously heterogeneous and is not this way despite its wholing but, rather, gathers without unifying. Additionally, as we saw above, a whole is a nested pattern of wholes and, therefore, contains within itself a perpetual multiplicity (i.e. the part is the whole within a whole or, to put it the other way, the whole is the part within a part). It is precisely this dynamism between the heterogeneous multiplicity of the network nodes and the unity of the networks that allows for, and fosters, the doing of politics. And, indeed, Latour himself seems to have some sense of this dynamism when he states that "the area 'covered' by any network is 'universal' but just as long and just where there are enough antennas, relays, repeaters, and so on, to

32 Latour, "Networks, Societies, Spheres," 5, emphasis in original.
33 Ibid., 15.

sustain the activation of any work. Thanks to the notion of networks, universality is now fully *localizable*."[34] But, of course, the universalities of res ecologia are localizable only because they already contain within them a fundamental heterogeneity and multiplicity. So, in this sense Latour is correct – this dynamism and potential for genuine localizability within universality is necessary for the doing of politics (as we will see below in this chapter). However, I am suggesting that the immanentism within Latour's ontological constructivism does not allow for the dynamism of simultaneous unity and multiplicity. Or, in other words, Latour destroys the possibility of politics in his decomposing of the transcendental.

Latour's compositionalism or neo-nominalism leads him to spurn the search for a world beyond this immanent world and to instead content himself with simply deranging and re-arranging or decomposing and composing the world around us.[35] His concept of relationality, therefore, seems to be both too shallow and too atomistic. It seems too shallow because to be part of a whole is not to enter into a higher entity but simply to share attributes in common. This holds the danger of universalizing the attributes of various entities in an understanding that attributes are shared between entities as if they were transferable from relational set to relational set. Instead, attributes, just as much as the substances of substantialism, must be reconceived in relational terms; an attribute of one entity is not the same as an attribute of another entity because the attribute itself is best understood as part of a whole network of relations. To speak of a common attribute is to give up on the task of understanding the relationality of networks. Additionally, his concept of relationality seems too atomistic because, as we saw above, it is entirely appropriate to understand there to be wholes that are greater than their parts. Simply focusing on the parts in a kind of neo-nominalism holds the danger of obscuring the very real importance of wholes. He is correct to write that we should search for universality without believing that universality is already there, waiting passively to be discovered. However, as we have seen, there is no reason to suggest that wholes do not actively make themselves known to us as wholes. In the same way that things presence as wholes coming to us as gathered from beyond our perception, so too does society come to us as gathered from beyond.

The dynamism at work within a gathering without unifying ensures that the essential nature of res ecologia remains somewhat hidden for us. Or, to put it another way, the Being of beings remains beyond and presences

---

34 Ibid., 8, emphasis in original.
35 See Latour, "An Attempt at a Compositionist Manifesto," 474ff.

to us in beings that come from a plenitude that transcends our being. The political relevance of this plenitude and rejection of immanentism can begin to be seen in the notion of natural ordering and a contemplation of the significance of violations of this ordering.

There is no doubt that it is out of fashion to speak of a natural ordering to the world in this day and age. To do so in the context of a network ecology immediately raises questions regarding the grand narratives that are so derided by the prophets of postmodernism. It brings us very quickly into uncomfortable questions of how our own personal narratives or the narratives of our communities relate to the grand narrative of ordering in the world. As Charles Taylor and George Grant suggest, however, it is impossible to avoid all grand narratives because they are essential to our thought processes and our actions. Our behaviour depends upon narratives that contain considerations of what life is all about, what is taking place in human history, and how our lives might fit into this history.[36] In short, we inevitably depend upon assessments and articulations of how the movements of our lives map onto the movement of the world around us (i.e. what we will call "politicization" in the discussion that follows).

This kind of transcendental argument has purchase because it makes little sense to speak of movement without a background against which the movement can be perceived. Without a natural ordering in the world, all one can do is engage in self-referential, ad hoc negations that are perpetually immanent and, due to what I would argue is the persisting resonance of a grand narrative, continue to hold a vague promise of transcendence. The immediacy of deconstructionist immanentism seeks presence in the world as a self-exclusionary action but this reflexivity simply projects a negative image of its own self-limitation and, in so doing, obscures the beyond that allowed the reflexive projection in the first place.[37] I would like to suggest that the attempt to move away from speaking about a natural ordering in the world is not only ultimately futile, but can actually be quite harmful in its denial of the political. The safety and sterility of denying and undermining the dynamic interplay between grand narratives and personal narratives serves to obscure structural violence that comes from beyond ourselves. Let me try to explain this a bit more ...

We cannot help but speak of a natural ordering to the world and we are led into trouble if we attempt to deny that we rely upon it. This

36 Taylor, *A Secular Age*, 573, and Grant, *Philosophy in the Mass Age*, 14.
37 Blond, "Introduction," 1–66.

argument will take much more work but, first, what might we mean by "natural"? Does natural mean, as is so commonly suggested, the material world that exists independently (i.e. without the control or influence of humans) of human activity? Or, by "natural" do we mean the innate or essential character or quality of something? Certainly, "natural" can be technically defined in a number of ways. In everyday life, though, we typically understand something as natural if it possesses a kind of relative permanence or persistence. And, indeed, both of the definitions above rely upon this conception of natural. Existence that is independent from humanity is perceived by us humans who, in a sense, look outwards from ourselves at a kind of background or environment within which we are living our lives. In the second definition, we understand an essential quality of something as that which persists despite relatively superficial changes to a thing's character or environment.

So, naturally, change is a matter of perspective and the persistence that is "the natural" is no different. Persistence or permanence is relative; it is a stability that is relative to that which is changing around or in relation to it. Further, this relative persistence is only understood from our perspective as humans living as embodied, historical beings. Grand narratives, therefore, should be understood as narratives against which or within which we can perceive ourselves as moving through our own personal narratives (just as we can only perceive grand narratives relative to our own personal narratives).[38] The "natural" is what we understand to be relatively stable and persistent in ourselves and in the world around us. Finally, although we tend to categorize things into natural and unnatural, we should remember that the natural (a) is relative, (b) exists on a spectrum, and (c) is always contestable. In this sense, therefore, the natural is fundamentally political.

It seems quite clear that folks like Latour and Gilles Deleuze – being, themselves, part of a rapidly changing technological society – no longer perceive a deeper persistence that we used to perceive. The exercise of self-determining freedom is the highest meaning that can be found by immanentists because all differentials between a personal narrative and a grand narrative have been eclipsed by a fixation upon one's personal narrative manifest in techniques of control. A vision of the differential has dissolved into the quest for technique that will advance one's personal

---

38 We should also note that a grand narrative such as "natural ordering" is only seen – and only makes sense – to the degree that we view it in relation to ourselves. It is nonsensical, in other words, to speak of a kind of freestanding grand narrative. Indeed, to do so is actually to obscure the grand narrative – i.e. a grand narrative cannot be approached directly, it is always relative to the one approaching it, it is always political, it is always negotiated ...

narrative independently of any other narrative. In other words, the internalization of this quest for freedom has disallowed the perception and articulation of narrative differentials among immanentist philosophers.[39]

If there is ordering or patterning that makes up our world and we can recognize (at least to some degree) the ordering, we are well placed to recognize and articulate structural violations of this ordering. We are better able to identify structural violence at work within our world. This new approach to focusing on structural violence, in turn, allows us to better address four core problems facing us in liberal capitalist countries – social isolationism, colonial relations with indigenous peoples, ecological destruction, and the cosmopolitan search for perpetual peace.

First, this network ecology holds the potential for giving us a lens through which we might recognize the violence of the liberal state-market collusion and begin working towards the densification of reciprocal social relations, the development of social capital. The loss of resilient, reciprocal communal relations in America and Britain since the 1960s has been thoroughly chronicled by Robert Putnam in *Bowling Alone* and by Philip Blond in *Red Tory*.[40] A combination of market liberalism and state liberalism built upon an ontological and political individualism has created a social crisis in liberal capitalist countries. As Philip Blond writes, "we can see and feel the effects of this social crisis all around us – our receding trust in others, the normalisation of antisocial behaviour, our fear of children in the streets, our political and civic disengagement, spiralling rates of drug and alcohol abuse, high levels of dependency on state income and personal debt."[41] This social crisis has been fostered by a political ontology and political economy that oscillates between the individual (individuated subject) and the state (totalized subject). Alasdair MacIntyre also picks up on the problem of this individual-state dualism when he notes that "the continuously reestablished dominance of markets, factories and finally bureaucracies over individuals, themselves sometimes conceived of as independent, rational beings, prescribing their moral standpoint to themselves, and sometimes as anomic products of circumstance, whose happiness must be contrived for them."[42] Therefore, a network ecology approach will hopefully allow us to develop a political ontology and economy that avoids the dualism disintegrating the civic middle and undermining democratic community.

39   Grant, *Technology and Empire*, 139.
40   Putnam, *Bowling Alone*; and Blond, *Red Tory*.
41   Ibid., 73.
42   MacIntyre, *After Virtue*, 212.

Second, we can begin to see the opportunities for creating resistance to imperial violence when we consider anew the central reason behind our belief that imperialism is immoral. The classic liberal tale we are told is that imperialism violates an inherent right to self-determination. So, under the liberal model of self-government, there is a tendency to understand the reason for the liberty as simply being that which supports more liberty. For example, as James Tully writes, "self-government enables Aboriginal peoples, just as it enables non-Aboriginal peoples, to participate in governing their societies in accord with their own laws and cultural understanding of democracy, to overcome alienation and to regain their dignity as equal and active citizens."[43] It should certainly be noted that liberal communitarians who tend to be skeptical of liberalism's atomistic ontology will resist the notion that the *only* thing wrong with imperialism is that it violates and inherent right to self-determination. Quite the contrary. They will contend that there is a fundamental link between negative and positive freedom such that collective self-determination is not achieved simply by doing away with (political, moral, or material) restraint, but is only achieved by allowing healthy cultures and communities to develop. In other words, there can be no collective will being exercised in self-determination without the existence of a collective to exercise its will. Civic self-determination, therefore, is a primary good but vibrant communal relations (and perhaps healthy relationships with the earth) are necessary means to this end. Or, put another way, liberalism depends upon the existence and persistence of a community that develops the background context from which judgments as to the relative importance of obstacles to action can be made.

The network ecology approach, however, provides us with an approach to political ontology that enables us to turn this logic on its head such that civic self-determination is understood not as the end, but as the means to another end. Namely, that of being good, of being in non-dominating relation with each other and the earth. And, not only that, but self-determination is neither a necessary nor a sufficient condition of being good. So, not only does it rule out the romantic notion that "each person's [or community's] form of self-realization is original to him/her, and can therefore only be worked out independently," the negative liberty approach in which "it is a sufficient condition of one's being free that nothing stand in the way," and the republican approach "according to which men's ruling themselves is seen as an activity valuable in itself."[44]

43 Tully, *Democracy and Civic Freedom*, 252.
44 Taylor, "What's Wrong with Negative Liberty," 212–13.

It also rules out the liberal notion that freedom itself (whether negative or positive or some combination of both) is an inherent good. Imperialism is a wrong, therefore, not because it denies indigenous peoples control, but because it poses an existential threat to indigenous peoples – it takes away their ability to be good people. For example, as Johnny Mack makes clear in "Hoquotist," the Nuu-chah-nulth people have become deeply disoriented as a result of no longer knowing their storied traditions.[45] This disorientation that continues to take place through colonial relations represents an existential threat because the denial of the ability to be good – the denial of the ability to understand and fulfill their responsibilities to the land as Nuu-chah-nulth people – means the Nuu-chah-nulth people are unable to be true to who they are. Becoming reconnected with the perceptual orientation and responsibilities that flowed from the traditional stories, then, is not a *means* to an end (e.g. a means to self-determination), but it is the end itself.

If we understand ourselves and our world as res ecologia as outlined above, we will see the notion of self-determination as an attempt to avoid vulnerability and, therefore, as incoherent as a normative end. If we are able to focus on processes of pattern making and what this does to the integrity of wholing patterns, we can better recognize standardizations that undermine the deep pluralism of network ecology. If we put the good of resilient communities foremost in our analysis and back it up with a robust ontology of interconnectedness, we will be better placed to undermine the structural domination of imperialism. Putting the right of liberal procedures foremost will, despite attempts to avoid an atomistic ontology, blind us to the structural shifts present in twenty-first century imperialism manifest through standardizations of communications processes and normative evaluations. Further, one of the implications of the network ecology approach is that imperialism is understood to be bad for not only those who have been denied self-determination, but also for those who have colonialized as a part of their self-determination. So, imperialism is bad not only for those on the outside of the power flow (i.e. indigenous peoples – "the determined"), but also for those inside the power flow (i.e. settlers – "the self-determining").

Third, there is an opportunity for creating resistance to the structural violence of ecological destruction through the development of the political ontology of network ecology. As Michael M'Gonigle has so aptly pointed out, the legal and political discourse rooted in liberal values and institutions have been propping up an unsustainable political economy

---

45 Mack, "Hoquotist," 287–307.

that is rapidly leading to, for example, climate change, species extinction, loss of agricultural land, collapsing fisheries, and the destruction of habitat. He argues, therefore, for a green legal theory that "eschews the limited focus of environmental law on the physical environment in favour of a critical and more complete understanding of the social and institutional dynamics of unsustainability."[46] Network ecology represents a political ontology in keeping with this challenge to burst the discourse of liberal political theory that upholds an unsustainable political economy. As we saw above in our discussion of Polyani and C.B. Macpherson, the connection between liberal political ontology and liberal economics is significant, and a political ontology that is focussed on the rates of change in pattern formation holds the potential for fostering a political economy rooted in sustainable thought and practice. Indeed, it is one step toward the "common, integrated framework for the critique of both human domination and the domination of nature" that Plumwood has called for in *Feminism and the Mastery of Nature*.[47]

Fourth, a network ecology allows us to reaffirm the importance of a historical approach to political ontology. As should become clear in the discussion that follows, the dualistic logic of normativity underlying the liberal approach to ontology and political economy operates as a denial of history and presents itself as permanent order. It is, in this sense, in keeping with the logic of rule outlined by Michael Hardt and Antonio Negri in *Empire*. As they write: "Empire presents its rule not as a transitory moment in the movement of history, but as a regime with no temporal boundaries and in this sense outside of history or at the end of history." Or, "in other words, Empire presents its order as permanent, eternal, and necessary."[48] Unlike the dualistic logic of liberalism, a network ecology is all about the changes in history that shape and reshape ourselves and our world. For, indeed, between the singular (subject) and the totality (object) everything is in flux and this relational flux disrupts all attempts to create a perpetual peace of absolute dualism.[49]

B. THE SELF AS RES ECOLOGIA

The network self is best understood in contrast to what has been described as the modern self. The modern self – clearly expressed by Kant – is a creature that is independent, rational, powerful, lonely, free, cold,

---

46 M'Gonigle, "Green Legal Theory," 35.
47 Plumwood, *Feminism*, 1–2.
48 Hardt and Negri, *Empire*, 11.
49 Of course, see Kant, *To Perpetual Peace*.

calculating, and emotionally detached. This confident, yet deeply misguided, creature is increasingly alienated from the world around him
because he is driven by a quest to avoid anthropocentrism or the subjectification of the world around him. Indeed, he is tragic in his futile struggle both to withdraw from the world and yet simultaneously grasp the
nature of the world. As Latour notes, the Kantian dream of formulating
a clear and distinct divide between subjective and objective was actually
a kind of science-fiction nightmare – "the outside world now turns
around the mind-in-the-vat, which dictates most of that world's laws, laws
it has extracted from itself without help from anyone else. A crippled
despot now ruled the world of reality."[50] The network self is dramatically
different than the detached and controlling modern self.

The network self is highly vulnerable to disruption and entirely dependent upon that which is outside ourselves. Further, this persistent vulnerability causes great anxiety and we seek, in numerous different ways, to
limit or even escape our fundamental dependence on the world around
us. There have always been attempts to mediate or control this deep dependence, but the modern era represents a new development in our
understanding of the relationship between ourselves and the world.
And, indeed, the modern self is probably best characterized by the idea
that we exist in sharp distinction from the rest of the world such that,
whereas the self is a subject and is to be known subjectively, the world is
objective and to be known objectively. Of course, though, this radical
distinction between subject (self) and object (world) and the idea that
the self can be self-determining, is no more than a myth. The modern
self is a mythical creature (albeit a powerful one) that has developed in
keeping with the increased anxiety stemming from the idea that the self
was fundamentally isolated or self-contained within a disenchanted universe. In other words, the modern self has developed to protect us from
our vulnerability through the myth that we are free in the sense that we
develop our values and purpose in life from within ourselves rather than
from our relation to the orderings of the world around us. The modern
self, then, became a mythical monster that seeks to dominate humanity
in order to stamp out the inhumanity of either mob rule or the evil dictator. The modern self is a benevolent dictator who uses the inhumanity of
the objective world to subdue any inhumanity within humanity itself.[51]

Turning to the network self represents a rejection of the Kantian fan-
tasy of humanizing (subjectifying) humanity by means of the inhuman

50 Latour, *Pandora's Hope*, 6.
51 Ibid., 15.

(objective world outside the self). It means, along with Latour, a rejection of the subjective/objective divide and an embrace of the vitality of the world within which the self lives and moves and has its being. In other words, things – both human and nonhuman – possess a persistent historicity by virtue of their ongoing presencing as beings-in-the-world (to use Heideggerian language) with a reality of existence that is relative to their place within network patternings of the world. The network self, as all things, does not simply exist or not exist but exists in various degrees through time and it articulates and is articulated in its relations with a whole ecology of res ecologia. The network self is, therefore, also itself understood as res ecologia – an ecological thing. The subject is best understood as not being one with itself or a complete whole in itself (contra Kant's account of the unity of consciousness in the transcendental unity of apperception), but is a plurality or multiplicity. In this sense, a search for a new political ecology rooted in the structure and processes of distributive networks means deconstructing the binary opposition between particularity and universality – i.e. in denying the dualistic logic of simultaneous individuation and totalization underlying the ontology and politics of liberalism. A purely particular singularity in a "subject position" is problematic because it contains within it the notion of a fixed position within a totality. The network self, as a nested network pattern that is in constant flux, has a position, but it is not fixed within a totality. Likewise, the self has no centre, but it is a patterning that has an integrity that comes from beyond perception.

The self exists as a pattern development process that is highly vulnerable to disruption and entirely dependent upon the not-self. The story we tell of political action-coordination – the coming together in political community or corporatization – in liberal political theory is a tale of attempted escape from our fundamental (i.e. existential) vulnerability as "selves." The myth of the autonomous will developed as little more than a kind of fairy tale told to hide the reality of a deep dependence. The central problem that political theory is meant to solve then becomes one of legitimacy in relation to this idea of the autonomous will. That is, how might persons come together in political community and still retain autonomous wills? The political theory project, then, develops as an attempt to provide a solution for an imagined problem. This failure to recognize the impossibility of escaping this vulnerability through the ideal of a transcendent self is the primary failure of modern political philosophy. The inability to recognize this inescapable vulnerability not only led to certain structures and processes of political organization, but was itself inspired and affirmed by these same organizational behaviours in a kind of vicious circle. Indeed the practices of nation building through the development of a common citizenry under common laws allowed blind spots to grow in our understanding of the self and its place in the world. For example, as Tully writes, "modern citizenship was nationalized as local citizenship was subalternised. Generations of 'locals' were gradually socialized by education, urbanization, military duty, industrialization and techniques of citizenisation to see themselves first and foremost as members of an abstract and disembedded imaginary community of nation, *demos* and *nomos* of formally equal citizens."[52]

The pattern of the self is active, it is a struggle of reconfiguration and this struggle is misguided and futile insofar as it represents a struggle for self-preservation through autonomy – i.e. preservation through an overcoming of vulnerability. The process of abstraction and the regulation of the relations between the self and the not-self will be discussed in more detail below in terms of protocolic control, but it should be noted at this time that I am not suggesting that the not-self is never in a domineering relation with the self (i.e. as if the relation of dependence were never problematic), it is just that the attempt to escape this domination – if it is to be more successful – must be more attentive to the inescapable nature of the dependence inherent within the self itself. What we are seeking is the development of political structures and processes that enhance the mutually creative process between the self and the not-self. This mutually creative process is also described as a process of legitimation – i.e. a projection of the imagination into the future or the development of a trajectory. Phenomenologically, this entails the building of hope for the future. So, at root, we are seeking the avoidance of excessive disruption (i.e. domination) in the relations between the self and the world.

What then does this mean for the self as an embodied being? In order to get at some idea of a localized or embodied self, we must consider our understandings of the good that arises from bodily instincts (i.e. arise from the nature of our bodies as a certain kind of organism) as well as habitual practices (i.e. arise from the nature of our lives within certain environments). What we might call instincts and practices form our understandings of our self and our place in the world that, in turn, form the foundation for politics as such. Not only *who* the "we" and the "they" are in our conceptions of community, but *how* we go about determining who the "we" and the "they" are is rooted in our notions of the self and its place in the world. Our instincts and practices (and their relation to the world around us) make up who we are – our onto-episteme, our

52 Tully, *Imperialism and Civic Freedom*, 255.

knowing-being. For, indeed, knowing-being is the potentiality for becoming political-being.

Immediately, doubts arise. Why say it holds simply the *potential* for being political? Is not *all* of our being political? In order to answer these questions, we need first consider the implications of the network ontology – res ecologia – outlined above for our understanding of the ontology of the self. That is, what do we mean by the "knowing-being" of the self?

First, we should acknowledge that our being is best characterized as simultaneously a unity and a multiplicity (it is, in this sense, in the image of the triune godhead who articulates us into existence by saying "Let Us Make Man in Our Image"). This deep complexity within our being means we will do well to follow the basic insight of Karl Marx, Søren Kierkegaard, Sigmund Freud, and Friedrich Nietzsche that the true nature of the self is not open and transparent to itself. Further, following the structuralist and poststructuralist more radical decentring of the self, we will do well to resist the inclination to view the self as a unitary subject, as an individual unit with a singular identity. As Alan How puts it, this means that "individuals are never fixed entities but always self-divided, they need to meet the needs of others to be themselves, but equally have an inner life, which pulls them away from being the stable product of socialization via others."[53] I do, however, make a difference between a "decentring of the self" on one hand (in which subjectivity is preserved – albeit as a fundamentally divisive subject) and a "destruction of the self" on the other hand (in which subjectivity is reduced to nothing more than an effect of a signifying system of discourse). I find the latter approach to be excessively reductionist and abstractionist in its own retreat from the real lives of persons in the world. On the one hand it is important, therefore, that we find an approach to understanding the self that does not become entrenched within a full-blown ontological description that would limit us to a singular idea of "the authentic self" that was inevitably based upon our current assumptions. However, it is also important that we do not reify symbolic patterns and disregard the social and material realities of our existence. Either approach – albeit in different ways – holds the danger of uncritically becoming satisfied with the current state of affairs in the world. Instead, we should focus upon a self (a self with real needs and interests) that exists, changes, and struggles to understand itself based upon the systemic conditions of society as a being that is both unity and multiplicity as a patterning process. This

53 How, *Critical Theory*, 150.

approach may be seen as a shifting balance that, due to its perpetual indeterminacy, means self-understanding is never fully satisfactory but is in
keeping with our notion of an active, developing network self.

There is, therefore, a "mode" of our being that is not political being.
And, to develop a better awareness of being that is not political being (or
the distinction between knowing-being and political-being), we can look
to the ontological hermeneutics of Heidegger and Hans-Georg Gadamer.
According to Heidegger, hermeneutics within the Enlightenment project was built upon a Cartesian conception of the self as an abstract and
disembodied thinker and therefore ignored the pre-scientific elements
of our being in the world. Heidegger suggested that ontology becomes
hermeneutics as this being produces the meaning of everyday life.
Understanding is a basic mode of being in the world and interpretation
is something that a person *is*, rather than an activity in which s/he con-
sciously does or does not engage.[54] This means, for Heidegger, that our
being is *fundamentally* hermeneutic and does not depend upon reflective
cognitive activity for an interpretative impulse. Gadamer, as a student of
Heidegger, then established this ontological turn in hermeneutics that
his teacher began and endeavoured to demonstrate the historical situatedness of human existence. Our historical situatedness means, to put it
very simply, that our understanding is determined within and through
history. As Gadamer writes, "reason exists for us only in concrete, historical terms, i.e. it is not its own master, but remains constantly dependent
on the given circumstances in which it operates."[55] This means that all
understanding is tradition-bound and even self-understanding and critical thought are coloured by the prejudices of our being-in-history.
Indeed, Gadamer argued that the Enlightenment thinkers' focus upon
independent reason and the denigration of prejudices sought to move
human understanding into the ideal realm of absolute reason. Habermas,
failing to recognize the depth of being active and present "behind" or
"beyond" understanding, seeks to understand all being. And, therefore,
he simultaneously seeks to politicize all being. But, we will do well to remember the connection Imre Lakatos draws between the truth and the
darkness in his correspondence with Paul Feyerabend. As he wrote,
"Lucifer is the chap who brings false light … I am shrouding you in the
darkness of truth."[56] And, truly, the network self transcends the division
between light and darkness.

---

54 See Heidegger, "Phenomenology and Fundamental Ontology," 215.
55 Gadamer, "The Historicity of Understanding," 260.
56 Lakatos, "Lakatos to Feyerabend," in *For and Against Method*, 313, quoted in
Motterlini, "Reconstructing Lakatos," 507.

Our understanding of our ontological situation is determined by preju-dices; they make up the horizon of a specific life-situation because they establish the limits of our being-in-the-world. But, this horizon of the present is under perpetual revision as prejudices are tested, in large part, by engagements with our past and our traditions. So, understanding, as a mode of our historical being in the world, involves a fusion of horizons – a testing of prejudices and perspective-building movement between see-ing the whole in terms of the parts as well as seeing the parts in terms of the whole (i.e. a "hermeneutical circle"). Understanding, like our exis-tence, always remains indeterminate and subject to revision – there is a fundamentally unshakable and ever-present ignorance. Our very exis-tence is caught up in the interplay between the past and the present or, in other words, our being is always less conscious being than simple being.

This notion of historical being is reinforced by Latour's idea of dis-tributive being. Latour suggests that we need to rethink our metaphysics of history such that a thing, a fact, a human, a non-human is understood to be persistently historical in its relative existence. What this means, to put it very simply, is that existence takes work, it takes a whole network of actions to exist and this existence is dependent upon, or relative to, these creative or supportive actions. As he writes, "an entity gains in reality if it is associated with many others that are viewed as collaborating with it. It loses reality if, on the contrary, it has to shed associates or collaborators (human and nonhuman)." There is, therefore, "no final stage in which historicity will be surpassed, with the entity *relayed into eternity by inertia, ahistoricity, and naturalness.*"[57] The history of being is brought to a halt when the self is solidified or reified as a self-contained beingness that self-perpetuates or self-directs its own being and identity. Without inde-terminacy in the self, there can be no continued history of the self. If we apply this basic insight of Latour we realize that the self too is persistently historical – it is an interaction that continues to take place as a succession of events, as an ongoing patterning of movements.

Importantly, the self is not simply historical such that if we dig deeper we begin to realize that our being is given to us, but our very continued existence is also dependent upon a network of actions. So, the historicity of the self goes down deep, deeper than our capacity for self-assertion, deeper than our understanding. The being of the self is knowable (by the self and the other), even outside the understanding, unlike the Kantian *Ding an sich*. I say it is knowable because understanding is best thought of as the articulation of thought by the mind and, in this way, as

57 Latour, *Pandora's Hope*, 158, emphasis in original.

akin to what is typically conceived of as self-reflective consciousness. The articulation of thought by the rest of the body (but not by the mind) is knowing without understanding – a kind of unreflective or unarticulated consciousness. This knowing without understanding takes place in our instincts and practices and their relation to the world around us. This relation between understanding and knowledge is why our thought and beliefs are often developed by the practices of the body without conscious thought. For example, we come to understanding after repeated practices or patterns of action with our bodies acting in certain patterns of relations with the world around us. So, the self is never *fully* known by the self; it is never fully *knowable*. Historicity, then, goes as far as our knowing-being and, beyond that, is rooted in the mystery of our being that comes from beyond ourselves.

To summarize, we have briefly discussed the notion that our being is not all political being. However, in this age of immanence, this is a bold claim that deserves more explanation. Let us go back, therefore, to the most basic explanation of res ecologia outlined above and, specifically, to the two central ways in which our existence transcends our understanding: ecologically and historically. In our discussion of res ecologia above we have outlined a portion of what is meant by "ecologically." And, with the help of Gadamer in this section, we have considered the historical nature of the self in its knowing-being. In order to understand political being, we need to now turn to consider what we mean by "the political."

By now, in the self as res ecologia we have clearly rejected out of the hand the modern conception of the self as a self-contained and self-directed being as well as the postmodern notion of the self as a purely political being. But where does the self as res ecologia leave us when it comes to questions of identity and the nature of the political? How might we conceive of the political if we were committed to a different political ontology? If we were committed to an ontology that is deeply relational rather than atomistic or simply antagonistic and if we viewed our relationality as extending beyond a bare social oppositionalism to encompass our social, material, and spiritual relations? If we understood ourselves as res ecologia?

The political of res ecologia is always present as a potentiality ready to be made incarnate because the political is a contestation regarding ourselves and our place in the world, a contestation of our being-in-the-world. There is always a latent or background politicization taking place insofar as we often understand ourselves and always act as beings-in-relation to others and the world. But this diffuse political being only becomes acute or definite – becomes truly visible to us – when a contestation becomes localized. Indeed, all politics is local because it is the move from the local to the global that is the making of something political; this translation is what reveals, what articulates that which is already latent and diffuse. Articulating the global or broader significance of things is the making of things public, it is politicization.[58] Therefore, the political is always at hand, it is always potentially made manifest. The political, then, is an "apocalypse" in the classic sense – a "revelation," "revealing," or "disclosure of what was previously invisible."

Importantly, the political is also an attentiveness to the relations in patternings; it is a politicization of ourselves in relation to things (both human and nonhuman). Things (in the substantively relational sense), therefore, are political to varying degrees depending upon how directly they are contested with reference to public being – depending upon the degree to which they are politicized. Because politicization always involves someone (or group of people) acting in relation to some thing, politicization always also politicizes the self. The making public of things is always also the making of oneself public in relation to a thing such that politicization is a threefold relation between things local, things global, and the self as local-global. It is not something achieved as the end of the story but is an ongoing relationship that is persistently historical in its relationality. Because politicization is a threefold relation, to the degree that a person is ungrounded, he is unable to make things public. He is unable to find the local in a way that he can articulate it sufficiently to translate it into the global in an ongoing revelatory relationship.

What then do I mean by the articulation of the local and how does it relate to the development of political identity? For, indeed, we cannot speak of the political and of politicization without also speaking of political identity. The political identity of the self takes place in and through the development of the relationship between knowledge and understanding that we just discussed. Identity is a manifestation of self-understanding and self-understanding is politicized knowledge – i.e. knowledge that is internalized and articulated by the mind such that it is (a) localized and then (b) conceived in relation to the transcendent (in relation to the world of the self). The process of politicization, therefore, means the translation of knowledge into understanding. The development of knowledge, and hence the articulation of knowledge, takes place through

58 Politicization is an apocalypse (a revealing or making visible) of a contestation between ourselves and the world that takes place through a movement from the local to the global and back again. It is an articulation of the broader significance of things – the making of res publica. The making of public things is always also the making of oneself public in relation to a thing such that politicization is a threefold relation between things local, things global, and the self as local-global.

communicative interactions (both human and non-human). What this means for the development of political identity, then, is that that which is outside the self (whether human or non-human) determines to a great degree the politicization of knowledge or the self-understanding of the self. In other words, the formation of political identity takes place within the interaction between the self and the world because knowledge is not possessed by the self, but accessed by the self in and through his acting in relation to the world around the self. Of course, then, the self can be known by the other or understood by the other in a way that the self is not known or understood by the self or, indeed, *cannot* be known or understood by the self. Self-understanding, like the political more generally, is always present as a potentiality but the one whose understanding is as extensive as his knowledge – a fully conscious being – we call God.

It should be clear by now that the ability to politicize is not the ability of an individual as an isolated, self-contained being. It is not about individual self-expression because the very actions of politicization are, by definition, the self-in-relation-to-the-world and this relation is deeply reflexive in its rearticulation of the relations of the self-world. Deviation from the givenness of patterning could, then, originate from either "within" or "without" the self – i.e. as an act of the imagination and will of the self or as a violation arising from a force of power working upon the self. What does it mean, in normative terms, to develop one's political identity or the identity of another being (either human or nonhuman)? For, according to the notion of political identity outlined here, identity is not simply a romantic ideal of self-expression but arises from and is dependent upon a process of interaction between the self and the world in a way that reveals the deep dependence and persistent vulnerability of the self. Identity is primarily given to the self (we are more being than conscious or self-directed being) so deviation from the givenness of identity ensures one's politicizations are (at least somewhat) disruptive of the existing patternings of the self and the world. It makes one's politicization violent – disruptive – toward the self and the world and, of course, this violation of patternings in the self and the world has normative import. What this means, of course, is that there is a kind of identity one *should* have, or at least there is a way one should have an identity. The historical/relational nature of political identity for the res ecologia means there is a *might be* as well as a *should be* in dependent relation to that which *has been*. Identity is not simply what *is* but what *might be* as a result of what is and has been. If it is too strong, the violence of politicization that disrupts existing patternings denies the possibility of making things public by denying a person or being's ability to locate things and translate them into contested things – there is a way of politicizing that takes away the ability of a thing to politicize itself in relation to the world around it. Democracy, then, is the search for a balance that allows for the politicization of all things – i.e. not the *actual* politicization of all things, but the *potential* for all things to be politicized. I don't believe, therefore, that one should politicize in a way that takes away a person's ability to politicize as they ought to. For the potential for deviation to arise from both "inside" and "outside" the self means that both the self and the world have responsibilities pertaining to the development of one's identity.

The connection between the *is* and the *ought* of this approach to political identity has been expressed quite clearly by Alasdair MacIntyre in *After Virtue*. As he writes: "I am never able to seek for the good or exercise the virtues only *qua* individual. But it is not just that different individuals live in different social circumstances; it is also that we all approach our own circumstances as bearers of a particular social identity. Hence what is good for me has to be the good for one who inhabits these roles. As such, I inherit from the past of my family, my city, my tribe, my nation, a variety of debts, inheritances, rightful expectations and obligations. These constitute the given of my life, my moral starting point."[59] This conception of a particular social identity has certain normative implications rooted in a historical conception of the self. MacIntyre continues to suggest that "I am what I may justifiably be taken by others to be in the course of living out a story that runs from my birth to my death; I am the *subject* of a history that is my own and no one else's, that has its own peculiar meaning."[60] He emphasizes the importance of the fact that being the subject of a lifetime narrative means that one is responsible for certain actions and experiences – i.e. responsible in the sense that local events and relational patternings are connected to larger or more global patternings. In this sense, then, being a subject of a history assumes a certain degree of politicization, but a politicization that is always purposive in the sense that its future will demonstrate a certain degree of continuity with its past. The self as res ecologia, therefore, has its identity shaped by its embeddedness and nesting within larger network patternings. This does not mean that, because the self has to develop its political identity in and through larger patternings, the self cannot (or should not) innovate through disruption. Yet neither is the self whatever it chooses to be. Nor, for that matter, is there a creation of identity (or inherent moral worth) in bursting the boundaries of particularity by moving beyond the "moral *limitations* of

---

59 MacIntyre, *After Virtue*, 204–5.
60 Ibid., 202.

the particularity of those forms of community" (e.g. MacIntyre)[61] or in the unrestricted ability to "*move around* within one's history and culture, to *distance oneself* from particular cultural roles, to *autonomously choose* which features of the cultural tradition are most worth developing, and which are without value" (e.g. Will Kymlicka).[62] Instead, the self is *always* and *necessarily* embedded within network patternings so there are no boundaries to be burst to create the self. The patternings are shaped by moral innovation, but they always persist despite the violence of pattern disruption through politicization. The patternings are, for example, ecological, spiritual, and economic and therefore go well beyond human community or cultural particularities.

Before moving forward, we would do well to consider some of the implications this network ontology might have for our understanding of law and political economy. Kymlicka correctly argues that liberal freedom means an individual subject can transcend culture and community – i.e. that the good life is one that is self-directed based upon our personal values and that each consumer-individual is free to question and rework these values as he see fit.[63] However, as Slavoj Žižek has noted, this notion of cultural transcendence is rooted in a highly problematic Cartesian/Kantian understanding of the subject. He writes, "this subject is conceived of as capable of stepping outside his particular cultural/ social roots and asserting his full autonomy and universality – the grounding experience of Descartes's position of universal doubt is precisely a 'multicultural' experience of how one's own tradition is no better than what appears to us the 'eccentric' traditions of others."[64] Based on this conception of the subject, justice is the setting of those conditions within society that will allow for individuals to engage equally in shopping around for values that fit their own understanding of the good life; the good of justice is transformed into the "right of moral independence."[65]

It is important to recognize that although Kymlicka is correct that the liberal idea of freedom is centred upon independent self-determination, he is fundamentally mistaken in his support for this approach to political identity. His seemingly attentive sensitivity to the pervasion of culture (and therefore the impossibilities of neutrality in governing institutions and processes) leads him to set aside the vision of the ideal demos in

61 Ibid., 205.

62 Kymlicka, "Liberalism and the Politicization of Ethnicity," 256.

63 See Kymlicka, "Liberalism and Communitarianism," 183–4.

64 Žižek, *Violence*, 121. A striking example of this kind of subject may be seen in Judith Butler's notion of gender identity as performative. For example, see Butler, *Gender Trouble.*

65 See Kymlicka, "Liberalism and Communitarianism," 184–5.

which all citizens are freely and equally united under a single common citizenry.[66] Instead, though, he advances a vision of a common citizenry at the sub-state level in a drive toward a kind of sectional homogeneity or fractured universalism that remains true to the ideal of equality. Culture then becomes little more than a context for individual choice within which each citizen has equal choice by virtue of their claim to a (now contextualized and multicultural) universal citizenship. However, as Andrea Baumeister notes, this kind of multicultural citizenship is not only problematic, but openly rejected by advocates of diversity who understand that his "emphasis upon liberal values will threaten the long-term viability of cultural groups who value autonomy and individual liberty much less than liberals." That is, these kinds of attempts "to ground a theory of group rights in equality of respect and individual freedom continue to be premised upon the Enlightenment principles of self-conscious reflection and individual self-determination" and are, therefore, highly problematic.[67] The politics of difference we see in theorists like Kymlicka is certainly a positive step forward beyond what he calls "liberal orthodoxy"; there should be little doubt that it represents a kindler and gentler liberalism. However, this conception of multicultural citizenship continues to be rooted in a deeper theoretical commitment in which the pursuit of the good life is conceived of as a fundamentally personal project in which each person has the same stake.

The issue, at the political level, seems to come down to one of incorporation. The liberal approach is to privilege universal (and, by extension, individualistic) incorporation while more traditional approaches to citizenship privilege consociational (and, by extension, pluralistic communal) incorporation. The "traditional liberal conception of citizenship has rested on the belief that differences, be they in terms of gender, race or ethnicity, should not affect our standing as citizens."[68] Differences between individuals are, therefore, perceived to be merely contingent and secondary to the characteristics all humans hold in common. This notion of justice rooted in subject-object dualism (i.e. a simultaneous individuation and totalization) at the theoretical level inevitably produces a homogenizing impulse at the political level in, for example, the notion of a common citizenry. Further, adherence to universal maxims (e.g. Kant's deontological or Mill's utilitarian or Rawls' hybrid) will inevitably lead to gross distortions of network patternings as they take place

66 For example, see Kymlicka, "Liberalism and the Politicization of Ethnicity," 239–56.
67 Baumeister, *Liberalism and the "Politics of Difference,"* 107, 171.
68 Ibid., 6.

in the lives of individuals (and these distortions dislocate so violently that they disallow people's ability to be good). Indeed, constructivist notions of justice cannot foster virtue as a wrestling with rules nor develop the morality of law needed for deep pluralism because, without understanding the teleological nature of life, morality is destined to be understood as embedded in the formal laws of the modern state. This drive toward statism takes place because if, as David Hume, Kant, Rawls, etc. suggest, virtues are simply dispositions toward following the rules, then we are in a bind because the rules must be determined before virtues can be determined. However, an atomistic ontology means that the development (rather than the discovery) of common rules is problematic and requires the top-down imposition of something like a modern state institution – i.e. the universal is understood to be pre-political. Thus, without understanding the narrative/teleological nature of life and political identity, the virtues lose their dynamic relationship with law and without this dynamism, law totalizes in its normativity.[69]

C. ACCELERATION

The central, overarching concern here is how this dualistic logic disrupts patterning processes of ourselves and the world. We cannot adequately understand this disruption, however, unless we consider the changing rates of change within the flux of these patterning processes. And, thus, we turn to the concept of acceleration ...

Our world is accelerating. Capital has become hyper-mobile. Our transportation systems are moving people and products around the globe faster than ever before. Mobile communication technologies mean that, for the most part, we no longer plan ahead, we simply coordinate in real-time.[70] But, our world is not the only thing speeding up. _We_ are speeding up, our very selves are accelerating. We not only hurry through life from event to event, meeting to meeting, task to task, but we are moving so fast forward that we are losing our connection with our past and this disconnection has existential and hence normative implications. Indeed, we are moving so fast that we are not even sure we have a history that defines who we are. We are going so fast we are experiencing a kind of tunnel vision that prevents us from recognizing the patternings in and around us. We can no longer see, hear, or feel ourselves and the world around us. We can no longer remember who we are and what we are doing on this earth.

---

69 MacIntyre, _After Virtue_, 216.
70 See, for example, Shirky, _Here Comes Everybody_.

We are analogue beings living digital lives. Our speed is fragmenting our very being with immanent pattern-shifts that hold us captivated by nothing more than a vague promise of transcendence. But this cannot last. We are not atemporal. Our being is historical and a digitalization of life disconnects us from our past, from who we are. In so doing, our speed fragments our very being, it detaches us from our historical being, it denies us the ability to politicize as we should.

Before digging deeper into this notion of acceleration, we should note that acceleration is the central concern that guides this work. The relational ontology of res ecologia serves as background for gaining perspective on the systemic violence of acceleration. A political ontology of network patternings aids us in assessing the connections between an atomistic political ontology and liberalism's political economy. In the chapters that follow, we will also begin to explore an understanding of structural causation in order to also gain perspective on the nature of the causes driving acceleration in the twenty-first century. But first, what do I mean by "acceleration"?

I mean the speeding-up of nearly all elements of our lives – computation, communication, transportation, resource extraction, manufacturing, consumption, increasing rates of change in familial relations, religious practices, sexual practices, vocations, fashions, and lifestyles.[71] Indeed, nothing remains untouched by this speeding up. And, it is important to remember up front that moving faster, acceleration, is not simply *more* movement – it is *different* movement. As Hartmut Rosa points out, just as "the acceleration of a sequence of pictures beyond a certain speed can suddenly bring it to life, in that a movie emerges from individual photos, or again as the accelerated motion of molecules alters at critical points the aggregate condition of matter (frozen, liquid, gaseous), so too the acceleration of social processes beyond certain speeds causes a transmutation of these processes themselves."[72] The ontology of res ecologia discussed above should make it clear that our being is historical and, therefore, changes in the rates of flux within patternings means fundamental, qualitative changes in who and what we are. Or, as Rosa explains, "individual as well as collective human existence is in its very essence temporal and processual; changes in temporal structures

---

71 As Hartmut Rosa writes, "rates of change themselves are changing. Thus, attitudes and values as well as fashions and lifestyles, social relations and obligations as well as groups, classes, or milieus, social languages as well as forms of practice and habits, are said to change at ever-increasing rates." Rosa, "Social Acceleration," in Rosa and Scheuerman, *High-Speed Society*, 83.

72 Rosa, *Social Acceleration*, 24.

are changes in individual and social existence."[73] Changes in our temporal structures transform our culture, economy, and understandings of personal identity, as well as our relation to nature. Hence acceleration is not simply a *quantitative* speeding-up, it is a *qualitative* change that takes place within material, social, and spiritual relations that make up our being-in-the-world.

So, everything in the world around us, and indeed, our very selves, is speeding up and not only is this acceleration pervasive, but it is transformative. The forward thrust of acceleration has very real material, social, and spiritual consequences.

In his 1970 bestseller *Future Shock*, Alvin Toffler described "the shattering stress and disorientation that we induce in individuals by subjecting them to too much change in too short a time."[74] Toffler was careful to emphasize the fact that the *rate* of change has implications and significance distinct from the *direction* of change. As he writes, "no attempt to understand adaptivity can succeed until this fact is grasped. Any attempt to define the 'content' of change must include the consequences of pace itself as part of that content."[75] However, although Toffler was certainly correct to focus on rates of change in his diagnosis of the ills of modern industrial society, he lacked the foundational ontology of interconnectedness in network patterning that is required if we are to understand the depth of the transformations taking place in acceleration. He was correct to point to the increased levels of anxiety and disorientation among individuals living within advanced industrial societies, but he did not offer a deep analysis or critique of the underlying logic behind the drive to accelerate.

Much like Toffler, William Scheuerman argues that a heightened rate of technological innovation, accelerated patterns of change in the workplace and family, and the rise of high-speed communication and transportation have produced the social acceleration of time. He notes that traditional institutions of liberal democracy (e.g. a separation of power) are grounded in temporal assumptions and, more importantly, "the legitimacy of liberal democratic rule is predicated on the necessity of wide-ranging but time-consuming deliberation and debate."[76] Therefore, he is concerned that our history has created a rift between our socio-economic life and our liberal institutions of deliberation and representation for self-governance. However, although Scheuerman correctly points us toward

73   Rosa, "Social Acceleration," 111.
74   Toffler, *Future Shock*, 2.
75   Ibid., 3.
76   Scheuerman, *Liberal Democracy*, 3, 4.

the problem of change he, like Toffler, lacks the perspective of structural change and therefore lacks a certain depth in both the diagnosis and remedy for the problem. So, for example, he seeks to protect the liberal democratic model of governance from the pressures of acceleration, rather than problematizing the ontology and economy of liberal democracy itself. Because they do not seek to dissect the logic of acceleration – to unearth the ontological and epistemological underpinnings of the drive to accelerate – neither Toffler nor Scheuerman offer us (a) a thorough diagnosis of the violence of acceleration or (b) a way of living and thinking that is resilient in its resistance to acceleration.

If we are to dissect the logic of acceleration, we need to be attentive to the high-speed global economy that forms our way of life by structuring the limits of our thought and action. For, as James Tully reminds us, "social action [or, for that matter, social theory] will be critical and effective only if it is based on an understanding of, and oriented in relation to, the specific relations of communication and governance in which it is situated."[77] And there can be little doubt that the liberal capitalist societies face some significant challenges as a result of globalized markets and rapid social change as we move into the twenty-first century. Dramatic advances in transportation and communications technologies have led to the creation of global markets that are high-speed, volatile, and driven by capital mobility unimagined even one hundred years ago. Additionally, the shifting demographics of more mobile populations and aging citizens is redefining the formal economy, straining the traditional models of social security, and undermining traditional ways of life. Changes in family, church, and gender roles have added further complications to regulation and public service delivery. These challenges are present within liberal, capitalist countries around the globe and have been developing rapidly since the middle of the twentieth century. What is very new, however, is the rise of the information age (e.g. the internet, mobile communications technology, etc.) and the redefinition of action-coordination that has arisen in response. No longer are organizational institutions necessary to reduce the transaction costs of action-coordination. With spectacular advancements in computation and communications technology, coordination costs have become dramatically cheaper. Communication networks, therefore, have formed and developed rapidly with user-generated content online and, indeed, as Castells notes, changes in communications have significant implications. "Networks constitute the new social morphology of our societies, and the diffusion of networking logic substantially

---

77 Tully, *Imperialism and Civic Freedom*, 186.

modifies the operation and outcomes in processes of production, experience, power and culture."[78] Therefore, acceleration may be understood
as a distinct feature of modern industrial, capitalist society and its inherent push to achieve ever-increasing levels of efficiency within processes
of interaction.

In the discussion of the self as res ecologia above, we noted MacIntyre's
explanation of political identity as historical being. The self, therefore, is
not simply a succession of psychological states or events (as the empiricists would suggest), but is a subject with a unique history – and this
subject can be held responsible for certain actions and experiences at
any time.[79] This responsibility can only take place, however, if the more
local relational patternings are articulated in connection with larger,
more global patternings. And, of course, this connection depends upon
both continuity throughout time and resonance between patternings.
The image I used above is that of the comparison between analogue and
digital – we are analogue beings living digital lives. The connection between patternings that makes up our identities, because it depends upon
continuity through time, relies upon a certain rate of change that begins
to fragment if it is accelerated too much. And, of course, this should not
surprise us given the fact that our lives are made up of biological processes that take place according to a certain rate of change and are limited in their speeds. Additionally, purposiveness in life is the imaginative
projection or extension of a trajectory into the future. If our rate of
change is so fast that we are unable to retain contact with the past and
our place within its narrative flow, however, we will likewise be unable to
project ourselves into the future. Purposive imaginings rely upon memo-
ries so if the patternings are so disrupted that we can no longer recognize them, we will be unable to extend or expand them into the future.
Without sufficient continuity and resonance, our being will be fragment-
ed and dominated by the tyranny of the now, we will be smothered by an
oppressive immanence.

It should be clear by now that acceleration does not refer simply to the
speeding up of, say, events in the daily lives of individuals caught up
in the rat race of career development. Nor is it simply a psychological
phenomena that irritates those within major urban centres; it is altering our very being by changing how we understand ourselves and our
relation to the world around us. But acceleration cannot be adequately

---

78 Castells, *The Rise of the Network Society*, 469.
79 See MacIntyre, *After Virtue*, 202.

understood and its significance for political and legal theory cannot be fully appreciated until we recognize the causal logic underlying its rise in modern industrial societies and the essential role standardization plays in this logic.

So, in conclusion, let us briefly consider one aspect of the underlying logic behind the acceleration of industrial, capitalist society by looking at the development of mechanized time. Theorists of time often begin their analysis of social acceleration with the development of the mechanical clock and its dramatic acceptance, use, and internalization around the globe. The "regime of the clock" or the "first empire of speed" during the modern, industrial era was a period within which "time was transformed from a mode of subjective experience into an abstract value."[80] Clock time was, therefore, the imposition of a kind of mathematical grid overlaid upon natural, more fluid, timescapes. As Hassan writes concerning the mechanical clock, "its strict analogue logic cuts through the weaved intersections of times that constitute our ongoing temporal becoming. Instead it grids social and natural timescapes with a mathematical logic that produces a synchronization of the world in accordance with a Pythagorean *kosmos* where all things may be conceived of as number."[81] The development of a common metric for measuring the movement of time meant the homogenization and universalization of an abstract evaluation process – hours, minutes, and seconds (all ordered across the globe since the introduction of Standard Time in the late nineteenth century). Without speculating too much, it is safe to say that this standardization of time measurement – i.e. coordination and universal synchronization – developed out of the human thirst for control. For without standardization (a process of abstraction away from the different temporal experiences of various locales) there could be no effective prediction of events and, therefore, no effective coordination of actions across vast distances. The abstract common metric embodied in the use of the mechanized clock, therefore, did not directly create the social acceleration of time; it created the means of standardization which in turn allowed for acceleration based upon a human drive for control and efficiency. Acceleration, in this way, is facilitated and fuelled by standardization. But more on this below.

---

80 Hassan, *Empires of Speed*, 55–6.
81 Ibid., 52.

CONCLUSION

In this chapter, I put forward a bold proposal: we need to re-imagine our political ontology in order to begin seeing how things and our very selves come to us from beyond ourselves. I led us into a discussion, therefore, of how we might best conceive of the nature of a thing and the nature of ourselves as res ecologia. We saw how things and ourselves are patternings that are vulnerable to disruptions that distort their nature or their network integrity. Rejecting a radical immanentism that decries all talk of structures or patternings that come from beyond ourselves, we began developing a way of speaking that is attentive to natural ordering processes in ourselves and the world. I suggested, therefore, that our politicization of things as well as our political identities are best conceived of as processes that we participate in rather than create. It is the integrity of these larger processes that gives us normativity and the capacity to make normative judgments regarding disruptions to relations within and between things and ourselves.

Although much more work needs to be done, we have already begun to recognize that a reworking of our political ontology is needed if we are to develop a language of political normativity that is not reproducing the violence at work within the liberal tradition. Now, although we may see how acceleration in patterning processes could alter the nature of these processes, we have yet to explore in detail why this is so and why this change should be of concern to us. It is to this end that we now turn in chapter 2.

2

Violence and Domination

A. STRUCTURAL CAUSATION
The pattern flux of networks produces a stability that persists through time and develops a kind of internal purposiveness.

B. POWER AND VIOLENCE
Violence is best understood as a violation of the patterning flux of networks.

C. RETHINKING DOMINATION
Domination is not dependence, but excessive violence that disrupts the nature of the networks.

INTRODUCTION

We concluded the last chapter with some discussion of the problem of acceleration and the fact that temporal changes in patterning processes are not simply quantitative, but are qualitative. Faster is not just more, it is different. Acceleration disrupts and displaces within the patternings to not just threaten their stability, but to change their very nature.

In order to understand better in what manner acceleration alters patternings, it is necessary to outline what is meant by "power," "violence," and "domination." That is, if we are to become more attentive to the violence of liberalism, we need to have a clear sense of what we mean by "violence." Only in this way can we begin to understand the injustices that are produced and re-produced by the liberal tradition.

In this chapter I will begin with a suggestion that we view causation within patternings as producing a stability that persists through time and develops a kind of internal purposiveness. I invite readers to consider premodern ways of thinking about causation and shift from thinking about relations between individual things to contemplating the shifting structures of things. Recent work in theoretical ecology then brings some focus to this discussion of structural causation, and network patternings are viewed from the perspective at which they are seen to be self-structuring. This self-structuring gives patternings a kind of integrity that is susceptible to disruption. Violence, then, is seen to be a violation of the patternings and domination is an excessive violence that causes a significant disruption of the integrity of network patternings.

This rethinking of violence and domination represents a shift in our understanding of some of the fundamental questions of political philosophy. Once we question the human and social ontology of the liberal tradition and begin to view ourselves as res ecologia – as deeply dependent and persistently vulnerable networks that are tied into the fabric of the world around us – we find ourselves drawn away from the liberal conception of domination that has become so prevalent in the political theory of our day. That is, instead of the problem of domination being understood primarily as a problem of dependence, disruption becomes the primary framework shaping and guiding our recognition of excessive violence in the world. We begin to get a sense that something is wrong when families, communities, and ecosystems are being disrupted and are less concerned when we see that an individual person lives in a deeply dependent relationship with others.

Before we dive into these definitions in more detail, it is interesting to note with Niklas Luhmann that our level of satisfaction with the current state of society will significantly determine the degree to which we open up the definitions of "power," "violence," and "domination." "If one is convinced in advance that the society in which we live is constructed improperly," he writes, "then one will choose a very broad, limitless concept of power. In this way one devises for oneself and others an addressee of criticism."[1] In other words, the problem of power, violence, and domination is articulated with at least some sort of a solution – say, some notion of justice – already in the back of our minds. I am happy to acknowledge that the definitions of "power," "violence," and "domination" that follow are developed with a view to what I take to be the central challenges facing a search for democratic governance in a liberal world. But, not only is the problem pursued with the solution in mind. As Steven Lukes points out, engaging in disputes regarding the nature of power – that is, how power should be defined – is itself to engage in politics. Definitions of power, violence, and domination – and, consequently,

---

1 Luhmann, *Political Theory in the Welfare State,* 156.

uses of these definitions in political philosophy – are inextricably tied into a set of value-assumptions that determine the range of applications available to the theoretical concepts involved.[2] But, if our definitions are value-laden and developed in keeping with the normative ideals we already possess, how much can we really expect from such definitions? Can they bring us any degree of theoretical clarity?

Perhaps our expectations regarding term definitions are best kept in check by learning from the shift that took place in Wittgenstein's thinking, specifically the evolution of his thought on the issue of analytic philosophy's quest for certainty. The analytic tradition in philosophy, with its roots firmly planted in the Enlightenment, places significant emphasis on precision in thought and language and tends to approach concepts of human nature, truth, and justice in somewhat ahistorical terms. Philosophers like Bertrand Russell, therefore, sought to develop a language of logic that would allow philosophers to conceptualize and communicate with what was understood to be a kind of scientific precision.[3] Ludwig Wittgenstein, although beginning his philosophical work with this same quest for precision (see *Tractatus Logico-Philosophicus*) soon became aware of the fact that it was a mistake to demand too much precision from human expressions (see *Philosophical Investigations*). The meaning of words, he realized, was found in their use within a variety of "language games," and it was philosophy's task to serve as a therapeutic activity (a "critical hermeneutics") to relieve persons from the bewitchment of language and the quest for hidden meaning.[4] Wittgenstein surely seems to be correct when he argues that the meaning of a word lies in its use. However, as Wittgenstein also suggests, although we might grasp the meaning of a word in a flash, we do not grasp its use extended through time.[5] It simply is not possible to comprehend the complete *use* of a word – and therefore it is not possible to comprehend the complete *meaning* of a word either. It is this perpetual and persistent indeterminacy within the meaning of words that ensures that pursuit of exactitude in or finality of definition is a wild goose chase. It is this indeterminate and value-laden nature of meaning then that makes the question of the meaning (and hence significance of) violence a democratic question.

2 Lukes, *Power*, 30.

3 See, for example, Russell, "Introduction to *Principia Mathematica*," 161–3, and Russell, "Vagueness," 84–92.

4 Janik, "Wittgenstein's Critical Hermeneutics," 63.

5 Wittgenstein, *Philosophical Investigations*, 46.

A. STRUCTURAL CAUSATION

In the process of outlining a political ontology of res ecologia we are inevitably led to consider our understanding of the nature of causation. For example, not only does the talk of diffuse agency in network ecology but the phenomenological discussions of the active gathering and presencing of things – the coming to us as wholes from beyond – raise questions regarding causation. Further, it is quite clear that any definition of power, violence, and domination involves a background set of understandings regarding causation. To put it simply, talk of power is, at root, talk of someone or something (A) acting upon or influencing someone or something (B) – that is, A affects or changes B in some way. And, if we are dissecting causation, we need to ask two fundamental questions: "How do things persist through history?" and "How do things change?" Underlying a concern for systemic power flows, as outlined in this project, is a set of assumptions regarding structural or systemic causation. How persons develop in and through history. How patterns of ecological, social, and spiritual interaction develop in and through history. How persons affect patterns of ecological, social, and spiritual interaction. Further, if the distributive networks we are discussing here are also understood to be in flux and persistently indeterminate, how are we to conceive of the notion of domination as "excessively disruptive"? Not only how is disruption caused, then, but how might we begin to understand "excessive" change within a process of structural development?

The ideas of force, resistance, and disruption employed in the following discussion on power, violence, and domination are rooted in an understanding of causation that can be viewed as somewhat of a return to a premodern approach. Aristotle, as is well known, proposed that we are able to understand why something is the case through an investigation into its four causes – material, efficient, formal, and final.[6] Put very simply, the *material* cause describes the material out of which something is composed. The *efficient* (or mechanical) cause is that (e.g. agent, event, or state of affairs) which initiates change or halts change. The *formal* cause is that form to which a thing progresses. In a real sense, then, the formal cause informs us as to the nature or essence of a thing; it tells us what is being unfolded within the historical existence of a thing. For example, the form of a chicken is present within the fertilized egg. The formal cause is an essential pattern that is made manifest throughout the existence of a thing. It is the macrostructure of the whole that causes

6 Aristotle, *Physics*, 129, and Aristotle, *The Metaphysics*, 115.

the parts to behave in a certain manner and may, therefore, be understood as a kind of internal cause. The final cause (the *telos*) is the purpose for which something exists or for which something is accomplished. For example, a war is waged in order to enhance one's position in this world or the next. Of course, these four forms of causation were part of Aristotle's understanding of place and order and reflect his hierarchical approach to the universe.[7] These forms of causation possess an intrinsic hierarchy within Aristotelian thought in the sense that each form is operating at a different scale. The material and efficient causes operate most frequently within a limited subfield (from which their effects are understood to propagate up the scale of action). The formal cause is a meaningful focal point of observation and knowledge in that it maps out the essential nature or structure of something or some action. The formal cause, then, takes place beyond the thing itself and structures the entire existence of something or some action in relation to the rest of the world. The events at a certain level are contingent upon, but not necessarily determined by, events at the lower levels.[8] However, all levels of cause are needed if one is to reach understanding because, as Aristotle writes, "we never reckon that we understand a thing till we can give an account of its 'how and why,' it is clear that we must look into the 'how and why' of things coming into existence and passing out of it, or more generally into the essential constituents of physical change."[9] In other words, Aristotle understands that we do not have understanding of the physical world until we understand the nature and purpose of things and for this understanding we need to see all the causes. I tend to agree.

As noted in the last chapter, the seventeenth century marked a dramatic shift away from this kind of "Aristotelian" conception of the universe. Place, order, and causation began to be conceived of in what we now describe as modern terms. As Charles Taylor writes, "the world was no longer seen as the reflection of a cosmic order to which man was essentially related, but as a domain of neutral, contingent fact, to be mapped by the tracing of correlations, and ultimately manipulated in fulfillment of human purposes."[10] This new conception of the universe, not surprisingly, meant significant changes in politics – changes tied into not only atomistic notions of place (i.e. individual atoms existing in relation to a fixed framework of space and time), but also mechanistic notions of causation. At the beginning of the seventeenth century, a clear

7 Aristotle, *On the Heavens*, and Durham and Purrington, *Frame of the Universe*, 53ff.
8 Ulanowicz, *Ecology*, 12–13.
9 Aristotle, *Physics*, 129.
10 Taylor, *Hegel*, 539.

division begins to the made between natural science and metaphysics. And, more importantly, natural science begins to be concerned exclusively with material and efficient causes and metaphysics with formal and final causes. For example, as Francis Bacon writes in 1605 in his *The Advancement of Learning*: "For as we divided natural philosophy in general into the inquiry of causes, and productions of effects: so that part which concerneth the inquiry of causes we do subdivide according to the received and sound division of causes. The one part, which is physic, inquireth and handleth the material and efficient causes; and the other, which is metaphysic, handleth the formal and final causes."[11] This twofold division between the four causes of Aristotle is a significant step into what is now known as the modern era. This step was furthered by Hobbes' emphasis upon material existence and by Descartes' emphasis upon mechanical causation in his 1644 work *Principles of Philosophy*.[12] The final step into the era of modern science, however, came with the publication of Isaac Newton's *Philosophiae Naturalis Principia Mathematica* in 1687.[13] The *Principia* solidified the paramountcy of mechanical causation in natural science and, therefore, established the positivistic assumption that "natural systems are at some fundamental level actually governed by purely abstract laws that can be specified in terms of mathematical equations."[14] In other words, this commitment to mechanical causation was a dramatic step forward in the objectification of the world and, importantly, this objectification extended beyond our natural environment to "englobe human life and society and the result is a certain vision of man, an associationist psychology, utilitarian ethics, atomistic politics of social engineering, and ultimately a mechanistic science of man."[15]

If we are to move beyond reductionist conceptions of power and causation that objectify the world and subjectify the self, we need to begin looking beyond the material and efficient causes that have for so long dominated the modern worldview. As Menno Hulswit points out, in the classical (Aristotelian) conception, "causes are conceived as the active originators of a change that is brought about for the sake of some end" but in the modern approach there was "a strong tendency to understand causal relations as instances of deterministic laws. Causes were no

---

11 Bacon, *The Advancement of Learning*, 114.

12 For example, see Hobbes, "De Corpore (Concerning Body)," 9.7, and Descartes, *Principles of Philosophy*, 14–15.

13 See Newton, *The Mathematical Principles of Natural Philosophy (Philosophiae Naturalis Principia)*.

14 Wolfram, *A New Kind of Science*, 859.

15 Taylor, *Hegel*, 539.

longer seen as the active initiators of a change, but as inactive nodes in a law-like implication chain."[16] Therefore, not only was the efficient cause held to be the fundamental means of understanding the natural world, but the classical emphasis upon formal causation (the nature or patterning of a thing) gave way to the notion of pervasive or universal laws of nature. Both were attempts to explain the stability of the world around us: the former centred upon the *structure of things* whereas the latter centred upon the *relations between things*.[17] Moving beyond the re-ductionism of mechanical causation means beginning to once again ap-preciate how the structure of things persists and how these structures change through history.

The problem with the modern approach, then, is not the focus on rela-tions between things in itself. Rather, the problem lies in the fact that this focus upon laws of nature leads to an objectivist approach to causation in which the relations between things are understood as universal laws. In other words, all agency of structures is denied within a totalized, deter-ministic universe; all action, and therefore the development of system processes and patternings, is reduced to mechanical causation in which the activity of the parts defines and determines the activity of the wholes (à la Latour). Causal relations, then, seem to be (at least in theory) re-versible – i.e. if we go back in time, the effects of the causation would be undone.[18]

The modern reductionist/objectivist approach to causation has led to an unrealistic, bottom-up approach to understanding complex systems such that the prediction of all systems (regardless of their complexity) is considered to be theoretically possible; prediction is possible if only we have sufficient information regarding the parts of the system and the rules governing their behaviour. This failure to understand complexity has meant that, as Stephen Wolfram notes, "in the existing sciences much of the emphasis over the past century or so has been on breaking systems down to find their underlying parts, then trying to analyze these parts in as much detail as possible."[19] In the last few decades, scientists have increasingly run up against the limitations of this approach in, for

16 Hulswit, *From Cause to Causation*, 42, emphasis removed.

17 Ibid.

18 Mechanical causation, according to Charles Peirce, involves three key properties: (a) the end is entirely dependent upon the beginning, (b) the end can only be reached through a single process, and (c) the process by which the end state is reached is com-pletely reversible. See Robin, *Annotated Catalogue of the Papers of Charles S. Peirce*, 26–7. Also see Hulswit, *From Cause to Causation*, 82.

19 Wolfram, *A New Kind of Science*, 3.

example, measurement in quantum mechanics, prediction in chaos theory, and singularities in gravitation theory. More importantly for our discussion here, though, the limitation has been seen in complex systems theory in what Wolfram calls "computational irreducibility." Computational irreducibility means, for Wolfram, that if one considers the evolution of a system as a computation, the evolution of a complex system cannot simply be predicted through an understanding of the underlying rules of behaviour governing the parts within the system – even if one knows all the rules. He writes: "even if in principle one has all the information one needs to work out how some particular system will behave, it can still take an irreducible amount of computational work actually to do this. Indeed, whenever computational irreducibility exists in a system it means that in effect there can be no way to predict how the system will behave except by going through almost as many steps of computation as the evolution of the system itself."[20] The reason for this irreducibility lies in the fact that our system processes of observation and analysis are not more sophisticated than the system processes we are observing. Or, put another way, our powers of observation and analysis cannot outrun the computations of complex systems in our environment with more sophisticated computations. If we are seeking to understand how complex systems both persist and change despite our limited abilities, we have reason to focus our attention upon the self-structuring processes of complex living systems – i.e. what I am calling structural causation. We have reason to turn to structural causation because the reductionism of mechanistic causation is not only extremely limited, but tends to blind us to these limitations.

Giving attention to structural causation may be understood as a reflexive process of observation: it is a more holistic combination of both the system processes being observed and the system processes of observation themselves. Importantly, by "reflexive" I do not mean simply a matter of turning our minds to the system processes of observation but, instead, reflection upon the connectivity between the two system processes. And this connectivity may be understood by considering the computation of system processes. Engaging in a kind of computational reductionism that we must excuse for now, Wolfram explains his "Principle of Computational Equivalence": "any processes that are not obviously simple are equivalent in their computational sophistication. So this means that even though a system may have simple underlying rules its process of

---

20 Ibid., 739. What this means, therefore, is that "there is absolutely no reason to think that the specific concepts that have arisen so far in the history of mathematics should cover all of science." Ibid., 860.

evolution can still computationally be just as sophisticated as any of the processes we use for perception and analysis."[21] We can observe a kind of formal causation within complex network systems because "once a rather low threshold has been reached, any real system must exhibit essentially the same level of computational sophistication" – i.e. "observers will tend to be computationally equivalent to the systems they observe – with the inevitable consequence that they will consider the behavior of such systems complex."[22] The phenomenon of complexity in system processes (e.g. complex network patterning) itself, in other words, arises as a result of the connectivity between the self and the not-self. This connectivity is important because, unlike modern mechanistic science in which perception and analysis of humans is idealized such that they are assumed to be infinitely powerful, we now understand that making helpful conclusions about complex network systems means including the processes at work within the network system that is making the conclusions – i.e. ourselves.[23] Focusing on structural causation, therefore, is a reflexive process of understanding ourselves as network systems deeply rooted in an environment of network systems.[24]

So, we have some reason to consider a structural approach to understanding causation – it holds the promise of helping us understand ourselves and our place in the world. And, indeed, as Aristotle noted, causation is about how we know and understand ourselves and the world. But, how do we develop an approach to causation that allows us to better understand network relations and, consequently, better understand the analysis of power, violence, and domination? I propose we do this by turning to the science of ecological systems. For the study of living systems represents an excellent realm within which to consider organizational principles and the causation at work in organizational patternings. However, before briefly setting out an approach to understanding the origins of order in living systems, it is important to recognize that we no longer need to retain the deterministic assumptions accompanying a mechanistic approach to scientific investigations. The mechanism of the modern approach to science led ecosystem scientists to "portray an

21 Ibid., 736.
22 Ibid., 737.
23 Ibid., 736.
24 That is, structural causation – compared to computational irreducibility or computational equivalence – is more of an approach to understanding metaphysics than a statement regarding the need for epistemic humility. I suggest that Wolfram is more concerned with epistemology because he seems to be very concerned with arguing against a strong rationalist tradition in mathematics with a theory of necessarily experimental mathematics. For example, see Wolfram, *A New Kind of Science*, 772ff and 863.

ecosystem as a grand machine whose working parts are its component populations and whose linkages are its trophic and physical transfers."[25] We will turn, instead, to something like Karl Popper's post-positivist concept of indeterminacy in an attempt to better guide our consideration of the emergence and maintenance of order within living systems.[26]

Popper is perhaps best known for his critical rationalism in which he rejects classic accounts of empiricism (and the observationalist-inductivist approach to science that developed out of it) in favour of a falsifiable account. However, Popper was also clearly in opposition to the determinism of previous philosophies of science and made this explicit later in his life. For example in *A World of Propensities* Popper argues for a fundamental incompleteness in the causality of the universe and suggests that indeterminacy can arise at any level of causation; he proposes a kind of diachronic and relationally probabilistic approach to science. In order to demonstrate this, he distinguishes his *propensity* interpretation of probability from the *classic* theory of probability. He describes the classic theory as relying upon the following definition: "The probability of an event is the number of the favourable *possibilities* divided by the number of all the equal *possibilities*."[27] He then notes, however, that it is quite inappropriate to understand possibilities as *equal* possibilities and we should not speak of probabilities in simply a numerical sense. Instead, all possibilities would be better understood as weighted possibilities; certain possibilities and probabilities are greater than others. What this means, then, is that "a tendency or propensity to realize an event is, in general, *inherent in every possibility*." More generally, he concludes that "all this amounts to the fact that *determinism is simply mistaken*: all its traditional arguments have withered away and indeterminism and free will have become part of the physical and biological sciences."[28] The future is not fixed, it is objectively open (i.e. regardless of our knowledge of the future) much like the computational irreducibility of Wolfram's complex systems. Past situations influence and change propensities that in turn influence future situations – but none of this influence determines situations in a unique way. Thus, the world is fundamentally open, but it is not unstructured; the world is not without stability because propensities provide form and structuration without determining events.[29]

25   Ulanowicz, *Ecology*, 3. Also see Ulanowicz, "Perspectives."
26   See Popper, *A World of Propensities*.
27   Ibid., 9, emphasis in original.
28   Ibid., 11, 17, emphasis in original.
29   See ibid., 18. Also see Ulanowicz, "The Propensities of Evolving Systems," 217–33.

If we accept that the universe is open with a tendency (a propensity) inherent within every situation or step in the evolution of a system, then we should understand that both Newtonian reductionism and Aristotelian hierarchicalism are approaches to understanding causation that are fundamentally incomplete. As Robert Ulanowicz notes, under the propensity interpretation of probability, reductionism is incomplete because indeterminacy can arise at any level and hierarchicalism is incomplete because moving up through the higher levels of causal forms will not allow one to discover all the sufficient causes – even the full causal spectrum will have holes in it.[30] In contrast, what we might call an "ecological approach to causation" allows for a greater emphasis upon flux and process rather than place and individual organism. It allows us to recognize the fundamental indeterminacy that affects our observations at any scale of analysis. It allows us to also recognize, correspondingly, that causes might be originating at any scale of analysis. This ecological approach, therefore, provides us with the ideal domain in which to study organizational principles related to networks, an ideal place to rethink the nature of causation within and between res ecologia.

But, if causes might be originating at any scale of analysis, where do we begin this study of organizational principles? It is no longer productive to simply move to the lowest level and trace the causation up through the multiple system levels. Instead, we will do better if we not only look for the level of analysis at which the efficient cause is most clear, but also *look for the level at which the network system (patterning) appears to be self-structuring,* the level at which there is a persistence of form beyond the constituent parts. As Ulanowicz writes, "in an open universe, any configuration at a given scale can be somewhat autonomous of what transpires at finer resolutions. It becomes permissible, therefore, to concentrate on description at the focal level, while keeping implicit most of the contributions from finer scales."[31] Our focal level, therefore, becomes one that is as much as possible attuned to the ordering agencies of systems. In ecological study, then, this is typically known as an autocatalytic cycle. A three-component autocatalytic cycle takes place when an increase in a process (A) has a significant propensity to increase a second process (B), process B then has a significant propensity to increase a third process (C), and process C then feeds back positively into process A. Therefore, in an autocatalytic system, the propensities for positive feedback are greater than the decremental interferences; there is a power

30 Ulanowicz, *Ecology,* 37.
31 Ibid., 56.

flow internal to the system as a whole.[32] In order to make the persistence of the system-form more explicit, we need to consider the selection pressure within the system in which the system "whole" exerts a pressure upon the system "parts." The system-whole influences the system-parts when, as Ulanowicz writes, "if a random change should occur in the behavior of one member that either (a) makes it more sensitive to catalysis by the preceding element or (b) accelerates its catalytic influence upon the next compartment, then the effects of such alteration will return to the starting compartment as a reinforcement of the new behavior."[33] Further, the selection pressure within a system's autocatalytic behaviour is inherently asymmetric – i.e. there is a definite direction to the system in which the system-parts are driven towards higher levels of performance. We can, therefore, begin to see an ontology of systems emerging in which the autocatalytic cycle is not simply taking place as a result of the system's environmental pressure. Rather, the system has its own identity that develops in an active relation to its environment. Again, as Ulanowicz writes, "although the system requires material and mechanical elements, it is evident that some behaviors, especially those on a longer time scale, are, to a degree, *autonomous* of lower-level events."[34] It is at this level of autonomous organizational development of systems that I would suggest we will find the most rewarding understanding of organizational principles and systemic causation. It is at this level that we are able to focus on patterning processes (and understanding flows as causes) rather than objects as self-contained, interacting beings.

How then does this brief discussion of causation in complex systems give us insight into the nature of power, violence, and domination? What does this outline of a systems ontology mean for understanding violence as a disruption (and displacement) of the other? Or, finally, how might we now speak about domination as the excessive disruption of a system's development?

First, then, how is disruption caused? As we saw above, the distributive networks we are discussing in res ecologia are in flux and persistently indeterminate; network structures are always shifting and pervasive power relations that ensure a perpetual displacement and disruption (socially, materially, and spiritually). Ecological systems are always existing, changing, and developing in relation to their environment as material and energy are transferred between their system-parts and the world

---

32 See ibid., 42–3. For more on positive interactions within natural systems, see Bertness and Callaway, "Positive Interactions in Communities," 191–3.

33 Ulanowicz, *Ecology*, 46.

34 Ibid., 49.

around them. As changes in these transfers take place, autocatalytic systems (which are dependent upon their material components, but not determined) exert pressure upon their constituent parts (or processes) to change and thereby enhance their performance. However, this natural development process in which the autocatalytic cycle merely induces competition within the system is not what we might mean by disruption. This approach to disruption would be based upon the object-interaction approach to causation rather than the ecological patterning approach. Instead, disruption is better understood as changes in a system's environment (or a sub-system's system) that induce a system to depreciate or replace a constituent part (or process) although the form of the system might still persist. For example, imagine there is an autocatalytic cycle comprised of three elements – A, B, and C – and a fourth element (D) is introduced. Now, D is both more sensitive to catalysis by A than B and more positively enhancing to C than B. In this situation, the introduction of D will disrupt the system as D either grows to overshadow B within the cycle or even entirely displaces B.[35] Or, more practically, the introduction of high levels of toxins in the water table may disrupt an ecosystem when some species in the area are forced out or replaced by other species in response to the harsh conditions, but the ecosystem as a whole does not necessarily collapse. The disruption of a distributive network, therefore, is best understood as either a natural or an unnatural process – and, likewise as positive or negative – depending upon the severity of the disruption.

Second, how are we to begin understanding what we might mean by *excessive* disruption? As Ulanowicz reminds us, "in the absence of overwhelming external disturbances, living systems exhibit a natural propensity to increase in ascendency. The word *overwhelming* quantifying *disturbances* implies that living systems are always subjected to disturbances ... some minimal disturbance is required in order for a system to continue developing."[36] That is, an excessive disruption – i.e. one that is considered violent – may be seen as the change in a system's environment that brings about a new form or pattern to the system as a whole. It is the kind of change that does not allow the autocatalytic behaviour of the system to persist. It does not allow the system to increase its magnitude of activity and the coherency and organization of its internal processes – i.e. its ascendency.[37] In socio-political terms, we see that cultures are alive by witnessing their change and adaptation through history.

35 See ibid., 48.
36 Ibid., 75, some emphasis removed.
37 See ibid., 8–9.

What is really significant about this dynamism within cultures, though, is not the fact that they change but that they retain their continuity through the dramatic changes. In fact, as Jeremy Webber has aptly noted, we must recognize not only the communal richness, diversity, and contestability of a society's cultural traditions, but understand that the conflicts within a society are one of the key crucibles within which a common identity is developed. Therefore, culture "can be conceived of as the set of references, the ways of framing questions and making arguments, that distinguish one language of public debate from another and that are always subject to growth and evolution."[38] If the continuity of this evolutionary growth is threatened, then it is clear that violence is being done to a culture. The continuity of a living system like a culture is threatened when, for example, the system's internal complexity is reduced such that it can no longer adapt and change in response to pressures and disturbances within its environment. When the complex living system becomes machine-like in its singularity it loses its adaptability and, consequently, becomes increasingly vulnerable to threats.[39] Power becomes violent in its disruptive force when the thing upon which the power is acting is altered at a fundamental level; its identity or place in the world is shifted. Of course, there is a correspondence between the disruption of a society's culture and personal disruption. As Michael Chandler and Christopher Lalonde write regarding suicide rates within indigenous communities in Canada, "because it is constitutive of what it means to have or be a self to somehow count oneself as continuous in time, anyone whose identity is undermined by radical personal and cultural change is put at special risk to suicide for the reason that they lose those future commitments that are necessary to guarantee appropriate care and concern for their own well-being."[40] But, given this background discussion of structural causation, let us now go on to consider power and violence in more detail and in more political terms.

B. POWER AND VIOLENCE

One of the keys to deproblematizing difference lies in reconceiving the problem of violence and the ideal of non-domination. Liberal theorists like Hannah Arendt and Habermas, for example, tend to misunderstand the problem of violence. Consequently they develop systems of liberal

---

38 Webber, *Reimagining Canada*, 238.
39 Ulanowicz, *Ecology*, 77.
40 Chandler and Lalonde, "Cultural Continuity as a Hedge against Suicide in Canada's First Nations," 221.

democracy that perpetuate significant degrees of violence and, indeed, fail to provide a theoretical approach to governance that is thoroughly committed to the ideal of non-domination. In other words, I would suggest that Habermas sets out to build a system of depth hermeneutics – a theory of communicative action – that ends up providing a foundation for excessively violent politics. He understands ideology as inherently violent (or at least inherently prone to violence) and, consequently, works out a theory of rationality that is to provide us with a theoretical touchstone from which to overcome ideology – i.e. rationality essentially becomes ideological critique. However, if we are to avoid the finality of universalization present within liberal theory, it is much more appropriate to understand power (and violence) as unavoidably present and active within *both* ideology *and* rationality. As Mouffe writes, "according to the deliberative approach, the more democratic a society is, the less power would be constitutive of social relations. But if we accept that relations of power are constitutive of the social, then the main question for democratic politics is not how to eliminate power but how to constitute forms of power more compatible with democratic values."[41] Mouffe is correct to say (1) that relations of power are (at least partially) constitutive of social relations and (2) that democratic politics is not a way of eliminating power relations (i.e. flattening them), but of changing these relations to ensure they are more democratic. The problem, as we will see, is that Mouffe seems to misunderstand the nature of values that are thoroughly democratic. Her continued commitment to liberal ideals blinds her to the need for a more radical democracy. The goal in the rest of this chapter, therefore, is to develop the concept of democratic values in terms of violence and domination within the context of *pervasive* power relations within the structural causation at work within res ecologia.

Before moving on to talk about violence and domination, let us consider what we might mean by pervasive power relations. In order to begin the discussion in a way that will be helpful for the development of a network theory of democracy (a theory of governance that, hopefully, helps us reduce and prevent excessive violence), it is important to understand the structure of power as well as the immanence of power within social, material, and spiritual relations.

Power may be seen as change in network patternings. As we have just seen, these network patternings, although ever changing and subject to transformative reconfigurations, possess a kind of stability – a pattern of network formation that develops through time – such that change is

---

41 Mouffe, *The Democratic Paradox*, 100.

always met with a degree of resistance. In fact, due to the underlying and all-pervasive structural patternings of social, material, and spiritual networks that make up the world, there can be no such thing as absolute power just as there can be no such thing as absolute freedom. In this sense we may agree with Hegel's understanding of the destructive power of absolute freedom. Hegel's notion of absolute freedom was, as Taylor notes, "a conception of freedom which was sterile and empty in his eyes in that it left us with no reason to act in one way rather than another; and it was destructive, since in its emptiness it drives us to tear down any other positive work as a hindrance to freedom."[42] And, indeed, because of the prevalent structures of networks that make up the world, it is impossible to conceive of absolute power or freedom in this sense. Power and freedom simply do not make sense without an accompanying notion of resistance. But, importantly, power is also inherently active. That is, it is never possessed by a subject or an organization as if it were a self-contained object. Power *is* the change; it is inherently active because it *is* the activity of reconfiguration pushing against resistance.[43]

Power is a reconfiguring push against resistance; a disruptive force that changes patternings. In this sense, then, there is actually no such thing as symmetrical power relations. A power relation, by definition, involves an asymmetrical relation in which power is an active coercive push towards change within relations. As such, power is best understood in both quantitative and qualitative terms such that we see it as existing on a continuum with violence and domination but also as conceptually distinct. Violence is dramatic power (i.e. a notable differential in power relations) and domination is excessive violence. The qualitative distinction between power, violence, and domination may therefore be seen to be stemming from our negative normative judgment that the degree of

---

42 Taylor, *Hegel*, 557. As Hegel correctly noted, aspiration to this kind of freedom inspires and drives forward revolutionary impulses and inevitably leads to violent terror and totalitarianism. See ibid at 403ff.

43 Although he is mistaken to narrow the definition of power to the imposition of a will (and thereby seek to distinguish between human and non-human exercises of power), Max Weber is correct to note that power is a push against resistance. For example, he understands power as "the probability that one actor within a social relationship will be in a position to carry out his own will despite resistance, regardless of the basis on which this probability rests." Weber, *Economy and Society*, 53. The resistance in power use need not be explicit, but it must always be present. The resistance often festers below the surface as moral outrage and condemnation until it breaks out in open acts of rebellion or mental illness and mood disorders.

power is "excessive."[44] This agonistic conception of power is somewhat different from the non-coercive model of power that has grown up within the liberal democratic tradition of thought. For example, Hannah Arendt made a sharp delineation between power and violence, and suggested that "power corresponds to the human ability not just to act but act in concert. Power is never the property of an individual; it belongs to a group and remains in existence only so long as the group keeps together."[45] And, following Arendt's sharp delineation between power and violence, Habermas develops the notion of "communicative power" in which political power is produced through the coming together of beliefs (e.g. almost akin to the power produced in nuclear fusion). Habermas interprets this to mean that the roots of power are to be found in uncoerced communication – i.e. "the power of communication aimed at mutual understanding."[46] In order to have democratic legitimacy, then, Habermas argues that all manifestations of political power must derive from communicative power and law serves as the medium for translating communicative power into administrative power.[47] Because power is understood as uncoercive in the ideal, Habermas and his followers struggle to bridge the divide between the non-violent ideal and the political realities of asymmetrical power relations. That is, the ideal of uncoercive power is so otherworldly that it cannot be patriated or acclimatized to political society. Further, because it is akin to Hegel's absolute freedom in its impossibility and sterility, his uncoercive notion of power is destructive in its blinding us to its own power use. Practically speaking, then, Habermas seeks to work out an institutional solution to the problem of transforming communicative power into administrative power. However, as Scheuerman rightly suggests, Habermas struggles (unsuccessfully) to adequately analyze how deliberative processes rooted in mutual understanding can effectively guide decision-making within the administration itself.[48] It should become clear in what follows that an agonistic or coercive understanding of power provides us with a more productive framework for moving toward a theory of democratic governance that is inspired by genuinely democratic norms – i.e. norms that facilitate their own critique and, hence, help minimize excessive violence.

44 Our judgment concerning excessiveness, of course, is itself rooted in a certain understanding of the causation inherent within the development of network patternings.

45 Arendt, *On Violence*, 44, emphasis removed. Also see Arendt, *The Human Condition*, 199–207.

46 Habermas, *Between Facts and Norms*, 147–8. Also see Arendt, *On Revolution*, 175.

47 Habermas, *Between Facts and Norms*, 169, 192.

48 Scheuerman, "Between Radicalism and Resignation," 78–9.

Power can not only be understood structurally as reconfiguring shifts in network patterns (i.e. change taking place against resistance), but also as immanent within both citizens and society.[49] Power as immanent within society means that, as Manuel Castells notes, power is "no longer concentrated in institutions (the state), organizations (capitalist firms), or symbolic controllers (corporate media, churches). It is diffused in global networks of wealth, power, information, and images, which circulate and transmute in a system of variable geometry and dematerialized geography."[50] In previous times, power could be seen primarily in the relationship between a governor and the governed such that power acted upon subjects from outside their own actions. However, "what the theories of power of modernity were forced to consider transcendent, that is, external to productive and social relations, is here formed inside, immanent to the productive and social relations. Power, as it produces, organizes; as it organizes, it speaks and expresses itself as authority."[51] In addition, power as immanent within citizens means power relations (i.e. power differentials) work in and through persons to develop a certain kind of subject. As Tully (following Michel Foucault) explains, "every form of social ordering also has distinctive relations of power by which the conduct (roles) of those subject to it is ordered (governed). Furthermore, being subject to these relations of governance ... and acting in accordance with them over time gradually brings about and instils a corresponding form of subjectivity or subjectification."[52] Cognitive and behavioural patterns are developed in and through modes of relations whose shifts are internalized over time. Network selves are developed "through immersion in immaterial labour, of knowledge acting on knowledge, with its creativity, flexibility and openness, its compressed sense of time and space; its particular communicative and interactive skills of information processing, analysis of symbols, reduction of complex phenomena to an underlying and manipulable code, and problem-solving; its experience of being able to belong to contingent virtual communities and cultures and to modify or disconnect from them as one pleases; and its overriding sense of 'creative destructiveness' – that everything can be programmed and commodified."[53] A network approach to democracy means, therefore, a focus primarily upon production through power flows: both the production of objects for subjects (commodification) as well as the produc-

49 Tully, *Imperialism and Civic Freedom*, 183.
50 Castells, *The Power of Identity*, 359.
51 Hardt and Negri, *Empire*, 33.
52 Tully, *Imperialism and Civic Freedom*, 175.
53 Ibid., 176–7.

tions of subjects themselves (subjectification). In both areas, it is a *process* of production that is important.

It is important to note that, with its focus on structural processes and the deep dependence of political subjects, the ontology of res ecologia leads us into a conception of power that is somewhat different than that which we find in Foucault or Tully. As will become more clear in our discussion of protocol in chapter 3 below, Foucault understands the subject as being free to the degree that he faces an unrestricted field of possible actions – and power is a restriction on the field of possibilities open to a subject.[54] This emphasis upon self-determination is, of course, quite out of step with our own quest to understand structural violations and, especially, the disruptions of rapid change in the patternings of the world. To be fair, Foucault does understand there to be a dynamic interplay between the subject as agent and the world as governing processes – i.e. he does not develop an essentialist conception of freedom.[55] Thus, we arrive at a kind of immanent power that Tully describes as the governance of communicative relations in which power does not exclude the exercise of freedom (i.e. as self-determination) or impose upon passive subjects. Instead, power works in and through active and interactive agents as they alter communicative and material relationships.[56] However, this approach too is still somewhat lacking because, within this perspective – even if we are seeking to be attuned to changing rates of change – one may still conceive of power as a degree of change in which the agency of the person is becoming diminished. That is, power takes place in and through relations between agents that have some set of options available to them in response to the pressures of change. As these options diminish – say through an overwhelming pressure – power becomes violent in its disruptive force.[57] In the approach to power I am outlining here, however, the reduction of possible actions is not necessarily significant because there is no assumption of self-determination. In other words, the opening up of options can be at least as disruptive as a restriction of options when we believe there are patternings already at work in the world, patternings that make up ourselves and our world. Within the ontology of res ecologia, therefore, disruption itself rather than disruption that restricts an agent-subject is the focal point – power that dramatically either restricts or unrestricts will be problematic and violent by virtue of its disruption.

54 See Foucault, "The Subject and Power," 790.
55 Ibid.
56 Tully, *Imperialism and Civic Freedom*, 185.
57 Tully, *Democracy and Civic Freedom*, 23.

Given our understanding of power as reconfigurative action operating against resistance, violence may be best conceived of as power that is forceful enough to *significantly* alter network patterns of social, material, and spiritual relations. Again, from a structural perspective, violence may be best understood as taking place through rapid/dramatic change of network structures and processes. There is always change and flux in network patternings, but *dramatic* change is violence – it is doing violence to the integrity of the network system as a pattern of relations existing and persisting through time. For example, when discussing distributive networks, a change in the network pattern – i.e. to make a centralized or decentralized pattern – should be seen as undermining the integrity of the system. Likewise, movement toward Cartesian grid-like structures would be excessive change not only because it would be fundamentally altering the network pattern, but because it would remove a network from its nesting within larger distributive networks (or isolate a distributive network with a grid-like pattern).

In keeping with the network approach to democratic politics and the importance of interconnectedness within this approach, violence should be understood as inherently relational and taking place in the displacement and disruption of the other and/or the not-self. Or perhaps more correctly, violence should be understood to take place in a *deep* disruption and displacement of the other and/or the not-self. As we saw above, network structures are always shifting and pervasive power relations ensure a perpetual displacement and disruption (socially, materially, and spiritually). What then do we mean by "deep"? Although we will explore this question of qualitative assessment further in the last part of chapter 3 below, in very general terms deep disruption means power that is manifest in a violation of social, material, and spiritual network structures and processes such that the speed and degree of change threatens the stability of the patterning through history. Our ability to assess both the speed and the degree of change, of course, will depend very much upon our own patterning processes and relation to the patternings in question. But, as mentioned, we will return to this question in chapter 3.

For now, if we take the approach to understanding power and violence outlined above, it becomes quite clear that agonists such as Mouffe are correct to argue that every creation of a "we" is accompanied by the creation of a "them."[58] Two basic conclusions follow from this insight: (1) the violence of agreement takes place internally and externally and (2) there can be no thoroughly non-violent political action - i.e. poli-

---

58 For example, see Mouffe, "Deconstruction, Pragmatism and the Politics of Democracy," 9.

tical actions are disruptive by definition and, consequently, violent by definition.

The violence of agreement may be seen within the creation of the "we" (internal political relations) as well as the creation of the "them" (external political relations).[59] When we encounter an other, we do so from a certain contextual perspective – a human perspective that is not simply meted and bounded by presuppositions but, more accurately, lived in and through patterns of life. Therefore, when we do come together in agreement, what we are doing is developing a kind of *modus vivendi* (a way of living with some enhanced degrees of commonality). Likewise, when we disagree, we take up or continue in differing ways of life. An appropriately non-dominating politic, therefore, is not to be found in agreement or consensus (which would be excessively violent insofar as those with dramatically different patterns of life would be deeply displaced), but in a certain *way of disagreeing* – i.e. in a certain kind of lived opposition within one's form of life in one's economy and spirituality. In the process of creating a "we," patterns of life are transformed to come into greater accord. Also, in the process of creating a "we," patterns of life are transformed such that they begin to take on a significantly different role within broader patterns of social and material existence. The nesting patterns of society could be seen as becoming more fractal as those within the "we" become more and more similar. In contrast, the patterns of those within the "we" become increasingly unlike (or disconnected) the patterns of those within the "them." Indeed, the patterns of the "we" are created and nested in order to align those within the "we" in opposition to those within the "they" and thereby transform the patterning beyond the self.

The violence inherent within political action may be seen within the teachings of Mohandas Gandhi. According to Gandhi, satyagraha is a holding on to truth and this holding on to truth excludes violence because humans are finite and unable to know the absolute truth (and, consequently, are not competent enough to punish those who might oppress or abuse them).[60] However, it is precisely this "holding on to truth" that makes Gandhi's political philosophy of satyagraha violent. Indeed, although satyagraha involves the renouncement of all forms of physical violence towards others, it demands a significant degree of violence enacted upon his initiates (e.g. fasting, restrictions upon the diet, active embrace of physical violence enacted upon oneself, etc.) and upon others (i.e. through the coercion – be it the force of moral, psychological, etc. pressure – used to transform the other). A simple example

59 Sen, *Identity and Violence*, 2.
60 For example, see Gandhi, *Non-Violent Resistance*, 3.

of the kind of violence present within satyagraha may be seen in Gandhi's autobiography where he recounts a story of how he dealt with his wife Kasturba's illness. He suggested that she stop eating salt and pulses (i.e. high-protein legumes such as beans and lentils), in order to facilitate healing. And when she disagreed he vowed to give them up for one year whether or not she did. She was deeply disturbed and eventually promised to abstain. He notes that this made her very sorrowful and that she sought relief in tears. However, he also stated that he "would like to count this incident as an instance of Satyagraha and as one of the sweetest recollections of my life."[61] He then went on to admit that medically there were two opinions regarding the value of a saltless and pulseless diet but morally it was always beneficial to engage in self-denial.

The political philosophy of satyagraha is rooted in the *active* engagement of oppressors in order to transform the relationship between the oppressor and the oppressed. Instead of seeking to destroy the oppressor as if he were an enemy, the satyagrahi seeks to appeal to the goodness within the oppressor and redeem the relationship. In order to achieve a thoroughly non-violent way of life, one must become as passive as possible (the non-resistant passivity of those within the Mennonite tradition might come closer to achieving a more thoroughly non-violent approach to "political life"). For, indeed, it is the active pursuit of political engagement to fundamentally transform power relations – i.e. the force of restructuring network patterns – that ensures politics remains violent by definition. This explanation is not, of course, intended as a critique of Gandhi's political strategy or ethics. Far from it, in chapter 6 below, I will go on to argue for a politic and ethic much akin to Gandhi's as being the only genuinely democratic politic. Instead, this example is meant to reveal the nature of violence and its relation to power (as well as its moral neutrality). It is important to note that under the definition given here, violence is (like power) morally neutral in itself. So, although it holds the potential to be excessive in its disruptive power, it is also a part of political action and requires additional normative input (i.e. a judgment regarding what constitutes excessive) if it is to be moral or immoral.

C. RETHINKING DOMINATION

If we are at least somewhat sympathetic to the political ontology of res ecologia outlined above in chapter 1, we will need to rework our conception of domination in political theory and how it relates to the

---

61 Ibid., 5.

conception of violence we just outlined. That is, if we understand persons as deeply dependent and perpetually vulnerable patternings that politicize themselves and the world around them in a purposive articulation of their relationship to their world, we will need to reimagine domination in terms of pattern disruption rather than simply in terms of interference. And, in order to do this, we will need to move somewhat beyond the republican ideal of non-domination.

Neo-republicans such as Philip Pettit have argued that domination should be understood as the capacity to arbitrarily interfere. He writes that "someone dominates or subjugates another, to the extent that they have the capacity to interfere on an arbitrary basis in certain choices that the other is in a position to make."[62] Pettit then makes it clear that he wants to distinguish interference and domination and contends that one may suffer domination without interference. For example he writes "I may be the slave of another ... without actually being interfered with in any of my choices. It may just happen that my master is of a kindly and non-interfering disposition. Or it may just happen that I am cunning or fawning enough to be able to get away with doing whatever I like. I suffer domination to the extent that I have a master; I enjoy non-interference to the extent that that master fails to interfere."[63] Importantly, Pettit also suggests that the concept of domination depends upon the intention of the dominating party (at least to some degree). This means for him, then, that the domination cannot come from a system or network – the dominating party must be a personal or collective agent.[64] Pettit is very clear in his explanation but, as I hope to show below, his concept of domination – and therefore his concept of non-domination – is reliant upon a number of mistaken ontological and normative assumptions and is, consequently, quite unhelpful when seeking to develop what I understand to be more genuinely democratic norms of governance.

The republican notion of domination as the potential for the arbitrary imposition of negative consequences mistakenly assumes:

(a) the autonomy of persons,
(b) the need for an intention to dominate, and
(c) the kind of imposition is what determines whether or not there is domination – i.e. it is the *kind* of imposition rather than both the kind *and degree* of imposition.

62 Pettit, *Republicanism*, 52.
63 Ibid., 22–3. Also see Skinner, *Liberty before Liberalism*, 50–3, and Skinner, "A Third Concept of Liberty," 237.
64 See ibid., 52–3.

These three assumptions may be seen in the republican concern regarding dependence. Neo-republicans like Pettit and Quentin Skinner might argue whether or not republicans are concerned with domination or if they are concerned about both domination and interference,[65] but at root both – I would argue – are (mis)concerned regarding dependence.[66] Indeed, the shared notion that domination and interference can be separated is itself rooted in the misunderstanding that dependence is closely tied into domination. This misunderstanding is expressed by Skinner, for example, when he writes that "it is never necessary to suffer this kind of overt coercion in order to forfeit your civil liberty. You will also be rendered unfree if you merely fall into a condition of political subjection or dependence."[67]

Dependence, for the neo-republican, is the ultimate concern but exploring this concern a little more will allow us to tease out the three mistaken assumptions noted above before going on to develop what I am calling a network conception of domination stemming from an ontology of res ecologia. Let us begin with a consideration of three scenarios that give us hints regarding the misplaced concerns within the neo-republican notion of domination. The first demonstrates that the neo-republican definition is too broad, the second and third demonstrate that the neo-republican definition is too narrow. All three show that the neo-republican concerns regarding dependence are misplaced.

First, consider the loving father of a child (or, for that matter, God within Judaism, Christianity, and/or Islam) who possesses the capacity to interfere on an arbitrary basis in certain choices that the child or devotee is in a position to make – but the father or God refrains from doing so. Instead of harming the child or devotee, the father or God provides for the child or devotee and even ensures that they are protected from violence at the hands of enemies or potential enemies. The neo-republican conception of domination applies in these situations – i.e. the child and devotee are dominated because of the father's and God's

---

65 For example, see Pettit, "Keeping Republican Freedom Simple," 339.

66 This uneasiness regarding dependence has very deep roots in Western thought and, indeed, may be understood as a key concern underlying the rise of modern philosophy. As Philip Blond notes, the notion that God and his creation are distinguishable simply on qualitative terms (e.g. God has an absolute plenitude of being while creatures have finite quantities of being), once mixed with an analysis of power, allows those after William of Ockham to stress the utter defenselessness of creatures before God and the potentiality of his malign will. The moderns, therefore, seek to escape this potentiality through the self-assertion of humans in constructivism – i.e. an attempt to find an existential footing outside the continued benevolence of God. See Blond, "Introduction," 8–9.

67 Skinner, *Liberty before Liberalism*, 69.

capacity for arbitrary impositions.[68] However, despite their dramatic degree of dependence upon their father and God, surely neither the child nor the devotee in this scenario should be considered persons who are dominated. Something beyond dependence is needed for us to make the negative normative judgement of domination because the father and God are not disrupting and/or undermining the healthy development of the child and devotee. Rather, they are affirming the development of the child and devotee and providing protection from those who would seek to do violence. Now, if the father or God had either (a) a history of making negative impositions upon the child or devotee or (b) something in his nature that inclined him toward negative impositions, then things might be different. In other words, for there to be domination, those who are potentially subject to negative impositions must have a real sense of danger or a kind of pessimism concerning their relationship to the one possessing the capacity for negative impositions.

Second, consider an indigenous tribal community that has lived as hunter/gatherers for thousands of years, has traditions and laws that are rooted in a specific area of geography, and has only engaged in limited trade with similar tribes from time to time. Now, imagine a significant number of European capitalist settlers immigrating into the lands around this community and beginning to engage in trade and commerce with members of the tribal community. The settlers have every intention of engaging in extensive and fair negotiation with the community and ensuring not only that traditional lands and customs are unharmed, but that the community sees significant material benefit as a result of the trade. Despite the settlers' continued adherence to their initial positive intentions, over a couple of generations the indigenous community is pushed away from its traditional ways of life and gradually integrated into the capitalist economic system of the settlers. This movement, although it means a loss of traditional economic systems and a loss of their traditional legal system, allows the community, by any standard of the settler society, to grow materially wealthy from the trade. Would we not call this domination even if the impositions of the settlers were neither arbitrary nor based upon any intentions to harm. In other words, can we not quite easily understand systemic violence (in which there is no intentional agent, but a highly disruptive clash of two systems of

68 This same point may be made with the more counterintuitive example of a benevolent slavemaster. For example, as Pettit writes, "I may be dominated by another – for example, to go to the extreme case, I may be the slave of another – without actually being interfered with in any of my choices. It may just happen that my master is of a kindly and non-interfering disposition." Pettit, *Republicanism*, 22.

economic exchange rooted in dramatically different worldviews – one system dramatically more powerful than the other) as domination?

Third, consider the development of biotechnologies and intellectual property laws that allow corporations to build economies in which uniformity is produced through ever expanding monocultures. The development of biotechnologies and the creation of intellectual property laws facilitating the commodification of life are intended to allow for "fast-growing species" in forestry and "high-yielding varieties" in agriculture that are to increase productivity.[69] However, as Vandana Shiva has rightly argued, "corporate strategies and products can lead to diversification of commodities, they cannot enrich nature's diversity."[70] Instead, "biotechnologies are, in essence, technologies for the breeding of uniformity in plants and animals" because the commodification of life means that biodiversity becomes simply an input into an industrial machine rather than "the basis and foundation of production and economic activity."[71] In other words, the commodification of life forms and biodiversity means that "our relationship with the rest of the living world is no longer that of partner, but one of consumer and, for the corporations, that of creator."[72] Surely this abusive relation to the natural systems of the earth is one of domination and is relevant to political philosophy.[73] Importantly, this relationship of domination with the earth is not unidirectional – the earth also dominates human communities through the imposition of storms, droughts, and disease. Of course, as humans dominate the earth more and more, the earth will correspondingly dominate humans more and more. There is a cycle of domination that takes place between humans and the natural world.

What are we to conclude from these three scenarios? The first scenario reveals that the neo-republican definition of domination casts the net too wide and takes in healthy relationships of dependence based upon the mistaken assumption that persons should be politically autonomous

---

69 Shiva, "Biodiversity, Biotechnology and Profits," 48.

70 Ibid., 45.

71 Ibid., 44–5, emphasis removed.

72 Shiva, *Earth Democracy*, 41.

73 Pettit rejects the notion that political philosophy should be concerned with relations between humans and the earth. For example, he writes, "were non-intentional forms of obstruction also to count as interference, that would be to lose the distinction between securing people against the natural effects of chance and incapacity and scarcity and securing them against the things that they may try to do to one another. This distinction is of the first importance in political philosophy, and almost all traditions have marked it by associating a person's freedom with constraints only on more or less intentional interventions by others." Pettit, *Republicanism*, 52–3.

(i.e. either that they are already autonomous (ontologically) or should be made to be autonomous). The second scenario reveals that the neo-republican definition of domination is too narrow and fails to capture destructive relationships between systems of economic exchange and their corresponding worldviews. The third scenario also reveals that the neo-republican definition of domination is too narrow insofar as it fails to capture destructive relationships between humans' industrial economic activity and the natural bio-systems of the earth. All three scenarios demonstrate that the neo-republican conception of domination fails to provide us with an adequate basis for developing norms of non-domination. The mistaken assumptions regarding dependence (and, therefore, autonomy of persons, the role of intentions, and the nature of negative impositions) are rooted in concerns regarding totalitarian state powers that impose upon subjects primarily from the outside. The primary concern regarding domination in this day and age, however, is power that works in and through the social, material, and spiritual patternings of life to destroy social and biological (i.e. political) diversity. Domination from the perspective of the relational ontology or res ecologia, therefore, is not dependent upon assumptions regarding the autonomy of persons, the need for negative intentions, or the nature of negative impositions. And it is to this relational approach to domination that we now turn.

In the discussion above, we began to understand power as reconfigurative action operating against resistance and to see violence as power that is strong enough to significantly alter network patternings. Domination is, then, an excessive alteration of network patternings. For example, the violent push towards singularity – e.g. when a distributive network becomes Cartesian grid-like – may be understood as a primary example of domination within liberal capitalist societies. The singularity of regular grid-formation is found in its finality. As such, domination is excessively disruptive in its power-push against the stability and diversity of network patternings always shifting and changing in asymmetrical relations. Because networks and nested patterns of networks are constantly in flux, the introduction of a singularity represents dramatic or violent change.

Within the modern framework, the singularity of domination was imposed upon agents as if from the outside (e.g. in totalitarian regimes) through confinement. Within a network/control society, however, this singularity is introduced within the agents themselves through the protocolic drive toward harmonization and universalization. The "problem of diversity" has always been a problem for those who have the domineering perspective whether through a totalitarian regime or through a common protocol. The domineering perspective is rooted in norms that are tied into ideal abstractions that push toward a singularity. Further, the singularity of totalitarian regimes, I would argue, is actually less insidious than that which is at work in the modulations of protocolic control if we take the diachronic patterning nature of res ecologia seriously. For, indeed, there is something more deeply violent about a restructuring of systems of meaning and action – i.e. existential development – compared to external violence and the impositions of a top-down regime.

In order to understand the significance of domination and the extreme violence of this push toward the totality of singularity, we might benefit from a brief look into Emmanuel Levinas' conception of the transcendent other. It is a conception of the other as beyond containment that will provide us with a conceptual touchstone for understanding the dangers of domination in liberal capitalist societies and how we might reenvision political norms such that they help us develop and economy that is resilient to protocolic domination.

Levinas' primary concern lies in moving beyond a conception of being tied up in the concept of totality and he seeks a new approach through the development of a phenomenology of the other. He understands there to be two basic approaches within the history of philosophical approaches to morality and politics – egoism and totalism. In the former, the individual is a mere projection of the self or an *alter ego* (e.g. Jean-Paul Sartre's existentialism). In the latter, the individual derives meaning from the totality; the self relates to the other as if s/he were an object that is best understood within a universal system (e.g. Hegel's dialectic of Spirit). Levinas understands both of these approaches to be egocentric and reductive and, importantly, out of step with our experience of other persons – Sartre reduces the other to an object and Hegel reduces the other to an extension of the self. He also understands both perspectives to involve an inappropriate conception of persons as historical beings. For the egoist, the individual is wholly outside history and, for the totalist, the individual is wholly within history. He turns, therefore, to embrace an eschatological approach to understanding the self and the other. For him, "eschatology institutes a relation with being *beyond the totality* or beyond history, and with being beyond the past and the present. It is a relationship with *a surplus always exterior to the totality*, as though the objective totality did not fill out the true measure of being, as though another concept, the concept of *infinity*, were needed to express this transcendence with regard to totality, non-encompassable within a totality and as primordial as totality."[74] Thus, the

74 Levinas, *Totality and Infinity*, 22–3, emphasis in original.

eschatological vision "institutes a relation with the infinity of being which exceeds the totality."[75]

The transcendent "beyond," to be clear, is not simply a negative concept. Rather, the "beyond" is reflected within experience, within history insofar as being overflows history. In this manner, he hopes to submit all of history – not simply the totality, but each instant – to judgment because it is within and through history that the living and breathing individuals are judged. Individuals have their identity before the fullness of time in their relationships with each other rather than in their relationship to history as a whole. But, how do we come to understand this eschatological vision? We cannot prove it through philosophical argumentation. This kind of argumentation is born out of a thirst for evidence of a totality that exists beyond the individual – a universal that ultimately explains all the particulars. Instead, "without philosophically 'demonstrating' eschatological 'truths,' we can proceed from the experience of totality back to a situation where totality breaks up, a situation that conditions the totality itself. Such a situation is the gleam of exteriority or of the transcendence in the face of the Other."[76] This transcendental method does not lead to dogmatic content for Levinas, but creates a space for thought in the idea of infinity.

Further, the eschatological vision is made manifest in and through discourse because it is dialogical, face-to-face encounters that allow a relation with the absolutely other that always overflows thought. Utilizing signs (e.g. a phrase or sentence) allows the self to render things offerable – i.e. to detach them, alienate them, or render them exterior and place them in the perspective of the other. Language puts possession into question and, indeed, places the subject at a distance from himself. Consciousness, then, does not lie in squaring being with representation but in overflowing the immediate phenomenology of the subjective self and accomplishing events whose meanings perpetually contain mystery.[77]

The self and the other are locked in a perpetual intersubjective relation in which independence and difference always remain and prevent either the self or the other from being drowned in a fusion or torn apart in an absolute polarization. However, the self is driven to seek out the face of the other by an unquenchable desire for the infinite. This desire provides the connection between the self and the other. And, this

75 Ibid., 23.
76 Ibid., 24.
77 Ibid., 27–8.

desire is too great to be fulfilled or satisfied – it represents an infinite task of responsibility toward all others.[78]

What then does this responsibility entail and how might it be manifest? Specifically, how might it be manifest within collective actions such as those taken up through governing bodies? In order to answer this question, consider how Levinas would deal with the suggestion that his intersubjective dualistic philosophy leads to chauvinistic politics – i.e. that one is to have consideration only for those in one's immediate presence. According to Peperzak, Levinas suggests that in the other's face, I see the virtual presence of all other persons. That is, "the situation makes it necessary for me to gather all others by means of a universal category that allows me to speak about them in general terms."[79] In other words, Levinas seems to be suggesting that universal norms are appropriately developed as analogies of the face-to-face encounter with the other. Peperzak continues to note that, for Levinas, politics has its "true source in the high esteem of individuals for other individuals. All social tasks are consequences of, and preparations for, the possibility of adequate face-to-face relationships and good conversations. If they are not directed toward this end, collective measures lose their human meaning because they have forgotten or masked real faces and real speech. This forgetfulness is the beginning of tyranny."[80] So, not only does the face-to-face encounter with the other form the foundation of our universal norms that encompass all persons but the face-to-face encounter also provides a kind of critical reference point from which to evaluate our bodies politic. There is, however, a kind of ironic tragedy to the pursuit of justice within the collective action-coordination of politics. As Levinas suggests, "the origin of the meaningful in the face of the other, confronted with the actual plurality of human beings – calls for justice and knowledge; the exercise of justice demands courts of law and political institutions, and even, paradoxically, a certain violence that is implied in all justice."[81] Politics is to be rooted in the face-to-face intersubjective engagement and held accountable to that experience but, at the same time, it is, by definition, erasing the faces of those within its reach.

What then does this mean for our understanding of domination? Levinas accurately touches upon the notion of domination within modern liberal capitalist societies when he writes that "violence [i.e. what we have come to describe as domination] does not consist so much in injuring and

78 See Peperzak, *To The Other*, 22.
79 Ibid., 31.
80 Ibid.
81 Levinas, *Alterity and Transcendence*, 172.

annihilating persons as in interrupting their continuity, making them play roles in which they no longer recognize themselves, making them betray not only commitments but their own substance, making them carry out actions that will destroy every possibility for action."[82] There are, therefore, two key points we can take from Levinas in order to understand domination in more socio-political terms: (a) values such as non-domination should be understood based upon the interaction between the self and the other – i.e. dialogically, and (b) domination takes place in the excessively violent displacement and/or confinement of the other. Excessively violent displacement and confinement stem from reductionist approaches to ethics in which the other is located and grasped within a universal metric of normativity (i.e. simultaneously individuated and totalized within dualistic logic).

Domination is excessive violence. It is a speed and degree of change that disrupts and displaces so much that it creates, for example, an existential threat. As should become clear in the discussion of protocolic domination below in chapter 3, we can see three key, interrelated features within this definition of domination: (a) an interruption of continuity, (b) a denial of self-recognition, and (c) a prevention of projection into the future. Disruption, therefore, should be understood as an interruption of patterning processes already taking place. Displacement as a denial of self-recognition insofar as the patternings of the self no longer can connect with the patternings of the past and the patternings of the family, tribe, community, and land. In this sense displacement denies the recognition of the self – the ability to continue patterning and recollecting what has gone before. And, finally, an existential threat can be found in disruption and displacement, but it means – when it comes down to it – a prevention of a future. A future is not something that simply begins in the new; a future only exists with a past as a projection of a trajectory forward beyond the now in an imaginative extension of the will. Disruption and displacement that prevents this looking-forward threatens the existence of that which is dominated. How do we know when these three elements are at work within patterning processes? They are identified through a combined empirical and normative judgment such that the question of excessive violence itself is a democratic question – it is dependent upon negotiation through the exercise of political resistance.

This conception of domination and, of course, the corresponding conception of non-domination will become clearer in the discussions

---

82 Levinas, *Totality and Infinity*, 21.

that follow but it should be noted at this point that an appropriate conception of non-dominating political relations is rooted in an understanding of human nature and our relation to the world (much of which is already contained in the notion of res ecologia). We may seek to avoid talk of human nature – e.g. as many poststructuralist thinkers do – but any and all attempts to develop political norms ultimately rest upon some conception of human nature. To speak of human nature is to (unfashionably) raise questions of natural ordering and grand narratives that are so derided by the prophets of postmodernism.[83] It brings us into uncomfortable questions of how our own personal narratives or the narratives of our communities relate to the grand narrative of ordering in the world. As Charles Taylor and George Grant suggest, however, it is impossible to avoid all grand narratives because they are essential to our thought processes and our actions. Our behaviour depends upon narratives that contain considerations of what life is all about, what is taking place in human history, and how our lives might fit into this history. In short, how the movements of our lives map onto the movement of the world around us.[84]

Without going into great detail regarding this problem of narrative differentials and human nature, I think we can take it that there are two fundamental drives within persons: a drive toward individuality and autonomy, and a drive toward collectivity and solidarity. The first is a seeking of immanence or presence in which the self is established as the focal point for understanding and relating to the world. The second is a seeking of transcendence within which the self moves beyond itself to connect to the world and, in a sense, to become other than itself. These two drives within humans create a kind of forward-moving impulse. These two drives are in tension and when both are present as they are in humans, create a disquieting or even intolerable situation that must be left behind. This situation is somewhat comparable to Hegel's contradictory starting point for his historical and ontological dialectics. The forward-moving impulse of these drives has the potential to lead toward a political association that is non-domineering in an appropriate balancing of these two basic impulses.

The appropriate balance between these two basic impulses is important – i.e. attention to the social psychology of humans is important – because domination is a certain relationship between persons or between persons and their social / material / spiritual environment. What this

83 For example, see Lyotard, *The Postmodern Condition*.
84 Taylor, *A Secular Age*, 573, and Grant, *Philosophy in the Mass Age*, 14.

means, therefore, is that it is unhelpful to try to objectify the notion of domination as if domination could always be seen from outside the relationship in question. Domination takes place in and through the relations and is therefore not adequately understood without concern for the intersubjective nature of the relationship. The objectification of domination in republicanism is also a kind of individualization of the concept of domination. That is, republicanism leads to individualism when dependence is understood as domination regardless of the nature of the dependence. In a network approach to democracy rooted in the ontology of res ecologia, however, dependence is essential – the issue is: *what kind of dependence* and *dependence upon whom/what?* William Paley is correct to point out that freedom as non-domination "places liberty in security; making it to consist not merely in an actual exemption from the constraint of useless and noxious laws and acts of dominion, but in being free from the *danger* of having such hereafter imposed or exercised."[85] Of course, though, dependence can serve as protection against the danger of domineering power relations. Dependence itself allows for a kind of transcendence beyond the self and, if it is a healthy kind of dependence, that transcendence never uproots the self. The network patterning of the self, we could say, is nested within a larger patterning that reinvigorates and reinforces the patterning of the self-network. Dependence may thereby provide protection from the danger of excessive disruption and displacement – protection from domination.

In seeking to come to a more nuanced understanding of relations of dependence and more aptly identify domination (or, rather, more effectively engage in political action to undermine relations of dominance), we can build upon the ethical relation between the self and the transcendent other. For example, as Todd May points out, Levinas' ethical relation between the self and the transcendent other (the infinite obligation to the other) does not allow for the thoroughgoing solidarity or singularity of egalitarianism. As May writes, "the relation between self and other in Levinas' approach is grounded on a double asymmetry rather than equality. Instead of a community of equals, there is an inequality running from other to self and back from self to other. In this double asymmetry, there is never a *we*. The *you* and the *I* in our double asymmetry are never surmounted into a community of equals."[86] Whereas Todd May suggests that, from the perspective of Jacques Rancière, this infinity obligation is problematic, from a network democracy perspective, we might

85 Paley, *The Principles of Moral and Political Philosophy*, 357, emphasis in original. Quoted in Pettit, *Republicanism*, 45.
86 May, *The Political Thought of Jacques Rancière*, 150.

understand this asymmetry of mutual inequality to be appropriate and, indeed, a helpful non-egalitarian approach that avoids the violent push toward singularity.

CONCLUSION

It is important to note that, in a network approach, power, violence, and domination are understood as existing on a continuum – i.e. violence is excessive power and domination is excessive violence. The distinction between these concepts, however, is not simply quantitative. We distinguish between these concepts because we see something qualitatively different between violence and mere power or between domination and violence. That is, the use of the term "excessive" means we are making a negative normative judgment regarding a quantitative increase (i.e. an increase in coercive power). Our distinctions between power, violence, and domination, therefore, should be viewed as both quantitative and qualitative in nature. Further, our understanding of power, violence, and domination – if developed with the complexities of embodied existence in mind – will necessarily lack precision and will inherently be worked out with an eye to the normative ideals we already possess. In other words, we can sketch out a basic conceptual framework for understanding power, violence, and domination, but the lines of this sketching will always blur as we attempt to make definite distinctions apart from real-life situations. And, indeed, even in real-life situations, our understanding of these three concepts will always be dependent upon our position within, or relation to, the situation itself. In a sense, then, we may do best to think of power as the basic concept and both violence and domination as different ways of conceptualizing power relations. That is, as we saw, there is no reason to make a value judgment regarding power, or indeed violence *in itself.* However, as power becomes increasingly intense, we begin to get more and more concerned. So, it seems appropriate to say that violence can be morally acceptable or unacceptable depending upon the level of violence (which is dependent upon the relations in question) but domination is always morally unacceptable. Qualitative interpretation, however, remains a democratic art rather than a theoretical science.

3

Protocolic Modulations

A. PROTOCOL AND DUALISTIC LOGIC
Protocol is a set of standardized procedures that governs processes of interaction between units / agents. The development of protocol fuels acceleration through a destruction of the resistance found in specificity and asymmetry.

B. PROTOCOLIC MODULATIONS
Protocolic Modulations are shifts in protocol – synchronized violations of asymmetrical network patternings that continually disrupt the structural causation within the patternings of the world.

C. PROTOCOLIC DOMINATION
Protocolic Domination is the excessive (illegitimate) violation of the structural causation at work within the patternings of the world.

INTRODUCTION

If we accept, at least tentatively or provisionally, the ontology of patternings and the notion that structural causation gives patternings a self-structuring or autocatalytic integrity that can be disrupted, we are now in a place where we can begin to problematize a hidden structural violence at work in the world. This structural violence I am calling "protocolic domination." It is an excessive violation of the structural causation at work within the patternings of the world; it is excessive because it is such a dramatic degree of disruptive violence that it cannot be legitimized. Further, as we saw in our discussion of the integrity of patternings, structural causation develops resilience as an autocatalytic process built upon partial, asymmetrical disruption. Some degree of change and disruption is needed to allow living systems to advance and enhance their performance as a system, but this kind of positive disruption is one that alters through piecemeal changes. It does not undermine the autocatalytic process itself. The protocolic domination that we will discuss in this chapter, however, disrupts patternings in such a fundamental manner that it undermines the integrity of their structural causation.

Protocolic domination is a disruption that takes place through modulations of protocol – i.e. through standardized processes that rapidly shift in a synchronized violation of structural causation. Protocol is a central feature of the technological society that is our world in the twenty-first century; it is a restless, multi-layered set of procedures that governs interactions between and within both material and immaterial networks. Protocol's power to govern processes is found in the dualistic standardization that allows it to engage in synchronized shifts or modulations. The rapid shifts of protocolic modulations taking place in our world today are disrupting the structural causation of patternings at such a furious rate that they are best understood as protocolic domination. The modulations of protocolic control are taking place at an increasingly rapid rate due to the acceleration that is fuelled by protocol's dualistic logic. That is, the standardization of protocol has a simultaneous individuating and totalizing effect upon the patternings of the world and this simultaneous individuation and totalization is constantly restless and unresolved. The resilience that characterizes the autocatalytic processes of patternings is built upon genuine dependency and an asymmetry that is undermined by the rapidly shifting individual-universal polarity of protocol.

Although the discussions in this chapter will quite likely be somewhat odd to readers, the terms and ideas worked out in the following pages will form a key part of the analysis of liberalism to come. The theoretical language needed for describing the violence of protocolic domination continues to be developed and clarified throughout the remainder of the book but this chapter will set the stage for a turn to the more political discussions of liberalism in the next chapter. And, it is hoped that our ability to begin problematizing the structural violence of protocolic domination, will allow us to better perceive and protect a deeply pluralistic politic. Our discussion of protocolic domination in this chapter will allow us to better understand the dangers posed by standardization processes in the modern world and the importance of specificity within the political. We will begin to develop a perspective that allows for a radically different process of politicization than that which occurs within the liberal worldview.

The importance of specificity arises when the political is understood to be an articulation of the relations between oneself and particular entities persisting and patterning through space-time. There is an inherent immediacy in the politicization process itself that cannot be standardized without destroying the relations that make up the political. This kind of standardization through a dualistic logic, however, is exactly what is taking place in the development of protocol – i.e. shifts in the procedures for interaction that, by virtue of their homogenizing impulse, deny the localized embodiment that is necessary for politicization. The relationship between the dualistic logic of protocolic control and liberalism will be discussed in the next chapter, but first let us begin with a discussion of protocol and a consideration of the dualistic logic through which it lives and moves and has its being.

A. PROTOCOL AND DUALISTIC LOGIC

Although I will set out in a somewhat different direction, our discussion of protocol should begin with an understanding of Deleuze's notion of control and a recognition of its usefulness in understanding the nature of governance within modern, network society. Deleuze builds upon Foucault's historio-critical social analysis of disciplinary society in, especially, the eighteenth and nineteenth centuries and seeks to turn our attention to the power processes of "control society" in the twentieth and twenty-first centuries.[1] The following breakdown outlines the basic historical mapping that provides the framework for Deleuze's analysis.

PERIOD	DIAGRAM	MANAGER
Sovereign Society	Centralization	Hierarchy
Disciplinary Society	Decentralization	Bureaucracy
Control Society	Distribution	Protocol[2]

Whereas Foucault focused primarily (at least in his earlier works) on the key characteristic of disciplinary society – confinement – Deleuze seeks to explicate the key characteristic of control society and contrast it with disciplinary society. He writes, "we're definitely moving toward 'control' societies that are no longer exactly disciplinary ... We're moving toward control societies that no longer operate by confining people but through continuous control and instant communication."[3] Protocol is the manager of modern society and operates as a set of procedures that govern interactions within and through complex network patternings. In general terms, a protocol is a standard or convention that enables connections and interaction between network nodal-points. We might, for example, begin thinking of the standardizations of protocol in terms of

1 Deleuze, *Negotiations*, 174ff.
2 For this mapping, see May, *The Political Thought of Jacques Rancière*, 27.
3 Deleuze, *Negotiations*, 174.

the design and functionality of computer interfaces. Browser updates ensure an interface is efficiently allowing a user the opportunity to access the internet. However, these updates do not simply "allow a user the opportunity"; they alter the governing processes of interaction between the machines and users involved by periodically shifting the patterning of the interface. Further, updates affecting millions of users around the world reveal the standardization within the processes of interaction that has been achieved in order to facilitate more efficient communication between consumer-users and their product-computers.

In complex network systems, protocol is typically not singular but multi-layered and tailored to effectively control the processes of network development. In a distributive network system, we should not be surprised to see multiple layers of protocol – layers that exist as mixes of social and physical standardizations. A complex distributive system is a system that consists of multiple (relatively) autonomous nested nodal connections that nonetheless communicate and interact to coordinate actions. However, it is also important to notice that protocol, if it is to be effective in governing interactions between units / agents and coordinating their actions, will homogenize through standardization. As Alexander Galloway writes, "in order for protocol to enable radically distributed communications between autonomous entities, it must employ a strategy of universalization and homogeneity. It must be anti-diversity. It must promote standardization in order to enable openness."[4] Protocolic control, therefore, is a set of standardized procedures that governs processes of interaction between units / agents and fuels acceleration through the destruction of the resistance found in specificity and asymmetry.

Life involves multiple levels of physical, social, and spiritual interaction and these interactions pattern in such a way as to give rise to both simple and complex things. Protocol is what governs the changes within the interactional patternings of things. Or, put another way, processes and procedures are patterns of interaction; protocol is what governs the way these patterns shift and change. Analogously, then, we might think of protocol as a second-order language (or code) that determines the systems of meaning (the syntax, semantics, etc.) that are *possible* within our first-order languages. Protocol is a domain of discourse that includes and transcends the entities within our domain of discourse, system of meaning, or normative ordering. In this sense it is akin to the kind of government that Foucault defined in "The Subject and Power" because

4 Galloway, *Protocol*, 142.

it structures and determines "the possible field of action" as action acting upon the actions of others.[5]

A kind of protocol can be seen, for example, within the frameworks of information processing that translate human language into computational coding and back again. The interface of a computer allows for what seems to be very natural movements and instructions on the part of the user. This interaction, however, involves multiple levels of rule-governed translation to ensure the actions of the user have the desired effect in the computational processes of the computer machine. In a basic sense, a computer is a machine that manipulates data (coded items combined with organizing variables) in keeping with a sequence of instructions designed to perform a task. And programmers develop this set of instructions – a computer program – using source code that is written with a certain syntax and semantics that allow for the efficient development of algorithmic processes (rules to determine linear patterns of discrete actions). Source code, in turn, is itself a translation of machine code that is a set of atomic or singular instructions executed by the central processing unit of the computer in rapid succession. The challenge for programmers, then, is to develop the source code in a way that the algorithms of the programs allow users to access computational resources through a set of discrete entry-points – interfaces. In other words, the challenge is to develop points of access to computation that is as natural and intuitive, as user-friendly, as possible without losing precision in computation.

Protocol, therefore, arises as a determining factor in multiple locations throughout the communicative processes involved in programming and using computers. For example, machine code is developed in a certain fashion in order to effectively *compute* – atomic instructions that can be interpreted by a central processing unit of a computer operating in a systematic, linear fashion. Source code determined by a certain kind of syntax and semantics to ensure adequate precision in the development of *rules for computation*. These rules of computation (programs) are then designed within a certain set of constraints (e.g. usability, marketability, etc.) that determine the kind of interface a user encounters. The nature of the interface, in turn, affects how one's own thought processes develop and pattern when communicating with and through a computational machine. Protocol governs at all these points of translation or interaction between information systems.

Protocol is a management system or set of procedural determinants that may appear to be detached from or unrelated to the interactional

5 Foucault, "The Subject and Power," 790.

processes or the communicative content that it affects. For example, protocol has been described as information wrappers that "tend to be ignorant of their contents" and "encapsulate information inside a technically defined wrapper, while remaining relatively indifferent to the content of information contained within."[6] However, there should be no doubt that protocol has a significant effect upon the content of information flows within information systems. This effect, though, is hidden by a dualistic logic at work within protocol that facilitates the eclipse of its qualitative input. As Galloway has aptly noted, protocol is a kind of standardizing determinant that develops best in contexts where there are two, radically contrasting processes at work – strict hierarchy and radical decentralization. In the internet, for example, Transmission Control Protocol / Internet Protocol (TCP / IP) model of establishing communications between computers "uses an anarchic and highly distributed model, with every device being an equal peer to every other device on the global Internet."[7] On the other hand, the Domain Name System (DNS) that associated information with domain names for each entity (computer, service, etc.) connected to the internet is hierarchical and top-down with a strict "inverted-tree" model of control.[8] Within the internet itself, therefore, the protocols develop within a dualistic logic of standardization that not only allows protocol to control information flows but also helps facilitate the erasure of protocol's political implications or an eclipse of its qualitative input.

Let us begin with what I mean by "dualistic logic." Then, we can consider the way in which it obscures its own effects. Although it will be examined in more detail in the following chapter, we can note here that dualistic logic is a process of simultaneously individuating and totalizing through multilayered standardizations. And, in its simultaneous parsing and uniting, dualistic logic is constantly restless; it is never resolved and persists as a continuous polarization between two extremes. Dualism denies all genuine dependency in the relationality of the units / agents it governs because interdependency represents an asymmetry that is at odds with the symmetry of the individual-universal polarization. We might even say that dualism persists in and through its extremes as a symmetrical dependence and that this kind of radical dependency manifests a polarity that dominates or disrupts all the partial relations of dependency that make up ourselves and our embodied relations in the world. That which lies between the extreme poles of singular and

6 Galloway, *Protocol*, 81.
7 Hall, *Internet Core Protocol*, 407, quoted in Galloway, *Protocol*, 8.
8 Ibid., 9.

universal is stripped bare as those things participating in asymmetrical relations of dependence are transformed into individuals-in-relation-to-the-universal. Dualism's domination can be seen in this restless undermining of asymmetry in relations of partial dependency.

This notion of the restlessness within polarization of dualistic logic is in keeping with Deleuze's description of control society that is characterized by its "ultrarapid forms of free-floating control that replaced the old disciplines operating in the time frame of a closed system."[9] As such, protocol may be understood as "a system of distributed management" that is "robust, flexible, and universal," "can accommodate massive contingency," and "facilitates peer-to-peer relationships between autonomous entities" while controlling through "inflection, connectivity, contextualization."[10] This decentralized flexibility, of course, is only effective when coupled with a totalizing universality that facilitates the contingent coordinations of interaction between decentralized units / agents. Due to the nature of our bodies, our ways of life, and our history of life on this earth, our systems of meaning and normative orderings can only take on a certain range of defining characteristics. Our communicative processes are bounded by our physical, social, and spiritual existence such that, although we can (to some degree) know about things we have never experienced, our knowledge is inescapably linked back to our experience. There can be no knowledge without a history. Our politics, therefore, are naturally bounded and temporally restrained by the locality of our being-in-the-world. There are numerous natural constrains upon our political activity that persist in and through our bodies and environment, but protocol is a set of controls that governs in standardized processes of interaction. However, in its ultra-rapid and flexible forms of control, protocol is radically unnatural and rests not on tradition but simply on previous procedural shifts. It universalizes and then moves and modulates too fast to remain in sync with or to resonate with lived and embodied traditions or normative orderings.[11]

I have described protocol as the ways in which processes and procedures that govern interactions change; the rules that, say, govern the patterns of communicative action that make up our systems of meaning, the semiotic ecology in our industrialized world. "Rules" are patternings imposed or layered upon differing patterns that have their own

9 Deleuze, "Postscript on the Societies of Control," 4.

10 Galloway, *Protocol*, 81–2.

11 Compare with Jacques Ellul's description of technique which "no longer rests on tradition, but rather on previous technical procedures; and its evolution is too rapid, too upsetting, to integrate the older traditions." Ellul, *The Technological Society*, 14.

distinct developmental structure. In this sense protocol is, by definition, an imposition upon what we earlier described as a natural ordering within the world. And although protocolic imposition is not simply a linguistic matter, as an example we could speak of this imposition in linguistic terms to highlight the depth within us at which protocol can operate – i.e. the degree to which we have "naturalized" protocol in our modern world. Protocol in communication could be seen in as pattern shifts (modulations) within four kinds of rules: semantic, syntactic, pragmatic, and systemic. Semantic rules determine the ways in which we are able to symbolically represent or indicate things in the world around us. If we are to articulate the relative significance of a thing, we rely upon a set of symbols that we might use to refer to a thing. Indeed, we might even say that a thing only possesses a partial existence for us insofar as we have an unclear definition of that thing. Of course this partiality only becomes known in retrospect – the owl of semantic rules flies at dusk. Syntactic rules determine the ways in which we are able to combine symbols in order to enunciate relations between ourselves and the world. Grammatical patterns allow for certain connections and disconnections to be made and, like semantic rules, the exclusionary nature of these patterns can only be seen to the degree that that which was excluded begins to be included – i.e. second order syntactical rules are always and necessarily accompanied by first order syntactical rules. Pragmatic rules determine the ways in which the context within which articulations are made affects the meaning of the articulations. For example, the locutionary, illocutionary, and perlocutionary acts taking place in an utterance are all shaped by the context within which the utterance takes place. And, further, it is often the context that allows a sentence to shed its ambiguity and become a concrete utterance between two or more communicators. Systemic rules determine the ways in which the use of symbols or systems of meaning affect those who use them or participate in them. In other words, there is a set of patternings that determine how participation in a system of meaning adapts one to further participation in that system. These four types of rules change the means and mediums of communication; they make some things visible and others invisible. Ultimately, these rules greatly affect the way we can or cannot develop hierarchies of variables, the way we are able or unable to politicize ourselves and the things around us.

These four rules are in turn developed or altered in a few key ways: altered *rates* of information flows and altered *spatial* patterns in information transmission. That is, changes in the rates of information flows alters the significance of the information and transforms the ecological, social, and spiritual effects of the information patterns. Throughout the communicative processes, for example, intermediate gatekeeping (e.g. a throttling or suppressing of the spread of a message rather than the outright denial of the message) and / or flooding (e.g. an acceleration of associated messages that diversify and distribute the potential impact of a clear and distinct message) can develop patterns of communicative action that perform rule-like functions within the production and reproduction of communication technique. Additionally, changes in the spatial patterns within an environment (symbolically and physically) affect the transmission of information and, hence, the nature of the information itself. Thus, protocolic advancement as seen in the four rules outlined above is also developed through changes in both the nature of the sequential procession as well as the spatial layout pertaining to information production and reproduction.

It may be thought at this point that protocol sounds quite like Pierre Bourdieu's notion of habitus, or at least sounds like a certain kind of habitus. However, there is a significant difference. Whereas Bourdieu seeks to explain the production and reproduction of behavioural habits generally, my goal is to explain the production and reproduction of certain interactions particular to modern industrial life and to consider the political implications of these interactions. We should also note that protocol is not simply about human behaviour, it is about patterns of interaction in modern industrial society more generally. Examples such as communicative action are used simply to make the concept more approachable and more easily tied into the notion of politicization. There are, therefore, a couple key differences between habitus and protocol. First, Bourdieu is careful to note that describing social habit formation as rules, grammar, law, etc. is misleading because these things govern behaviour in quite different ways than habitus.[12] Bourdieu's concern applies, albeit to a lesser degree, to protocol. For, although protocol is inculcated in largely unrecognized ways through bodily practice and repeated / reinforced actions, it is by definition an imposition in a way that habitus is not. Therefore, whereas it is problematic to describe habitus in terms of rules, protocol functions much more like rules. Second, protocol is also somewhat different than habitus in the sense that protocol is defined by the homogenizing impulse within it whereas habitus is the transmission of social behaviour more broadly. As we have seen, to the degree that it is effective in governing through coordinating action between decentralized units / agents, protocol homogenizes through standardization. For, in order for protocol to transcend the variations and

12 Bourdieu, *Outline of a Theory of Practice*, 19.

deep diversity within the patterns of the world, it must universalize; it must develop a kind of homogeneity. It must develop standardization in order to open up interaction and ensure effective coordination.

So, protocol may be understood as related to habitus but as a standardizing process that develops and reproduces within modern industrial societies to disrupt and displace us in and through our being-in-the-modern-world. It is a kind of power at work in the world or a patterning imposition upon the patternings of the world. It is an active homogenizing impulse that pushes toward synchronization and coordination across great naturalized differences and divisions and these patterns of behaviour develop in the cosmopolitan society of advanced industrial nations such that practices are produced and reproduced in synchronization regardless of the physical location. We encounter protocol *within and through* people, machines, computational interfaces, markets, and institutions of the modern welfare state rather than as an objective system or set of rules against which we are explicitly measured. So, it is like habitus in the sense that, "if agents are possessed by their habitus more than they possess it, this is because it acts within them as the organizing principle of their action, and because this *modus operandi* informing all thought and action (including thought of action) reveals itself only in the *opus operatum*."[13] In other words, protocol is made manifest for us as a certain kind of objective patterning in and through our practice (and through the interaction between humans and, especially, their machines) rather than through the conscious intentions of individual actors. It is the historical development and propagation of modern industrial life as it becomes more and more naturalized.[14]

The patterning of protocol produces inherent censorships within persons living in modern industrial society such that it can never be fully revealed or understood by those who live modern lives – i.e. in the thinking and naming of protocol, we moderns *ipso facto* reproduce protocol that is unthinkable and unnameable. So, like the habitus of Bourdieu, discussion of protocol may be conceived of as an outsider-oriented discourse that requires a stepping-outside the behaviour to even recognize the patternings that govern behaviour.[15] It is unthinkable and unnameable to the degree that we engage in the practices that are governed by protocol because it develops in and through us as protocolic beings to the degree that we live as beings-in-the-modern-world. The structures of

13 Ibid., 18.
14 Compare with Bourdieu's description of habitus as "history turned into nature." See ibid., 78.
15 Ibid., 18.

the technological society produce and reproduce protocol which, on one hand, opens up types of mental, physical, and spiritual knowing while simultaneously producing ignorance in our mental, physical, and spiritual being. In addition, because it is produced and reproduced within our behaviour as beings-in-the-modern-world, we can articulate it only to the degree that our behaviour is out of sync with its patternings. It is like habitus in that it is a *learned ignorance* (*docta ignorantia*), a mode of practical knowledge not comprising knowledge of its own principles. It follows that this learned ignorance can only give rise to the misleading discourse of a speaker himself misled, ignorant both of the objective truth about his practical mastery (which is that it is ignorant of its own truth) and of the true principle of the knowledge his practical mastery contains.[16] Put simply, the eclipse of protocol takes place within the inculcation and reproduction of protocol itself. The reason for this lies, as we have seen above, in the restlessness of protocol's dualistic logic. This restlessness we will discuss further in our description of protocolic modulations below.

B. PROTOCOLIC MODULATIONS

As I noted at the beginning of this chapter, my purpose in turning to the idea of protocol lies in my desire to open up and theorize regarding the violence taking place in the modern world – i.e. what Deleuze refers to as "control society" in his "Postscript on the Societies of Control."[17] And, in order to better understand the kind of violence taking place within protocolic control, it may be helpful to remember and contrast it with Foucault's notion of spatial distribution in a disciplinary society. For example in *Discipline and Punish* he writes that "discipline proceeds from the distribution of individuals in space" such that (a) a specific space is enclosed (e.g. prison, school, monastery, barracks, etc.), and (b) partitioned such that each individual has his own space, and (c) the space is functionalized such that each space corresponds to a certain use. Discipline through distribution, therefore, acts as a kind of molding that shapes and defines the development of one's subjectivity, an "architecture that would operate to transform individuals."[18]

As Deleuze notes, this disciplinary architecture of control acts upon an actor "to allocate, to classify, to compose, to normalize" and to regulate through a logic in which the "different internments or spaces of enclosure

16   Ibid., 19.
17   Deleuze, "Postscript on the Societies of Control," 3–7.
18   Foucault, *Discipline and Punish*, 141ff and 172.

through which the individual passes are independent variables."[19] In our current technological or control society, these enclosures are no longer distinct but inseparable variations that control through perpetually shifting modulations. Or, in other words, "enclosures are *molds*, distinct castings, but controls are a *modulation*, like a self-deforming cast that will continuously change from one moment to the other, or like a sieve whose mesh will transmute from point to point."[20] Protocolic control is like a self-transmuting molding that is continually changing from one moment to the next. It operates as a standardizing set of norms and practices constantly reforming and reorganizing to govern and transform not only ourselves but also the world in which we live. It is the violent imposition dualistic standardizations enact within and upon complex natural patternings. Control society, therefore, is characterized by structures and processes that continually reorganize and reform to ensure standardization in simultaneous individuation and universalization.

We will discuss this further, but it should be noted up front that the key to understanding the significance of modulations in protocolic control lies in contemplating anew our assumptions regarding power and freedom and in reorienting them away from the self-determinism of liberal conceptions of freedom. For example, as we noted, Foucault understands the subject as being free to the degree that he faces an unrestricted field of possible actions. In "The Subject and Power," he writes that government is the exercise of power or modes of action that act upon the possibilities of action of others. However, he is also clear that "power is exercised only over free subjects, and only insofar as they are free" and "by this we mean individual or collective subjects who are faced with a field of possibilities in which several ways of behaving, several reactions and diverse comportments, may be realized."[21] Power, for Foucault, is a restriction of the field of possibilities open to a subject; it dissolves freedom wherever it is exercised.[22]

If this Foucauldian approach represents our conception of power and freedom, then we will likely see little significance in the shift from governmental enclosure to protocolic control. Both enclosure and control

19 Deleuze, *Foucault*, 25, and Deleuze, "Postscript on the Societies of Control," 4.

20 Ibid., 4, emphasis in original.

21 Foucault, "The Subject and Power," 790.

22 To his credit, Foucault is also quite keen to note that the workings of power upon the freedom of the subject should be understood as dynamic interrelations. For example, he writes that "rather than speaking of an essential freedom, it would be better to speak of an 'agonism' – of a relationship which is at the same time reciprocal incitation and struggle, less of a face-to-face confrontation which paralyzes both sides than a permanent provocation." Ibid.

restrict the so-called self-determination of subjects. However, if our conception of freedom centres more upon notions of stability and security than self-determination (and upon the behaviour of both individuals and systems rather than simply individuals), the difference between enclosure and control becomes significant. First, in this approach to power and freedom, enclosure is not always problematic. We are concerned about disruption rather than containment. Second, if we see freedom as groundedness, we are in a much better position to highlight the destructive and domineering nature of control through protocol. We are able to recognize the dualistic logic at work within protocolic control and its violence at work in eclipsing the political being of res ecologia.

So, if we are attune to the behaviour of complex systems and the dynamic interplay between persons *qua* patternings within patternings, we can begin to recognize the problematic nature of the dualistic logic at work in the modulations of protocolic control. As noted above, protocol is best conceived of as a set of governing standards that develop in and through two, radically contrasting processes – individuation and universalization. In other words, protocol layers universalized processes that are designed to coordinate and synchronize self-directing individuals and, in so doing, disintegrates the intermediate or localized processes of partially dependent coordination. It operates according to a dualistic logic that simultaneously individuates and totalizes and, if it is to be effective in coordinating action, will homogenize through standardization. Standardization is needed to bring about synchronization between heteronomous entities and this standardization depends upon a process of abstraction away from the different ways of being in the world that differ between various embodied locales. It is only in the abstract that the universal coordination and symmetrical synchronization of standardization can take place. In this manner, the standardizations of dualistic logic collapse space and time through universal coordinations and symmetrical synchronizations that are only possible through a kind of abstraction away from the difference and diversity of patternings that make up ourselves and the world (hence my saying earlier that protocol cannot accord with tradition and moves too fast to remain in sync with lived and embodied normative orderings).

But why should we be concerned about the layerings of protocolic control that develop within the dualistic logic of simultaneous individuation and totalization? In short, protocolic control is harmful because it modulates at such high speeds and these rapid modulations do violence to the ecological, social, and spiritual patternings of the world – the natural ordering of the world. Rapid change violates relational patternings and creates a kind of protocolic domination through systemic processes of destabilization, disruption, and displacement. In other words, proto-colic control "controls" through a perpetual re-making of relational pat-ternings to undermine interrelations of partial dependence. Modulations are standardized and synchronized violations that continually disrupt the internal pattern-developing or pattern-reinforcing changes.

The instability of protocolic control is taking its toll. We described domination above in chapter 3 as an interruption of continuity that de-nies, for example, self-recognition and a projection of oneself into the future. In other words, it is disruption that undermines the past-present-future trajectory within a self-patterning – and this disruption manifests in deviant and unhealthy behaviour and can even lead to existential threats. Detachment and disorientation have become widespread as a deep, underlying sense of purposelessness pervades liberal capitalist soci-eties. The symptoms appear with dramatic frequency as more and more people are struggling with depression, disassociation, narcissism, health and eating obsessions, sexual frustration and deviance, stress, and anxi-ety. Rapid protocolic modulations destroy social cohesion and oppose individuals against each another by dividing each person within.[23] This kind of division creates irrational behaviour as well as harmful patholo-gies such as disassociative disorders where there is a sense of alienation and dramatic internal conflict. In other words, protocolic modulations perpetually displace and remake the self such that the self does not know what it is or for what purpose it exists. Transformative modulations are continuous, always immanent with a vague promise of transcendence but the closest many in today's world may come to transcendence is a fleeting sense of the sublime as they reach the end of themselves and see nothing beyond.[24] The modulations, in other words, undermine tradition and disrupt enough to give rise to a widespread nihilism.

Due to its dualistic logic that abstracts away from the relational pat-ternings that make up our being-in-the-world, protocolic control tends to cover over its own political tracks. The political – as we have defined it above – takes place in the spaces between totality and individuality. It is a process of articulating a normative reorganization of relational pri-orities between the local and the global but there can be no genuine (i.e. non-paradoxical) relations between individuality and universality. The prevalence of this dualistic logic, therefore, has led to a widespread depoliticization in social theory or, more accurately, an obscuring of the depth of normative orderings in contemporary social theory. And, as

23 Deleuze, "Postscript on the Societies of Control," 5.
24 Cf. Blond, "Introduction," 14–16.

should become clearer in our discussion of liberalism's proceduralist turn, the depoliticization of social theory means that social theory fails to provide the tools needed for building resilience into our communities that can withstand the domineering disruptions of protocolic control. For example, this obscuration of depoliticization can be seen in Latour and Mouffe's understandings and theorizations regarding "the social" or "the political."

To put it simply, Latour's immanentism obscures the patternings of the world (as we saw in our discussion of res ecologia in chapter 2) and, in so doing, facilitates the modulations of protocolic control. Because he flattens all reality into one immanent plane, Latour argues that the social is only seen in the discreet moment where things are reorganizing, regrounding, recomposing, etc.[25] Focussing on viewing the social as Latour suggests makes us susceptible to the modulations of protocolic control because we are left with no options other than being swept along by the transforming movements of the social; we have nothing outside the immanent that we might look to for stability or resistance against the modulations. This is problematic because, as we just noted, protocol modulates rapidly and creates dramatic instability within the world. As constantly modulating layerings of patterning upon the deeper patternings of the world, protocol disrupts, destabilizes, and displaces at increasing rates of change.

This immanentism affords us no resistance to the modulations of protocolic control because if we are on an immanent plane, how can we see a shift in associations? Do we not rely upon some background assumptions of order or patterning in order to recognize the change taking place within the shift? And, moving beyond this more epistemological problem with immanentism, what is the more ontological concern with this notion of the social? Put simply, viewing all as an immanent plane plunges us into the change that is taking place. Without the means of recognizing and articulating order in the world (i.e. patternings that exist and persist beyond our recognition of them), we have no way to resist the change – we simply become part of the change. We are moved along in a reorganization of association and interaction according to the governing protocol. The underlying orderings do not guide us or hold us back. We descend to a plane of immanence where we are smoothly guided along according to shifting protocols without resistance. As Wittgenstein writes in *Philosophical Investigations*, "we have got on to slippery ice where there is no friction and so in a certain sense the conditions are ideal, but also, just

25 See Latour, *Reassembling the Social.*

because of that, we are unable to walk. We want to walk: so we need *friction*. Back to the rough ground!"[26] Moments of disorganization are moments open to deconstruction for Latour, but this deconstruction takes place according to the protocol that controls as a layering upon everything – construction, deconstruction, and reconstruction.

For an agonist like Mouffe, the social and the political are conceived of somewhat differently but, I would argue, no less problematically. Following in the steps of contrarian theorists Carl Schmitt and Jacques Rancière, Mouffe understands the political as "the dimension of antagonism which [is] constitutive of human societies."[27] The political is developed within a we-they dualism; it is constituted by the interplay between two extremes. For example, Mouffe argues that "all forms of political identities entail a we / they distinction" such that "every consensus exists as a temporary result of a provisional hegemony, as a stabilization of power, and that it always entails some form of exclusion."[28] Further, her notion of identity is wrapped up in the creation and recreation of difference or, in other words, she contends that "the affirmation of a difference is a precondition for the existence of any identity, i.e. the perception of something 'other' which constitutes its 'exterior.'"[29]

Although Mouffe is certainly correct to argue against the totalization in the liberal rationalists' ideal of a "universal consensus" in her work, she does tend to essentialize antagonism in her understanding of the political and thereby fall into the individuation / totalization trap of dualistic logic. In other words, my concern is that her conception of the political as an antagonism that constitutes a society is, in a sense, excessively Schmittian. She is careful to note that the we / they distinction does not *necessarily* mean a friend / enemy distinction as Schmitt argues, but she does maintain that there is always a possibility that the we / they relation could become a friend / enemy conflict if the "they" threatens the identity of the "we."[30] Not only does this persistent possibility of friend / enemy antagonism define the political for Mouffe, but the antagonism itself seems to rest upon a somewhat simplistic friend / enemy dualism.

Mouffe falls into this dualist approach because she denies the deeper patterns of persistence that allow relations between oneself and others / other things to exist and become articulated outside a simple binary

26 Wittgenstein, *Philosophical Investigations*, 40e.

27 Mouffe, *On the Political*, 9. Political questions, therefore, "always involve decisions which require us to make a choice between conflicting alternatives," 10.

28 Ibid., 16, and Mouffe, "Deliberative Democracy or Agonistic Pluralism," 17.

29 Mouffe, *On the Political*, 15.

30 Ibid. and Schmitt, *The Concept of the Political*, 35.

friend / enemy distinction. Then, in order to avoid the friend / enemy antagonism, she must assume an abstract (i.e. non-political) unity in order to allow us to perceive and articulate political behaviour. In other words, by resting the concept of "the political" upon the we / they distinction, she sets up a requirement that there exist a deeper unity that brings together and guides the way we make the we / they distinction. This abstractionism takes place because, if she invests her notion of the political in the localized consensus of binary antagonism, she has little choice but to either:

(a) move into Schmitt's friend / enemy distinction and the mortal enemy model that follows from it (and thereby forsake democracy altogether), or

(b) assume a higher unity that guides the way the we / they distinction itself is created and recreated (i.e. rely upon the universalisms of political liberalism).

She picks the latter approach by seeking a certain way of drawing the we / they distinction and, in so doing, seeks a unity that transcends the distinction itself (i.e. in the legitimization of one's opponents). So, for example, Mouffe writes that members of democratic societies, "while in conflict, they see themselves as belonging to the same political association, as sharing a common symbolic space within which the conflict takes place."[31] In so doing, she falls back into a kind of abstract standardization characteristic of liberal proceduralism that facilitates rather than restricts the modulations of protocolic control.

Agonistic liberals like Mouffe, therefore, are putting forward an important critique of rationalist liberalism, but are unable to mount a radical critique due to their somewhat superficial conception of the political. By understanding the political world as sheer contingency, the agonistic liberals view political identity in simple, oppositional terms. Like the immanentists above, the agonists deny the depth of transcendence in natural ordering and therefore are caught in the awkward situation where they are left with little choice but to both posit and obscure the background ordering within which political identity exists. It is within this obscurity and inability to find the stability of patternings that protocolic control is able to flourish and develop in its domineering modulations.

31 Mouffe, *On the Political*, 20.

C. PROTOCOLIC DOMINATION.

As outlined in the last chapter, I understand domination as an excessive violation of patternings in the world – a speed and degree of change that disrupts and destabilizes so much that it cannot (or should not) be considered legitimate. Further, we noted that the domination of humans can be understood as an interruption of continuity such that persons can no longer recognize themselves or project themselves and the things around them into the future from within the trans-temporal trajectory of tradition. Those who are dominated are, in this way, inhibited in their ability to politicize themselves and the things in the world around them. How, then, might we begin to understand the particular features of the logic at work within *protocolic* domination? Further, how might we best understand its relation to, and distortions of, the politicization process?

Protocolic domination is the illegitimate violence caused by disruptive power taking place through the modulations of protocolic control. It is the excessive violation of structural causation within the patternings of the world – a kind of violence that has been simultaneously enhanced and obscured by the dualistic logic of normative theorizing exemplified in liberal conceptions of justice. The rapid modulations of protocolic control, I would argue, are therefore the most problematic and under-theorized domination at work in the worlds of the market state. In chapter 2 above, we discussed how politicization is a threefold relation between things local, things global, and the self as a local-global being such that the making of things public is always also the making of oneself public in relation to a thing. And, because politicization is this threefold relation, to the degree that a person is ungrounded as a result of standardized modulations in protocolic control, he is unable to make things public. He is unable to locate and lock onto the specificity of the local in a way that he can articulate and translate it into the global in an ongoing revelatory relationship. So, simply put, by talking about protocolic domination we are interested in widespread violations of patternings within the market state that are illegitimate due to their undermining of the very capacity for politicization. By focusing in on protocolic domination, we are seeking to become more attentive to a kind of violence that is active within our own systems of meaning and action-coordination, disturbances to the patternings that make meaningful action such as politicization possible for us as beings-in-the-modern-world.

Although if we are seeking to identify and describe violations in our systems of meaning and action coordination we should immediately be struck by the kind of question George Grant raised in *Technology and Empire*. With his piercing insight into the illnesses of our modern world,

Grant highlights the difficulty we have in recognizing and acknowledging what our modern technological society has deprived us of. Indeed he not only notes the difficulty, he also helps us understand the depth of this difficulty through his process of lamentation – and, in so doing, allows us to better understand the problem we are facing. He writes:

> We can hold in our minds the enormous benefits of technological society, but we cannot so easily hold the ways it may have deprived us, because technique is ourselves ... It is difficult to think whether we are deprived of anything essential to our happiness, just because the coming to be of the technological society has stripped us above all of the very systems of meaning which disclosed the highest purposes of man, and in terms of which, therefore, we could judge whether an absence of something was in fact a deprival ... All coherent languages beyond those which serve the drive to unlimited freedom through technique have been broken up in the coming to be of what we are. Therefore it is impossible to articulate publicly any suggestion of loss, and perhaps even more frightening, almost impossible to articulate it to ourselves. We have been left with no words which cleave together and summon out of uncertainty the good of which we may sense the dispossession.[32]

Grant laments the difficulty we have in sensing the loss of what we have forgotten when we cannot form the thoughts needed to consider what it is that we have forgotten. How do we recognize the losses caused by our systems of meaning when it is these very systems that make us who we are and shape our normative orderings as beings-in-the-modern-world? Our systems of meaning have been stripped of certain patterns of thought regarding the good life and it seems impossible to even imagine how we might restore them if we cannot normatively contextualize them.

Although Grant is dealing with a somewhat different set of problems, we face an analogous problem with regard to protocolic domination. How do we recognize modulating violations of structural causation in the world if we are ourselves being shaped and changed by the same modulating patterning-shifts? Or, more to the point, how do we recognize a violation of patterning as something more problematic than simply a *different* patterning than that to which we are accustomed? If we accept the network ontology of res ecologia outlined earlier, I think we have to admit up front that we are poorly placed to understand such matters and, no matter how well we are able to gauge structural violations,

---

32 Grant, *Technology and Empire*, 137, 139.

we will never arrive at anything more than a provisional estimation of patterning-shifts that we evaluate from our own localized time / space perspective. In other words, our ontological situation should give us great epistemic humility. This is not to say, however, that we *cannot* identify protocolic domination at work within ourselves and our world whatsoever. But, as with all domination, protocolic domination is identified through a judgment that combines both *empirical and normative* elements such that the question of excessive violence is a question to which any answer will always be contingent, contested, and negotiated. Indeed, we might say that the question "what is excessive violence?" is a fundamentally democratic question such that no final answer or universal definition can be given.

We should note, however, that the process of recognizing protocolic domination is somewhat different than the process of politicization (i.e. local-global-local). The political is latent and diffuse and only becomes acute or definite – is made truly visible – through a process of localization. The revealing or disclosure of politicization takes place as one moves from the local to the global (i.e. manifests the broader significance of things in an apocalypse) and then back again to the local (i.e. articulates the relation between the res publica and oneself as res ecologia). In politicization, this process involves a historical (diachronic) threefold relation between things local, things global, and the self as local-global. At least two capacities are therefore needed for someone to engage in the politicization process (a) the ability to localize oneself in relation to the thing and (b) the ability to project this relation of localization outward in relation to a res publica. In this manner, the broader significance of a thing can be articulated or made manifest.

This apocalypse of politicization, however, does not work when we are seeking to make the domination of protocolic modulations visible. Why is this? Why can we not simply politicize protocolic domination and thereby make its significance visible to ourselves and the world? I can point to a couple of key reasons – reasons that give us further insight into what I mean by both the "protocolic" and the "domination" elements of protocolic domination: (a) it cannot be politicized because, unlike things that whole, protocolic domination cannot be localized in relation to the self and (b) to the degree that we are able to politicize those things that are affected by the power shifts of protocolic domination, we are actually shielding those things from domination. Protocolic domination cannot be politicized because it cannot be localized in relation to the self as res ecologia. Just as politicization cannot be accomplished insofar as one is not grounded in specificity (one is unable to localize), so too the politicization of protocolic domination cannot take place due to its fundamental non-locality. Indeed, this is what protocolic means – protocolic modulations violate the structural causation of the world but do not themselves localize within any wholing thing. Protocolic domination is itself not a thing and, therefore, does not whole or present but simply disrupts the wholing and presenting of things as res ecologia (and res publica). There is an immediacy or specificity in the politicization process that cannot be standardized without destroying the relations that make up the political. This kind of destructive standardization, however, is what takes place in the development of protocol – i.e. shifts in the procedures for interaction that, by virtue of their homogenizing impulse, deny the localized embodiment that is necessary for politicization. We can see dualistic logic at work in the attempt to universalize normative relations (which, of course, cannot be universalized or they lose their relationality and hence their normativity). This push towards universalization undermines our ability to localize within the politicization process. In contrast, the revealing of res ecologia and its manifestation as res publica, therefore, actually serves to temper the excessive violence of protocolic domination by reinforcing the patternings of the thing.

Despite the fact that protocolic domination cannot be made visible through politicization, we can nonetheless to some degree recognize its disruptive effects within ourselves and the things around us. As we just noted, protocolic domination is identified through the combination of an empirical and a normative judgment because, like all domination, it is by definition an excess of violence – and what we mean by "excessive" requires not only empirical but also normative judgment. Further, much like how we cannot remember what we have forgotten, we cannot form judgments regarding protocolic domination directly. We can only form judgments regarding those things in the world that are disrupted by the modulations of protocolic control – i.e. form judgments regarding those things that are registering the effects, those patternings that are being violated. So, in this manner, we can form partial judgments regarding those things that we perceive to have a dualistic logic at work within them even though we cannot politicize the logic itself. And, as we proceed in the discussion that follows, we will focus upon understanding the patternings that are disrupted by protocolic modulation and those things within and around us that are shaped and driven forward by its dualistic logic. We should also note that, to the degree that we are able to direct our judgment concerning diffuse disruptions of structural causation toward some thing that is being disrupted, we are simultaneously obscuring another patterning disruption just outside the gaze of our judgment. Our judgments therefore remain *inescapably* partial.

Before we continue to outline the nature of pattern disruption taking place in protocolic modulations, however, let us consider the differences between protocolic domination and structural violence more generally. Or, in other words, why am I not describing this kind of patterning disruption simply as structural domination? Put simply, I am not referring to structural domination because if it is structural, it can be localized; if it is structural, then we are not talking about something that is driven forward by the dualistic logic at work in the modulations of protocolic control. Dualistic logic denies dependency in its abstraction away from the relational patternings that make up our being-in-the-world. There is, therefore, no structuration process or patterning at work within this polarity, it is inherently unstable and nonlocal in its reductive simplicity. Through its abstraction, it covers over or hides the normative and political effects it leaves in its wake of patterning disruptions. Protocolic control not only shapes the ways we are able to understand and articulate violence, but it obscures the structural violence it causes because it hinders our ability to politicize the violence. The power of protocol is most deeply disruptive in the continual transformations that displace the self in its being-in-the-world and undermine the processes of politicization. The transformations are perpetual: always immanent through standardized and synchronized modulations that abstract away from the embodied relations of res ecologia. The rapid modulations of protocolic control disrupt and dislocate us such that we lose our ability to politicize violence. So, in obscuring violations and preventing politicization, protocolic control fosters further violations that dig down into our very nature as beings-in-the-modern-world.

Before going on to consider some of the violence of standardized modulations in more practical terms, how might we understand the causation that is taking place in the domination of protocolic modulations? Quite recently, domination was typically viewed as the imposition of singularity from outside through confinement (e.g. a totalitarian regime). In the network / control society that is liberalism manifest in relation to the market state, however, this singularity arises in and through agents themselves as they are guided into standardized and synchronized patterns of interaction. Domination, in this sense, has become internalized within and through the diverse patternings of modern life. This internalization can be seen as taking place in at least two related ways. First, persons are guided into standardized and synchronized modes of interaction through a layering of uniform, albeit multi-layered, representations and interpretations of the self and things in the world around them. These modes of interaction are standardizations layered upon patterns of bio-material diversity. Through representations and interpretations of the spatial relations and patterns of connect / disconnect in the bodies and eco-systems of the material world, protocolic control acts to lift us out of our finite bodies and into an abstract realm of rationalized unity. Second, persons are guided through a layering of techno-mechanistic standardizations upon diverse familial and socio-political patterns of interaction. The standardization of the material mediums of interaction guide the patterns and substance of thought and action. Through the common use of mechanical appendages or tools and mediums of communication, the patterns of socio-political thought and action – as well as our understanding of the bio-material patterns of life – are shaped and reshaped.

Protocolic domination in a network / control society can be viewed as a kind of power at work in relation to both formal and final causation. Both of these causes are simply examples of causation or causal contexts that help us better understand the perpetual displacement of protocolic control. In relation to formal causation, the standardization of protocol works to homogenize not simply from the bottom up – i.e. from the parts (e.g. genes, persons) to the whole (e.g. persons, society) – but within and upon the whole in a way that shapes and determines the constituent parts. This is not a denial of bottom-up causation that takes place in terms of material and efficient causes, but a reemphasis on the nature of complex systems and their persistence and agency *as systems* or, of course, as res ecologia. It is a recognition that protocolic modulations are undermining the formal causation taking place within complex systems. In terms of final causation, the standardization of protocol works to homogenize the patterns of network formation and unify the power flows internal to the network systems. That is, the autocatalytic processes of complex systems are asymmetrical and thereby demonstrate a kind of final cause. However homogenization takes place as the purpose of life itself is altered and destroyed in synchronized modulations. Hence, final causation is also undermined. Put more broadly, structural domination serves to limit the internal diversity of complex systems – i.e. move them toward a decentralized (Cartesian grid-like) pattern – and thereby reduce the adaptability of the network patterning. In socio-political terms, this process is a kind of mechanization of society and, consequently, a mechanization of the self as the network systems become more machine-like. This push toward grid-like patterns with very limited formal or final causation is domineering in that it excessively disrupts the stability and resilience of distributive networks that relies upon a significant degree of internal diversity and complexity.

But, the question still remains – how do we recognize what violence is excessive such that we might call it domination? How do we make that normative judgment regarding the violence caused by protocolic control if we are ourselves swept up in the modulations?

The second part of the combined empirical / normative judgment for identifying the violence caused by protocolic control involves an articulation of the patternings of the self and the world and the relative values of these patternings. It involves coming to recognize the violence at work in the way in which the dualistic logic of protocolic control prevents politicization. An appeal to a universal normative metric, however, is inappropriate. It facilitates the universalization of relations – and, hence, the destruction of patterning relations – as well as a retreat from the real through abstractionism and idealization that obscure the violence being enacted. As we have seen above, an appeal to universal norms does violence to the inherent diversity and flux of network patternings through an appeal to the singularity of a universal finality. Further, an appeal to universal norms is dependent upon ontological commitments that obscure the violence of protocolic control. Indeed, we might say that by definition an appeal to universal norms is a furthering of protocolic control if one accepts the network ontology of res ecologia and the accompanying understanding of violence outlined in the previous two chapters. There is a domineering impulse of patterning disruption that develops through the ongoing interrelations between an appeal to universal norms and its corresponding ways of life such as a liberal political economy. If we are to recognize protocolic control at work, therefore, we will need to value the integrity of patterning systems and, perhaps most relevant for our concerns here, we will need to value the integrity of other persons and things as patterning systems that come to us as wholes from beyond. We will need to avoid universal normative metrics. The domination of the "empire of uniformity" promulgated by our universal norms (and manifest in the liberal political economy) may therefore be seen in the denial of the other as "the other" – i.e. the domination may be best seen in the *overcoming* of the other or the depatterning of the other.[33]

The domination of overcoming the other may be seen in an internalized domination in which the processes of identity formation is disrupted and displaced. Identity formation is so important in a network / control society because, as Manuel Castells writes, identities "build interests, values, and projects, around experience, and refuse to dissolve by establishing a specific connection between nature, history, geography,

---

33 By "other" I simply mean those who are not the self or, in a collective sense, not part of the group. The key point is that the other is different in some way. I do not use it in Schmitt's oppositional and violent sense where the other is an enemy, a stranger, or someone who presents an existential threat. See Schmitt, *The Concept of the Political*, 27.

and culture."[34] In other words, healthy identity formation is a process of putting down roots and developing a specificity or particularity; it is a process of localization through embedded interconnections that makes politicization possible. And it is this specificity that makes one a self and, simultaneously, an other to others. The "otherness" is overcome, however, by uprooting the process of identity formation from the interrelations of being-in-the-world and conceiving of and treating it as if it existed in some abstract realm detached from embodied ways of life. Of course, influencing and shaping identity formation (or participation in the construction of identity) is not problematic in itself. Our concern comes in the dualistic logic of simultaneous individuation and totalization at work within universal norms and liberal political economy. The domination of overcoming the other is born in the lack of reciprocity and therefore a lack of stability and resilience – for example, talk of equality involves a one-way or unidimensional positing of moral worth without the negotiation process of embodied relation. In this sense, then, the singularity of equality is illegitimate insofar as it lacks the dynamic interplay of dialogical relations. Its very logic is contrary to the reflexive logic of legitimation.

The process of identity formation should be understood from a number of different perspectives, but one of the most important approaches to understanding the nature of the self as res ecologia capable of resisting modulations of protocolic control will come about through the development of a new political economy. We need new techniques for ontological reframing that break from the domination of protocolic control and reconceptualize the economic self as a political self (and, likewise, the economic other as a political other). For example, as Gibson-Graham write, "where once we believed that the economy was depoliticized largely through its representations, we have more recently come to understand that its repoliticization requires cultivating ourselves as subjects who can imagine and enact a new economic politics."[35] Part of the re-politicization of the economy (i.e. the re-politicization of the self as economic-being) will surely involve movement away from a reliance upon talk of abstract (and mechanistic) laws in macro-economics and a conscious attempt to understand the embedded nature of economic transactions. Again, Gibson-Graham suggests that "as we begin to conceptualize contingent relationships where invariant logics once reigned, the economy loses its character as an asocial body in lawful motion and instead becomes a space of recognition and negotiation."[36] We will begin to develop a

34 Castells, *The Power of Identity*, 360.
35 Gibson-Graham, *A Postcapitalist Politics*, xxviii.
36 Ibid., xxx.

non-dominating discourse of political norms as we develop an approach to economic interrelations that has the processes of real-world economic lives as its focal point. That is, the patterning ontology of the self outlined above will need to not only be worked out as a theoretical touchstone for critiquing the individualism and abstractions of neo-liberal economics, but the real-world economic exchange-processes of communities existing outside the global, neo-liberal regime will provide a practical touchstone for developing the network ontology itself.

The understanding of domination as the disruption and displacement of identity formation processes not only involves a serious engagement with identities as economic relations but also involves a recognition of the fundamental incompleteness of persons and the perpetual vulnerability to which this gives rise. Kant is correct to note that persons are fundamentally incomplete (and cannot, therefore, be understood as ends-in-themselves in any absolute sense) but he is quite misguided in supposing that persons can be completed through an infilling of an abstract and universal moral law.[37] As we discussed in chapter 2, persons are best conceived of as network patternings that are developing in and through the relations of their ecological, socio-economic, and spiritual world. The self, therefore, is dependent upon the earth and others for this process of development. Just as a distributive network requires asymmetrical relations with its world to develop *as a distributive network*, the incomplete self is not only dependent upon the earth and the other, but is dependent upon relations with the earth and the other that are real-world relations (which are fundamentally asymmetrical) rather than idealized relations of abstract moral worth. To disrupt these real-world relations of dependency is to banish the patterning of the self, and hence the identity of the self, to a perpetual incompleteness with no genuine hope of development.

The kind of disruptive and depoliticizing domination we are looking at here can be seen in, for example, the ongoing struggle to create a common citizenry participating in a single market (i.e. the bringing of all persons under a single market state). These patterning violations of protocolic domination continue especially to be felt by indigenous peoples as universal normative metrics and a liberal political economy are "naturalized" within their ecological, socio-economic, and spiritual lives. In relation to settlers and their descendants, the other of specificity in indigeneity is overcome through seemingly virtuous ideals such as

---

37 For example, see Kant, *The Doctrine of Virtue*, quoted in Teuber, "Kant's Respect for Persons," 376.

equality, a common citizenry, and economic prosperity (i.e. participation in a common market in the commodification of land and labour). Those who find themselves outside the power flow of mainstream liberal society, however, resist standardization and its resulting homogenization and acceleration. Traditionalists seek a protection of their particularities against disruption and displacement while those who find themselves threatened by the standardizations of protocolic modulations seek areas of belief and practice where they can decelerate and stabilize their lives, their families, and their communities. For example, the problematization of difference outlined above is most explicit in the doctrine of egalitarianism where the abstractionism of an idealization driven by a logic of universalization and homogenization is made manifest. This homogenizing impulse involves a commitment to universality in its positing of a common normative metric. But, before going on to consider the violence of liberalization and its problematization of difference, let us first get our bearings by considering a little further the struggle for a common consumer-citizen.

Beginning with the first colonial explorers and settlers arriving on North American soil, there have been a number of prominent ongoing struggles against the homogenizing effects of idealized universal political norms in the Western hemisphere. Those indigenous and immigrant peoples who to this day find themselves outside the power flow of dominant governing systems very often resist the drive toward a common citizenry. For example, indigenous peoples have persistently pressed for self-preservation and self-government as a means of asserting their particularity. French Canadians have worked hard to preserve and protect their distinct place within an English North America and more traditionalist immigrants (e.g. Mennonites, Hutterites, Doukhobors, Amish, and conservative Muslims) have sought to live according to their unique traditions without disruption. Recently, too, we have seen the development of a critical reaction to the acceleration of society in the modern era through deliberate attempts to create unique personal identities that might slow down one's life and carve out shelters from the break-neck speeds of a monolithic hyperculture. These attempts to resist the accelerations of modern society, albeit often self-defeating behaviours, also represent a kind of struggle against the standardizations of protocolic modulations. Although we cannot go into the details of the struggles against homogeneity, it is important to note that these struggles continue to take place and that there is an important logic at work within these struggles that is significant for the restoration of conservative political ethics. The logic of resistance begins with a material, social, and spiritual environment divided by deep diversity and difference, moves into the introduction of the homogenizing impulse of a universal normative metric (and accompanying socio-economic standardizations), and then becomes manifest in defiance to the violence of universal normalization and a reassertion of difference. The logic of resistance, therefore, involves a push-back against the logic of homogeneity through a refusal to be individuated within a universal normative metric; it is an attempt to localize and embody the norms of political theory in order to bring the difference of diversity down into the very roots of our understanding of justice. Although the ideal of a common citizenry is most often pursued with the seemingly virtuous intention of building a just society for all, these struggles of resistance against a common, equal citizenry reveal the problematic nature of idealized universal political norms. These counter-struggles tip us off to the fact that there is a darker underside to the struggle for commonality in the name of justice.

One of the most infamous examples of the homogenizing impulse within egalitarianism (as well as the corresponding push-back from subaltern communities) may be seen in the Liberal government's "Indian Policy" of 1969.[38] Canada's federal government, under Prime Minister Pierre Trudeau and Minister of Indian Affairs and Northern Development Jean Chrétien, issued this policy statement as an explicit call for changes that were designed to bring about equality for all peoples in Canada. The federal government argued that "special treatment has made of the Indians a community disadvantaged and apart" and that "to be an Indian must be to be free – free to develop Indian cultures in an environment of legal, social and economic equality with other Canadians."[39] The problems of the past were not said to be rooted in policies and practices of cultural genocide or assimilation, but were instead presented as the result of *difference itself;* the problem was that indigenous peoples did not hold the *same* legal standing as non-indigenous peoples. In other words, "true equality presupposes that the Indian people have the right to full and equal participation in the cultural, social, economic and political life of Canada" and, indeed, "separate but equal services do not provide truly equal treatment."[40] It was further argued that "the treatment resulting from their different status has been often worse, sometimes equal and occasionally better than that accorded to their fellow citizens. *What matters is that it has been different.*"[41] Not surprisingly, many indigenous peoples across Canada were deeply

---

38 See "Statement of the Government of Canada on Indian Policy, 1969," Indian and Northern Affairs Canada, http://www.aadnc-aandc.gc.ca/eng/1100100010189/1100100 010191. Accessed 10 February 2016.

39 Ibid., 2.

40 Ibid., 7, 15.

41 Ibid., 4, emphasis added.

offended by this attempt to assimilate them into modern liberal society and began in earnest to organize in resistance.[42] Some, like Harold Cardinal, were explicit in stating that this push toward a common citizenry was "a thinly disguised programme of extermination through assimilation" in which "the only good Indian is a non-Indian."[43] One of the central problems with the 1969 White Paper, as identified by indigenous peoples, was the fact that the call for equality rests upon an assumption of a universal metric that is able to contain the other. In other words, indigenous peoples recognized that these egalitarian policies meant that "Indians are to become brown white men."[44] The deep cracks of cultural difference that made up life in Canada were to be covered over, sanded smooth, and polished bright; everyone was expected to join in celebrating the dazzling equality of the new just society.

CONCLUSION

In conclusion, it should be quite clear by now that there is no absolute or objective reference point from which to recognize protocolic domination. But of course this should not surprise us. We identify protocolic violence – or any kind of excessive violence – through a combined empirical and normative judgment because we need to (a) take stock of the current relational dynamics at work within and around us, (b) evaluate the relative importance of the patternings involved, and (c) evaluate the severity of the violations taking place. A conclusion arrived at through this kind of complex, reflective evaluative process will always be contingent upon not only our ability to recognize and articulate the nature of the violations taking place at a particular time, but also our place within relational patternings. And because others will always have different abilities to recognize and articulate violations that they employ from different places within relational patternings, the question of excessive violence is always changing and therefore is always subject to further negotiation. Indeed, as mentioned above, this should not be surprising because the question of excessive violence is itself a fundamentally (if not *the* fundamental) democratic question.

42 See McFarlane, *Brotherhood to Nationhood*, 108–21.

43 Cardinal, *The Unjust Society*, 1. Walter Dieter of the National Indian Brotherhood stated that this policy would be "the destruction of a nation of people by legislation and cultural genocide." Dieter, "Canadian Facts on File, 16–20 June 1968," 289, quoted in McFarlane, *Brotherhood to Nationhood*, 109.

44 Cardinal, *The Unjust Society*, 2.

4

The Logic of Liberalism

A. THE PROCEDURALIST TURN AND DUALISTIC LOGIC
Liberalism as a failed attempt to substitute "the right" for "the good."

B. LIBERALISM'S NORMATIVE STANDARDIZATIONS
Liberalism's normative ideals rooted in self-determination and equality contain standardizing impulses built upon a dualistic logic.

C. THE FREE MARKET, SCIENCE, AND COSMOPOLITANISM
The dualism within both a market-based political economy and the search for global politics.

INTRODUCTION

James Tully notes that members of culturally diverse societies negotiating their differences often appear to us as a "strange multiplicity." He suggests that, for those who have become accustomed to a singular notion of sovereignty, the persistence of numerous competing claims to authority causes us discomfort and even confusion. The multiplicity is strange to us because "the language of modern constitutionalism which has come to be authoritative was designed to exclude or assimilate cultural diversity and justify uniformity."[1] In this way Tully digs down through our political phenomena to reveal the underlying assumptions, regarding the constitution of society, that are giving rise to our discomforts. He unearths the homogenizing impulse within modern constitutionalism.

Taking up a similar methodology that seeks to uncover hidden assumptions behind our political discomforts, this chapter represents an archaeological exploration of a logic hidden within the liberal democratic tradition. Whereas Tully reveals a kind of constitutionalism that overcomes diversity through exclusion and assimilation, we can now begin to explore

---

1 Tully, *Strange Multiplicity*, 58.

the underlying patterns of our thinking and living – the hidden logic – that motivate this problematization of difference. Although its precise nature will require a thorough investigation and analysis, we can begin to detect the presence of this logic when we pause and reflect upon the concern and even revulsion we so often feel when faced with examples of socio-economic dependence and the vulnerability that comes with asymmetrical power differences. Why is it that inequality, vulnerability, and dependence so often appear to us as problems that are to be overcome? What hidden assumptions are lying behind and motivating this problematization of difference? How is our understanding of morality and political community being determined by these assumptions?

Anglo-American moral and political theory has become fixated with problems of overcoming inequalities and eliminating dependencies – what I am calling the "problematization of difference" – and almost all new PhD scholars and authors writing about politics engage in this problematization in some form or another. In what follows, I will suggest that this problematization of difference underlying modern moral and political theory stems from the fact that our thinking about justice and progress has been built upon a dualistic logic that simultaneously individuates and universalizes. This logic causes us to isolate political actors by viewing them as inherently valuable and self-determining while at the same time orienting them within a universal framework of moral action that determines what is morally acceptable for anyone anywhere. I believe this logic of isolation and universal orientation gives rise to a dangerous totalizing impulse that has been grafted onto our democratic theory at the root and runs through the very centre of our notion of justice. This grafting has lead to significant tensions within the liberal tradition and, importantly, has also led to some moral blind spots that are diminishing our ability to live in a more just and peaceful world.

A clarification and an apology should be made at the outset. First, my analysis of the logic at work within the liberal tradition is not intended to be a wholesale rejection of the practical workings of the liberal tradition. Although, for example, I contend that a commitment to freedom and equality as moral and political ideals has many inevitable negative consequences in practice, my concern is primarily with the nature of political theorizing that gives rise to this kind of ideal. Our striving for greater freedom and equality belies the fact that something has gone wrong in our broader approach to democratic theory and normative reasoning. Second, my analysis is not intended to capture the depth and diversity of the liberal tradition. I will move very quickly through a number of very different thinkers without seeking to deal with all of the details or do justice to the depth of their thought. This is because I am simply seeking to suggest one way of understanding what allows the liberal tradition to hang together – even as it manifests itself in numerous ways.

What then do I mean by "liberalism"? There is no doubt that liberalism has developed as a varied and complex tradition over approximately the past 400 years. It can be difficult, therefore, to determine and define its key characteristics without either slipping into gross oversimplifications and generalizations that distort the tradition or reverting to methods liberals have developed to describe themselves and their liberal interlocutors. In what follows I will do my best to avoid both of these traps, but will undoubtedly falter at times. Nonetheless, my goal will be to excavate the theoretical foundations of the central tradition that shapes and guides modern political thought in order to bring to light our hidden patterns of thought. Although I begin with a basic definition in order to initiate the analysis, the goal is not a definition of liberalism but rather a revealing of the inner workings of the tradition. In what follows, we will be looking for the mechanics of Western political thought. What are the hidden patterns of thinking that make liberalism tick?

Liberalism, like any tradition of thought can be understood in a very general sense as both a belief and a normative commitment. What makes it distinct as a tradition is the nature of this belief and normative commitment. It is the *belief* that a diverse multiplicity, if interacting in the correct manner, will come together into a singular progressive change. It is also a *commitment* to creating the right kind of procedures to make this progression a reality. I will suggest that the distinctive nature of liberalism's belief and normative commitment can most clearly be seen in an analysis of what I call the three interrelated "modes" of liberalism:

(a) the constitution of a universal public realm through proceduralism,
(b) the commitment to the ideals of self-determination and equality, and
(c) the cosmopolitan pursuit of progress.

The central mechanism for accomplishing progressive change – "the good" in liberalism – involves a refusal to search directly for it. Instead, liberals seek to substitute "the right" for "the good" by subsuming the search for the good under a primarily proceduralist account of normative obligations. As Charles Taylor describes it, liberals believe that "a liberal society should not be founded on any particular notion of the good life. The ethic central to a liberal society is an ethic of the right rather than the good. That is, its basic principles concern how society should respond to and arbitrate the competing demands of individuals."[2] This substitutionalism means that liberal thinkers deny outright that there is one single kind

---

2 Taylor, *Philosophical Arguments*, 186.

of procedure that is "the good." Inevitably, however, the three modes of liberalism actually do form a kind of definition and defence of a certain kind of procedures. So, as I will argue, not only do these three modes of liberalism all operate according to a common dualistic logic, but it is this logic that, in large part, constitutes "the good" of liberalism.

Dualistic logic simultaneously individualizes and universalizes and, in so doing, undermines deep pluralism by disallowing the acknowledgement of deep diversity. Dualistic logic causes us to be disturbed by inequality, vulnerability, and dependence – i.e. offended by patterns of asymmetrical relations that are inescapably built upon the specificity or particularity of non-interchangeable connections. However unwittingly, it causes us to seek a final resolution (in either atomism or universalism) while at the same time disallowing this very resolution by leading us into wild swings between individualism and totalitarianism in a kind of political schizophrenia. Against our best intentions, therefore, we are drawn into patterns of exclusion or assimilation in our attempts to find some relief from the discomfort of our strange multiplicities.

Before diving into this argument, let us give a little more consideration to the concept of liberalism. For, as Taylor has noted, in the last four hundred years liberalism has developed and diversified to include a wide range of values and priorities. When exploring the tradition, therefore, it is important to distinguish between what he calls "ontological issues" and "advocacy issues." Ontological questions may be thought of as those "terms you accept as ultimate in the order of explanation" whereas advocacy questions "concern the moral stand or policy one adopts."[3] Taylor is correct to also note that although the two types of questions are not independent of each other, taking a position in one area does not necessarily commit a person to a certain position in the other area. Although a person's ontological commitments do not directly determine his political priorities, they nonetheless form a kind of background language that determines the *means* of articulating political priorities. Therefore, at least two phenomena can arise from this dynamic connection: (a) a range of policy commitments can stem from any set of ontological commitments and (b) a person can have policy commitments that are out of sync with his ontological commitments. In other words, there is no direct or necessary one-to-one linkage between commitments to ontology and policy.

But if the liberal tradition includes such a wide range of perspectives on both ontology and policy priorities and there is no direct or necessary connection between commitments to ontology and policy, how am I justified in saying that it possesses a dualistic logic that problematizes difference? Am I being excessively reductionist? I do not believe so. First, there is

3 Ibid., 181–2.

something we call the liberal tradition that involves agreement and disagreement regarding both ontological and policy issues; there is some conversation that possesses enough consistency throughout history to identify it as a coherent tradition. And I am arguing that it is actually an acceptance of something like what I am calling dualistic logic that serves to hold the tradition together – that helps make liberalism a coherent conversation. Second, because there is a great deal of diversity within the liberal tradition, it is important to approach it from a number of angles if we are to tease out a common thread running through various strains of thought. This is the reason for my approaching liberalism through three "modes." Third, I am not suggesting that I am able to reduce the entire tradition down to one simple progression of thought. A tradition is fundamentally irreducible and its central logic is persistently negotiable. We have good reason, therefore, to seek a "logic of liberalism" but equal reason to remain always attentive to the need for epistemic humility.

With the challenges of identifying the central logic of a tradition in mind, let us move on to consider one of the ways we might approach liberalism. Let us begin with a discussion of liberalism's procedural turn and what the prioritization of procedure might mean for not only our understanding of the tradition as a whole, but also for how it fosters a persistent problematization of difference.

A. THE PROCEDURALIST TURN AND DUALISTIC LOGIC

Let us now turn to consider liberalism more directly. I would like to argue that it is in liberalism that we can best see the method of theorizing about political relations that facilitates the advancement of protocolic control. And, in so doing, liberalism also fuels the acceleration outlined in chapter 1 above. This should not be surprising on first blush, of course, because both protocolic control and liberalism depend upon the same kind of technological world – a world that divides and unites at the same time. But, before we get too far ahead, what do I mean by "liberalism"? Liberalism can be provisionally defined as a commitment to building societies that realize a vision of all persons as free and equal individuals. The central mechanism for accomplishing this within the liberalism that is dominant today is a substitution of "the right" for "the good" – i.e. the search for the good is subsumed under a primarily proceduralist account of normative obligations.[4]

4 The state is typically understood as possessing a legitimate claim to monopolized violence only if we can (at least theoretically) trace its origin back to a set of contractual procedures that granted individuals the opportunity to lose some individual liberty in

In "Cross-Purposes," Taylor rightly highlights the differences between issues of ontology (atomism-holism) and issues of policy (individualism-collectivism) in order to reveal the depth of the complexity involved in the debate between liberals and communitarians. However, there is yet another level of complexity that Taylor seems to miss in his analysis. A further category should be added to ontology (i.e. structuralism) as well as a further distinction to issues of policy (i.e. conservatism-liberalism). He focuses on the slippage between ontology and policy, but fails to recognize that there is actually a key distinction that is making, I would argue, an even greater difference between the way one understands the *changes* in the relations between individuals, collectives, and – importantly – larger patterning processes that shape the systems of meaning within which we live as historical beings. The political implications of one's understanding of these issues surrounding the various kinds of change in space / time are dramatic. Therefore, the variables involved in the debate could better delineated with an additional diachronic variable of relationality that allows us to draw attention to the difference between two different kinds of ontological analysis – what I would call "socio-phenomenological" and "eco-logical" ontologies – and highlights the nature of the methodology employed throughout the discussion of *res ecologia* above as well as the rest of this chapter.

By "socio-phenomenological" I mean a focus on the development of, and relations between, subjectivities or the social and cultural allegiances that might be described in inter-subjective, sociological terms. So, for example, Taylor focuses on the realm of socio-phenomenological ontology when he writes of a "we-identity" that is different from an "I-identity" and the consequent differentiation between common goods and convergent goods. This kind of ontological analysis sets out a language that determines a certain means of articulating political relations or the kinds of choices one can make in developing political priorities. For example, the "we-identity" accords more closely with a conception of positive freedom (e.g. participation in the public life of the republic) whereas the "I-identity" fits more closely with negative freedom (e.g. lack of restrictions).[5] Notice, though, that this experiential ontology captures *a certain kind of phenomena* – relations between persons and groups of persons.

---

order to gain some degree of collective security and prosperity. This kind of contractarianism is seen most explicitly, of course, in the work of Rousseau. For example, see Rousseau, *Discourse on Political Economy and The Social Contract*, 56–7.

5 Taylor, *Philosophical Arguments*, 192–3.

In contrast, by "eco-logical" I mean an eco-systems (embodied, relational, systemic) approach which, instead of focussing upon the experiences of subjects in social life, seeks to develop a language of the shifting patterns of being-in-the-world and endeavours to articulate, for example, how changes in bodies and environments change the nature of thought and action. Or, how changing rates of relational patternings shape the systems or structures of meaning within which we live and have our being. Like the discussion of res ecologia above in which we described ecological as the ordering principle of the spaces within which we dwell, so too does this approach focus us upon the patternings of ourselves and our world. This is, of course, in keeping with the kind of structural causation I outlined in chapter 2 above – i.e. a focus on the structure of things rather than simply the relations between things. The analysis of protocolic control outlined above, for example, is an attempt to engage in this kind of ontological analysis; it is an attempt to develop a language to recognize and assess changes in the rates of change within and around us. Ultimately, it is this kind of analysis that allows us to focus in on the real differences between conservatism and liberalism as well as the connections between liberalism (whether it is rooted in ontological atomism or holism) and the violence of protocolic modulations outlined above.

With this brief glimpse into the different methods of approaching political traditions and the impact these different methodologies have upon our understanding of political ontologies in mind, let us return to our discussion of liberalism. Let us consider the logic at work within liberalism's proceduralist turn and the dangers that arise when the ecological ontologies (the ordering principles of the structures and processes) of our political traditions go unexamined. Liberalism, in its most general sense, is rooted in the belief that either (a) there is no natural ordering process in the world, or (b) if there is a natural ordering process in the world, it is epistemically inaccessible with any adequate degree of certainty.[6] If this definition of liberalism is correct, substitutionalism (i.e. prioritizing the "right" over the "good") is the key identifier between liberalism and conservatism. Namely, liberals are those who engage in a substitution of the "right" for the "good" and conservatives eschew the taking of this proceduralist turn by putting the "good" before the "right."

But an important point of clarification should be made here. Conservatism also involves the use of "right" procedures (as, indeed, all political

6 Further, because liberalism is a political orientation (or a political outworking of ontological and epistemological beliefs), (b) tends to equate with (a) – i.e. if there is no meaningful epistemic access to the ordering, for all political intents and purposes it does not exist.

thought does). The question, then, is not *whether or not* one seeks to develop procedures for living together, but *how* one goes about developing these procedures and what relation they have to articulations of the good life. For conservatives, it is essential that procedures are directly derived from, and subservient to, a search for the good life. It is not a matter, therefore, of either completely abandoning the good and adopting a search for the right procedures or completely abandoning procedures in a bare, parochial, or chauvinistic assertion of one's conception of the good. What I am calling the "proceduralist turn" or "proceduralism" is a description of the logic behind the prioritization of the right ahead of the good and a recognition that folks engage in this turn to varying degrees.

If, as we discussed regarding the various methods of viewing political ontologies, liberalism includes such a wide range of varying perspectives and policy priorities, how can we draw a connection between liberalism and protocolic control? One can approach the relationship between the right and the good in different ways as a liberal but to the degree that one is engaging in the proceduralist turn one is becoming subject to a dualistic logic and, consequently, is unable to effectively articulate resilient ways of life that are able to withstand the rapid modulations of protocolic control. For it is my contention that the procedural turn is animated by the dualistic logic outlined above in chapter 3.

As we will remember from our earlier discussion, dualistic logic involves a simultaneous individuation and totalization. We can see dualistic logic at work within the proceduralist turn insofar as actors and procedures are defined and constituted in *direct and opposing relation to each other*. The actors to be governed by the procedures are individuated and, simultaneously, the nature of their participation is totalized in universalized procedures (or at least the universalized character of the procedures). Dualistic logic simultaneously individuates and totalizes in its abstraction away from the relational patternings that make up our being in the world. To the degree that we have abandoned the search for the good life in favour of the search for the right procedures that can govern behaviour sufficiently to allow everyone to live together, we have been led into the dualistic, individuate /
totalize (or assimilate / exclude) logic. In this manner, the dualistic logic at work within the proceduralist turn facilitates the eclipse of its normative input – i.e. an obscuring of the politics of procedural change, the politics of protocolic control. But, in order to understand this normative eclipse, let us briefly consider the underlying abstractionism of protocol and how this abstraction relates to proceduralism.

The simultaneous individuation and totalization – i.e. the mutual definition or constitution of the individuated actor and the totalized procedures – eclipses mediating relations of dependence and vulnerability that make up the normative worlds of beings-in-the-world. Individuation is a process of normative reasoning in which, at some point, it is necessary to consider a person or thing in isolation from its environment. Dualistic logic hollows out or dissolves the relations of dependence and vulnerability by setting up symmetrical relations between an individuated subject and a totalized subject (object). This symmetry denies dependence and, consequently, denies normative relations and, ultimately, the possibilities of searching for the good life. Normativity is a patterning that creates a history. However, there is no patterning in dualism, there is only abstract and ahistorical standardizations – the tyranny of the now. A patterning is historical and, because it has a past-present-future trajectory, allows for the projection into the future and thus a weightiness of normativity. As MacIntyre astutely notes regarding the historicity of our lives that gives us our ability to make moral judgments, "like characters in a fictional narrative we do not know what will happen next, but none the less our lives have a certain form which projects itself toward our future."[7] The moral view – rather than being a view from eternity, a view from nowhere, or a view from the noumenal self – is a view from within history, it is a patterning of being-in-the-world. Normative judgment, for good or for ill, is in this sense quite literally an exercise of one's historic prejudices rather than an individual operating under the constraints of impartiality.[8]

As we have seen in chapter 3, modern science was founded upon the elevation of mechanistic causation as well as the notion that natural systems were governed by abstract or objective laws that were deterministic in their causal connections. We also observed that this kind of reductionist approach to causation led to the idea that behaviour in complex systems could be predicted if one simply had enough information. In contrast, the structural causation approach to complex systems means that the past influences and changes propensities, but does not determine – the future is open. This indeterminacy, when it comes to speaking of normative relations, is rooted in reciprocity, a mutual giving of the self where the self is given without the certainty of return. This lack of predictability cannot be bargained or negotiated because it is fundamentally indeterminate in its asymmetry. Normativity, therefore,

7   MacIntyre, *After Virtue*, 201.
8   Sandel, *Liberalism and the Limits of Justice*, 180. Also, compare with Jeffrey Stout's explanation of Kant and Rawls' notion of the moral point of view in Stout, *The Flight from Authority*, 232.

is a trajectory without certainty – a relationality that is doubly asymmetrical and, consequently, dramatically out of sync with dualistic logic.

In order to govern or control in an environment of complexity and diversity, protocol must transcend the variations, must create symmetries to rise above the asymmetries of being-in-the-world. Relational patternings must be coordinated and synchronized. But this kind of synchronization can only take place by lifting us out of our finite, corporeal bodies into a realm of abstract, totalizing unity. If universal coordination and effective communication is to take place, the local and particular in ecological, social, and spiritual relations must be transcended through a process of abstraction. It is only in the abstract that universal coordination and synchronization can take place. So, if effective coordination is to take place through space / time, we must – at some level – move away from the lifeworlds of persons to minimize asymmetry and specificity while maximizing symmetry and universality. We must engage in a process of depersonalization, delocalization, deterritorialization, and atomization by simultaneously individuating and totalizing.

This kind of synchronization, for example, can be found in the requirement that we commit to liberal ideals if we want to engage in a process of legitimizing our political actions. In other words, liberalism does not allow for the recognition of any action as legitimate political action unless it is a part of a certain kind of proceduralism. However, as we will see, the proceduralism required for legitimate action is so demanding that it serves to either assimilate or exclude and this substitution of the right for the good allows no more than a thin pluralism. Liberalism, therefore, is fundamentally unable to develop a thick pluralism of the kind needed to avoid fuelling the domination of protocolic control at work in the modern world.

All too often, only those who accept liberal ideals – i.e. consider all persons to be self-determining individuals deserving of equal concern and respect – are understood to be engaged in projects of legitimizing their exercise of power. Leaving aside for now what *is* legitimate, within the liberal approach one cannot even begin to explain what *might* be legitimate unless one commits to these core liberal values up front. So, we can see a standardization already taking place in proceduralism as a requirement for legitimate political action – either you are some kind of liberal or you are simply unable to begin legitimizing power. This is the totalitarianism underlying liberalism – assimilate or exclude.

Much of liberal democratic theory has centred on trying to bring liberal ethical norms and popular sovereignty together in such a way as to establish a kind of deliberation that is thought to be both rational and democratic at the same time. In order to accomplish this, rationalist liberal theoreticians like Rawls and Habermas (and those who follow in their theoretical footsteps) employ various methods of limiting the deliberation to ensure that liberal ideals are adequately preserved throughout the deliberative process. That is, they seek an ideal theoretical realm that is not subject to the pluralism of values that we find in everyday life and where moral consensus can be reached without the exclusion of persons. This process of limiting deliberation, however, is highly problematic insofar as they are simply unable to find consensus without significant exclusions. In other words, Rawls' and Habermas' attempts to develop a meta-political position ultimately effects a process of depoliticization in which the limits of democratic political conduct are heavily policed.

One of the places where we can see this assimilate-or-exclude gatekeeping is in the requirement that all reasons for political action be undergirded by public reasons or open participation in public forums. Or at least, one must hold reasons that are translatable into public reasons should the need arise.[9] This is, in fact, a kind of gatekeeping that is used by liberals to cover their political tracks. In other words, a refusal to recognize the legitimacy of any political action that is not contributing to an overarching project of *constructing universal procedures* for living together in peace obscures the fundamentally political nature of a commitment to liberal substitutionalism.[10] And, the political nature of substitutionalism is made manifest when substantive disagreement about the good arising from, say, traditional communities is stretched and twisted into a process of universal comparison through "public reasoning." That is, "the good" becomes simply "one good among many" such that someone seeking to pursue "the good" must instead begin understanding themselves as pursuing "a good" within the terms of "the right." The right, however, always also represents the good no matter how much one attempts to deny the search for the good.

9   For example, for Rawls, public reason is: (1) "the reason of the public," (2) "its subject is the good of the public," and (3) "its nature and content is public." Rawls, *Political Liberalism*, 213. In this sense, his notion of public reason rests upon two key assumptions regarding commonality: (1) that it is directed toward the good of society (i.e. as a whole), and (2) it is engaged in by persons sharing a common / equal citizenship. See ibid., 213. Also see Rawls' definition of reasonable which is rooted in the same two principles of commonality. He writes, "persons are reasonable in one basic aspect when, among equals say, they are ready to propose principles and standards as fair terms of cooperation and to abide by them willingly, given the assurance that others will likewise do so. Those norms they view as reasonable for everyone to accept and therefore as justifiable to them." Ibid., 49.

10   As Mouffe has insisted, "drawing the frontier between the legitimate and the illegitimate is always a political decision." Mouffe, *On the Political*, 121.

For a hint of the good lurking behind liberalism's search for the right, consider the commonality (or should I say overlapping consensus) between Rawls and Habermas. For example, both Rawls and Habermas seek to use a certain method to arrive at a set of principles that are to guide us into an understanding of a just society. For Rawls, this means a thought experiment – the veil of ignorance. For Habermas, this means a transcendental uncovering of the structures of communication. But both Rawls and Habermas inevitably build the key principles of liberalism into their method itself. In other words, both develop a method upon the assumption that all persons are to be considered free, equal, and rational. Not only are they building the principles into the methods, but both of their methods also assume (or build in) the notion that the principles of a just society can be spoken of in abstract and impersonal terms – i.e. as if justice and moral worth were ascertainable apart from real-life relations of persons. It is behind this abstractionism that we can find their hidden Kantian metaphysics regarding human nature, their *de facto* metaphysics of persons as atomistic (i.e. interchangeable at core). And, interestingly, there is a deontic shift in their abstractionism that further belies their Kantian commitments. For, when we abstract away from embodied persons and their inherently messy political relations, interests and inclinations are emptied of their empirical content and thereby become universal duties – for liberals in the Rawlsian and Habermasian schools of thought, commitment to the principles of a just society (e.g. considering persons as self-determining and equal individuals) is a duty much like that produced by Kant's categorical imperative.[11] In other words, it is not the relationship between real persons that stimulates and shapes the political norms (indeed, both those who are theorizing and those who are being theorized about are considered free and equal individuals), it is the positive assertion that liberal principles hold true. Importantly, Rawls and Habermas did not suppose that their methods were neutral in an absolute sense. But they deem them appropriate because of the results to which they ostensibly lead – the principles of a just society. Of course, though, this is really a process of circular reasoning that is intended to justify liberal principles and preserve them against any doubt caused by democratic political thought. And the standardizing abstractionism this circular reasoning employs actually provides the foundation for structural domination through protocolic modulations.

Thus, proceduralism is problematic to the degree that one presumes that the demands it places upon people are pre-political or somehow

---

trans-political. For example, Rawls builds equality into his theory of reasonable pluralism such that uniformity and commonality are held to be unquestionable if one is to be considered reasonable or even dealing with a political rather than personal matter. Any request or demand for unequal treatment is, by definition, held to be unreasonable by Rawls and therefore not a request or demand that is up for political debate.[12] In short, genuinely political aspirations which are always requests / demands for differential treatment or some kind of distinction are disallowed and discounted from the outset because commonality is required for entrance into the realm of the political.

More recently, Anthony Laden has attempted to reconcile liberalism and identity politics with a Rawlsian version of liberalism termed "deliberative liberalism." He seeks a kind of liberalism that is more open to difference and to a deeper pluralism, and he looks to reasonable political deliberation as the basis for the development of a common political will. In outlining the notion of deliberative liberalism, Laden does not stray too far from Rawls for, by requiring "reasonable" deliberation, Laden means that deliberators "must exchange only public reasons" and (ironically) suggests that exclusion and assimilation undermine the reasonableness of deliberation.[13] In other words, political deliberation demands the giving of public reasons such that, if the identity of a public citizen does not square with some other aspects of a person's identity, the private elements of a person's identity must be abandoned, or at least fenced off in some manner. However, importantly and to his credit, his requirements of non-exclusion and non-assimilation also mean that the demand for abandonment or fencing-off cannot be overly burdensome to individuals.[14]

This attempt to deepen the very thin pluralism of Rawls is certainly a step in the right direction, a step away from standardization. However, the proceduralist turn in Laden's work continues to undermine the thickening of the pluralism in a denial of politics. We can see this in the restrictions he places upon deliberation which seem to be rooted not only in his status quo approach to politics, but also in his political

12 Rawls assumes equality as an ideal of democracy from the very beginning and builds his understanding of "public," "reasonable," "consensus," and "political" upon this assumption. It is not surprising, then, when he understands a well-ordered society to be one that is rooted in uniformity – i.e. "a society in which everyone accepts, and knows that everyone else accepts, the very same principles of justice." Rawls, *Political Liberalism*, 35. Further, in *A Theory of Justice*, he describes equality as "essentially justice as regularity" – i.e. it "implies the impartial application and consistent interpretation of rules according to such precepts as to treat similar cases similarly." Rawls, *A Theory of Justice*, 504.

13 Laden, *Reasonably Radical*, 12–13.

14 Ibid., 14.

ontology regarding citizenship. He outlines what he calls a "political conception of citizenship" – i.e. a concept of citizenship that is built upon a form / content dualism. Citizens have form features (elements of identity that are determined by social systems and, in turn, place limits on the development of content features) that are beyond the reach of politics and they have content features (elements of identity that are contingent features – the reasons an identity authorizes) that are deliberatively constructed.[15] Personal identities, then, are "identities with minimal form features" and social identities are "identities all of whose content features are determined by their form features."[16] However, not only are the form features determined outside politics, but the content features are constructed through a deliberative process that is highly artificial and limited to universal considerations. Therefore, Laden leaves us with a notion of citizenship that is excessively focused on public / universal features of identity and downplays collective identities that are social, but much narrower than universal. That is, the individual content of identity is said to be contingent and open to change by the form of identity that is common to all within society.

Laden sometimes seems to come close to addressing the problem I am raising here, but then goes on to write "since we are understood to be reasoning together as citizens, public reasons are the appropriate sorts of reasons to offer" and, further, "if we are to deliberate reasonably with our fellow citizens, we must regard them as equal."[17] But that is precisely the point – the assumption regarding reasoning together *as citizens* is what determines from the outset that the political engagement must be on liberal terms. He builds liberalism into his conception of deliberation and then attempts to demonstrate how pluralistic his notion of deliberation is. But, of course, it is only pluralistic insofar as everyone is already willing and able to be liberals. Further, the fundamental commitment to commonality underlying the procedural turn becomes quite clear when Laden describes a theory of reasonable deliberation is one that "analyzes the intrinsic character of deliberation rather than its reliability or the choices it yields."[18] This presumption of underlying unity within proceduralism has significant implications for his understanding of legitimate governance. For example, he writes, "a government that acts on nonpublic reasons as if they were public reasons requires that some citizens submit to its authority without consenting to it. It is thus not acting

15 Ibid., 108, 112–13.
16 Ibid., 110.
17 Ibid., 114.
18 Ibid., 75.

legitimately."[19] By arguing in this way, Laden is actually suggesting that only states committed to liberal values may be legitimate. Simply put, "the public" often seems to be another way of saying "the state." Thus, public reasons are reasons one gives as a citizen – i.e. as a member of a state made up of a common citizenry.[20] Public debate on political matters that is aimed at promoting or defending an interest narrower than the common citizenry within a state is not to be understood as serving a legitimating role through reasonable political deliberation. In addition, reasonable political deliberation must be directed toward questions of the good of all citizens and must be concerning the power of the state.[21] By demanding commonality in their proceduralism both Rawls and Laden build a kind of individual-state dualism (and state-centrism) into their systems of thought.

Those committed to liberal proceduralism feel compelled, as Jeffrey Stout explains, "to reify a sort of all-purpose, abstract fairness or respect for others because [they] cannot imagine ethical or political discourse *dialogically*."[22] There is, however, no reason why we should remain wedded to the Kantian notion of universal normativity we see at work in proceduralism. Indeed, for the expressivist, for example, norms are not universal abstractions but "creatures of the social process in which members of a community achieve mutual recognition as subjects answerable for their actions and commitments. The social process in which norms come to be and come to be made explicit is dialectical. It involves movement back and forth between action and reflection as well as interaction among individuals with differing points of view. Because this process takes place in the dimension of time and history, the beliefs and actions one is entitled to depend in large part on what has already transpired within the dialectical process itself."[23] In contrast, proceduralism operates within a conceptual framework that forecloses against the possibilities of "epistemological and sociological dimensions of discursive practices" that necessarily give us a multiplicity of norms and normativities.[24] The line between

19 Ibid., 105.

20 Ibid., 13, 101.

21 Ibid., 102–4. When the state is understood as uniting individuals in political community, the only justification for the despotic means of unification can be found in egalitarianism. However, the justification then becomes a further contribution to the problem in need of justification. That is, the more the social contract is justified, the more it needs to be justified. Hence, the modern welfare state, and now the reach of the market state, expands at a furious rate.

22 Stout, *Democracy and Tradition*, 74.

23 Ibid., 78.

24 Ibid., 74.

"political" and "non-political" is set out in advance through the process of developing the right procedures. Put another way, the proceduralist turn actually betrays an unwillingness to accept the politics of numerous communities and represents a search for the means to construct a shared, communitarian politic.[25] It is wrong, therefore, to pit communitarianism against liberalism; the proceduralism of liberalism ensures a search for a *universal* community united by common terms and practices.

The proceduralist turn leads inevitably to a thin pluralism. Perhaps the most interesting kind of thinker to consider here is the one who – using the variables outlined by Taylor and then modified by myself – is an ontological holist and a political liberal. Indeed, it should be quite obvious how one committed to ontological atomism and political individualism cannot be committed to a thick notion of pluralism. It is more difficult with one who, for example, understands that a person's political priorities are shaped within the interplay between a cultural environment that is not of their own making and a reflexive engagement with the political language that takes place in and through history.[26] This person, therefore, believes in the existence of irreducible social goods that are created along with the formation of what Taylor might call a "we-identity."[27] This kind of collectivist-liberal focuses on the socio-phenomenological ontology in an attempt to combat atomistic ontologies and extreme proceduralism but, due to this sociological approach, is nonetheless inevitably drawn into the proceduralistic turn as a kind of pragmatic liberal. The pragmatic liberal, therefore, imposes an artificial, formalized pluralism because the ability to develop a deeper, more authentic pluralism is destroyed to the degree that he abandons the primacy of the good.

I am suggesting that to the extent that one puts the right before the good, one is drawn into a totalizing logic that precludes a thick pluralism. There is a difference, therefore, between putting the good first and putting the right first when it comes to being a pluralist. This is because the difference between the right and the wrong operates through a different logic than the difference between the good and the bad. The search for the right is dualistic in a way that the search for the good is not – or, to put it another way, the search for the good can be dialogical in a way that the search for the right cannot be. Perhaps ironically (and surprisingly to the liberal), the logic of the right is a search for a universal or totalized community populated by individual actor-subjects defined in

25 Wolterstorff and Audi, *Religion in the Public Square,* 109.
26 Webber, *Reimagining Canada.*
27 See, for example, Taylor, *Philosophical Arguments.*

relation to the totality-object. The right must be totalized because, as soon as we are able to seek multiple procedures for negotiating the nature of the good (i.e. multiple "rights"), questions concerning the right procedures suddenly are seen for what they truly are – questions of the good. A substitution of the right for the good can only be thorough if one seeks *the* right (and, hence, *the* good). A search for the good – if properly understood as a dialogical endeavour – is actually governed by a discursive logic of multiplicity.

There is also a dynamic, two-way causation at work within the search for the good that facilitates a deep pluralism. The mind and the body change together in a dynamic, two-way causal relationship, and the abandonment of this mind-body causal connectivity has led to unhelpful (if not outright harmful) conceptions of pluralism that are thinned out on abstractions of common thought and practice. There is a two-way relationship between techno-environmental change and psychosocial change such that changes in our patterns of life change our patterns of meaning and vice-versa. Therefore, in order to keep pace with a rapidly changing world, we had to leave behind conceptions of natural law that rooted us in commitments to patternings outside ourselves (individually and socially). We had to move away from the idea that our environment and our very selves possessed a natural ordering that undergirds our conceptions of morality because this kind of thinking was out of sync with the rapid modulations of our modern life. Likewise, however, our abandonment of natural law as an attempt to adapt to change around us in turn served to inspired even greater rates of change. Without attention to this two-way change, we might be tempted to assume (a) that our ability to change our way of thinking is limited only by our imagination, or (b) that a change in our patterns of thinking is the primary cause in a change in our patterns of living.

The dualistic logic of the right stems from the kind of thinking Deleuze and Guattari have described as arboreal or tree-like, and it is unable to comprehend genuine multiplicity. As Karena Shaw explains, thinking like a tree "begins with the assumption of a strong central unity and proceeds through a binary logic of division. Through this process it achieves the appearance of diversity, multiplicity, and universality, but this appearance is always dependent on a primary unity."[28] There can, within this mode of thought, be no fundamental or deep articulation of multiplicity and no striving for an ordering outside of oneself because there is a persistent re-iteration of the original unity throughout the thought process.

---

28 Shaw, *Indigeneity and Political Theory*, 161.

The original unity controls or totalizes all along the way. As Deleuze and Guattari write, "binary logic is the spiritual reality of the root-tree. [And] this system of thought has never reached an understanding of multiplicity: in order to arrive at two following a spiritual method it must assume a strong principal unity."[29] Or, again, they write: "Multiplicities are rhizomatic, and expose arborescent pseudomultiplicities for what they are. There is no unity to serve as a pivot in the object, or to divide in the subject. There is not even the unity to abort in the object or 'return' in the subject. A multiplicity has neither subject nor object, only determinations, magnitudes, and dimensions that cannot increase in number without the multiplicity changing in nature (the laws of combination therefore increase in number as the multiplicity grows)."[30] Although Deleuze and Guattari go too far in their understanding of the implications of the falsity or artificiality of multiplicities in arborescent thought, their central point of critique is well placed. A dualistic logic of individuation and totalization cannot genuinely comprehend multiplicity. Or, in more policy-oriented terms, the individual-state logic at work within liberalism does not allow it to deproblematize difference.

The violence of dualistic logic and its politic of individual-state relations, when seen through this contrast between arboreal or network modes of thought, is revealed as a kind of violence that is difficult to pinpoint because it universalizes while simultaneously positing the legitimacy of its universalization. As Deleuze and Guattari note, this kind of state violence presents itself as pre-accomplished so "it consists in capturing while simultaneously constituting a right to capture."[31] The existence of multiple, horizontal communities of thought and practice will always stand in tension with the possibilities that a direct relation between the individual and the state will offer in seeking to create a society where all people are free and equal individuals.

The form of thinking underlying the proceduralist turn builds upon ontological assumptions by requiring all thoughts to be structured or standardized according to the individual and the totality. The entire structure of thought, therefore, stems from the base ontological assumptions in a kind of necessary fashion such that, if you accept the assumptions, the whole structure will follow. The foundational ontologies, then, are not held to be constituted as political commitments because the logic of structuration relies upon unidirectional or necessary causation. This form of life – it should be becoming clear by now – advances the standardizations

29 Deleuze and Guattari, *A Thousand Plateaus*, 5.
30 Ibid., 8.
31 Ibid., 447–8.

of protocolic control. The challenge, then, is to develop rhizomatic (or network) thought that resists this totalizing unity with multiple sites of localization, to deepen pluralism through a discursive logic of seeking the good in and through embodied, historical beings-in-the-world.

To conclude the discussion of the first mode of liberalism, let me sum up my argument so far:

(a) liberalism is characterized by proceduralism,
(b) proceduralism operates according to a dualistic logic,
(c) dualistic logic has a totalizing impulse that creates a normative eclipse,
(d) the totalizing impulse and its corresponding normative eclipse does not allow for a thick pluralism and therefore problematizes difference, and
(e) both dualistic logic and its totalizing impulse may, for example, be seen in liberalism's requirements of public reasoning.

Nevertheless, the dualistic logic of liberalism and its relation to the problematization of difference cannot be convincingly shown simply by looking at one example or one aspect of liberalism. More is needed. For example, we also need to reconsider the normative ideals that are guiding and shaping the liberal tradition. And, hence, it is to these ideals that we now turn.

B. LIBERALISM'S NORMATIVE STANDARDIZATIONS

In addition to the proceduralist turn itself, the central ideal of liberalism belies an underlying standardization at work – namely, the ideal that all persons be considered self-determining individuals deserving of equal concern and respect. So, what about the values that are guiding the proceduralist turn? In what way does a normative commitment to building a society in which all persons are considered to be free and equal individuals lead us into standardizations (and therefore cause acceleration)? Within even a brief overview, I believe we can already see this kind of standardization at work in both ideals – freedom and equality.

Before we begin, however, it should be noted that much like my analysis of the proceduralist turn above, the following explanations of freedom and equality are descriptions of the central thrust of the logic behind these ideals within the liberal tradition and we should therefore remember that folks are committed to this logic in varying degrees. Although we do not have time or space to dig down deep into anything resembling a comprehensive genealogy of liberal ideals, we can briefly sketch out the basic logic underlying the commitment to self-determination and egalitarianism as normative political ideals. Additionally, there are many sects and counter-traditions that should be explored, but we will only concern ourselves at this time with the orthodox notions of self-determination and equality as they have developed within the canon of liberal democratic theory. To begin, let me outline the central narrative of the story I would like to tell regarding the historical and conceptual development of these ideals.

In order to discuss self-determination as freedom, I think we need to go back to the basics. We live on this earth as beings that cannot escape our existential vulnerability and this fact causes us great anxiety. However, instead of overcoming this anxiety, we aggravate it by disenchanting the world through a struggle to control our environment.[32] This disenchantment is followed by the creation of a philosophical and political transcendent self that mediates between the self and the world by simultaneously individuating and totalizing the self (the kind of thing we have described above as dualistic logic). The false freedom of self-determination is thereby created in the space between individualized subjects and the totalized subject (e.g. the objective state operating under the rule of law). This self-determining freedom, however, is little more than a denial of the deeply vulnerable self in an eclipse of the in-between worlds through the polarization of this dualistic logic. But let us go through the details of this misadventure a little more carefully ...

First, as we have discussed in chapter 1 in seeking to understand the self as res ecologia, we exist as patterning processes that are highly vulnerable to disruption and entirely dependent upon that which is outside ourselves. But we persist in seeking to escape this vulnerability by simultaneously subjectifying ourselves and objectifying the world around us. Additionally, though, the story we tell of political action-coordination (the coming together in political community) in modern political theory is largely a tale of attempted escape from our fundamental or existential vulnerability. The liberal conception of freedom as self-determination represents the latest chapter in a story of civilization in which we attempt to build a transcendent self that will serve as a buffer between the direct and immediate relation of the self and the world. The development of the transcendent self reaches a new level as part of the rise of modernism in Europe when the political solution to vulnerability began to be seen in the formation of the demos as a universal self: a self that transcends

32 Note the work of Max Weber and Jacques Ellul in this regard. For example, see Weber, *The Protestant Ethic and the Spirit of Capitalism*, and Ellul, *The Technological Society*.

the immediate self and shields it from its direct dependence upon that which is outside itself.[33] This transcendent self, then, represents a kind of mediating interface between the self (understood both meta-physically and socio-phenomenologically) and the world; it is an attempt to see oneself and one's relation to the world from a universal position that is abstracted outside the lived realities of one's dependent relations. The transcendent self is a manifested projection of the self onto the world around the self through, for example, the instrumentalized practices of science, technology, and the state.

However, if we understand the depth of our dependence and our persistent vulnerability, we must wholly reject the classic (i.e. seventeenth- to nineteenth-century) notion of freedom as being a power manifest according to the determination of an individual's will. For example, Spinoza's notion of freedom as absolute or pure self-determination could also be mentioned in opposition to the freedom of the network self. He writes, "that thing is called free, which exists solely by the necessity of its own nature, and of which the action is determined by itself alone."[34] Then, as Algernon Sidney wrote in his *Discourses Concerning Government*, "liberty consists only in being subject to no man's will, and nothing denotes a slave but a dependence upon the will of another."[35] And as John Locke writes in his *Essay Concerning Human Understanding*, "Liberty ... is the power a man has to do or forbear doing any particular action, according as its doing or forbearance has the actual preference in the mind, which is the same thing as to say, according as he himself wills it."[36] Or, again, as Hume suggests in his *Enquiry Concerning Human Understanding*: "By liberty ... we can only mean *a power of acting or not acting, according to the determinations of the will*; that is, if we choose to remain at rest, we may; if we choose to move, we also may."[37] Although there is much more to be said about the subtle differences between these notions of freedom, there should be no doubt that these classic

33 As M'Gonigle notes, this philosophical transcendent self was advanced in the development of positivism and the "loss of the cultural duty to make society accountable to something outside of itself" – e.g. "a philosophy of social separation from nature." M'Gonigle, "Green Legal Theory," 37.

34 Spinoza, *The Ethics*, part I, definition vii. For Spinoza, God is free because God is pure self-determination. However, we should note that it does not make sense to speak of freedom in a manner so divorced from the real lives of people; it does not make sense to speak of God as free when trying to do democratic theory.

35 Sidney, *Discourses Concerning Government*, vol. II, 126.

36 Locke, *Essay Concerning Human Understanding*, 155.

37 Hume, *Enquiry Concerning Human Understanding*, 63.

conceptions of freedom are all centred upon the notion of independent or autonomous self-determination and self-expression.

We should note a few underlying assumptions at play in this classic conception of freedom that are made explicit in Locke's and Hume's philosophy. First, as Richard Schacht has noted, "what is at stake is the source of determination of some particular course of action."[38] Although there is more to be said about freedom, we can note that the freedom of the self as res ecologia is much less focused upon actions than it is upon actualizing potentials within the structures and processes of its patternings. Second, it is a person's own individual will that is the determining factor in the course of action to be or not to be taken. This notion of freedom as action undertaken according to an individual's self-determining will is a denial of the deeply vulnerable self in an eclipse of the localized in-between worlds of ecological, social, and spiritual dependence through the polarization of a dualistic logic. It is fundamentally out of step with an understanding of the self as res ecologia – i.e. deeply and persistently interconnected, indeterminate, and actualizing potentialities.

The ideal of freedom as self-determination (and self-expression) is developed through a deepening of the separation between facts (as the given) and value (as the constructed). This distinction makes possible the individuation of the self as a self-contained being that is universalized in political community through consensual value-construction (i.e. contractualism). Thus, the liberal tradition as it has developed over the past 400 years has viewed the individual as the foundational political unit who is only truly free when he is self-determining. For example, as we will see in our discussion of Habermas below, he argues that "the modern legal order can draw its legitimacy only from the idea of self-determination: citizens should be able to understand themselves as authors of the law to which they are subject as addressees."[39] To view all people as free in the sense of independent (i.e. rather than understanding freedom as security or peaceful participation) is, however, to understand the social, material, and spiritual constraints of living in community as a burden. That is, freedom *to* construct political values as individuals is necessarily freedom *from* the dependence and vulnerability of community. This is why I refer to it as an abstracted, universal position outside the lived realities of our existence.

Thus, there is no "natural" political community for the liberal but, rather, the individual is naturally in a state of opposition to all others. He

38 Schacht, "Hegel on Freedom," 291.
39 Habermas, *Between Facts and Norms*, 449.

must be pressed into political community from the top down by a universal political body – e.g. the state. The totalizing unity of the state is understood as being a necessity if we are to free the individual from those associations that inevitably restrict the flourishing of the individual *as an individual.* Freedom itself, then, is understood to be a bare kind of transcendence in which the self as an autonomous individual is able to ascend above the domineering interrelations and ties of nature, family, and tradition to delocalize as a universal self.[40] Of course, Rousseau and Kant represent the preeminent philosophers representing this kind of metaphysical groping for a transcendent, universal self that is meant to allow us reprieve from the existential domination of dependence upon the world.[41]

We might ask, however, why this individual-universal connection must be made and must, therefore, destroy the in-between worlds of localized dependencies upon nature, family, and tradition. Why can we not simply localize the contract to, in a sense, naturalize the political community of the free? To put it simply, if we universalize the individuation (understand all humans as individual persons), we are necessarily also universalizing the constitution of political community – political community becomes totalized as an all or nothing affair. In other words, if all are free and self-determining, then there simply is no reason or rationale for localized political community other than as a stepping stone towards the universal – nature, family, and tradition become instrumentalized as simply the means to a cosmo-political end. Therefore, although not all liberals will be wholeheartedly committed to the vision of freedom or the mechanisms employed to achieve it as outlined above, the logic underlying the attempt to escape the vulnerability of dependence should be quite clear. The simultaneous individuation and universalization of the self totalizes the constitution of political community and thereby eclipses the localized political communities rooted in natural, familial, and traditional dependencies.

Next, let us turn to the other central ideal of liberalism and consider the manner in which the logic of egalitarianism standardizes our normative relations and, in so doing, actually eclipses or disintegrates our normative relations much like the ideal of freedom as self-determination. Our Western democratic tradition has embraced egalitarianism wholesale, but

40 For example, this appears to be how Kymlicka understands freedom in "Liberalism and Communitarianism," 183–4.

41 We should also note that this same totalization is central to utilitarian thought insofar as individual agents are conceptualized as being neutral with regard to their claims on the good – i.e. the "good" is to be maximized in an impartial manner.

it is essential that we ask ourselves what we are actually committing to when we continue to cling to equality as a normative ideal. Once again, the explanation that follows is not intended to capture the full spectrum of egalitarian thought but to tap into the underlying logic of egalitarianism and the manner in which this logic standardizes our normative relations.

What do we mean by "egalitarianism"? Although a detailed definition could be developed, for our purposes here, we only need to refer to egalitarianism in a general sense. So, by "egalitarianism" I mean the promotion of equality as a normative ideal in which all persons are considered, at some basic level, to have the same moral worth or to be deserving of the same concern and respect. This fundamental normative ideal has, almost without exception, become an unquestioned presumption in modern Western political theory. Will Kymlicka, therefore, speaks of the fact that the core argument in contemporary political theory "is not whether to accept equality, but how best to interpret it" and describes the current consensus as an "egalitarian plateau."[42] Furthermore, not only has the ideal of equality become a fundamental assumption of democratic theorists across the board, but this normative ideal has been elevated to a place of preeminence by many democratic theorists. For example, Ronald Dworkin even goes so far as to argue that "no government is legitimate that does not show equal concern for the fate of all those citizens over whom it claims dominion and from whom it claims allegiance. Equal concern is the sovereign virtue of political community – without it government is only tyranny."[43] It is safe to say, then, that equality is now understood to be the foundation or prerequisite of justice in modern industrial societies.[44] There is a nearly sacred assumption that all persons should be afforded equal concern and respect.

42 Kymlicka, *Contemporary Political Philosophy*, 4. Or, as Sen explains, "a common characteristic of virtually all the approaches to the ethics of social arrangements that have stood the test of time is to want equality of something – something that has an important place in the particular theory." Sen, *Inequality Reexamined*, ix. This egalitarian consensus is certainly tied to the rise of liberalisms and its ascendency to the level of meta-ideology.

43 Dworkin, *Sovereign Virtue*, 1. In other words, equal concern and respect for all citizens is actually "a precondition of political legitimacy." Dworkin suggests that equality is "a precondition of the majority's right to enforce its laws against those who think them unwise or even unjust." Ibid., 2.

44 For example, the Preamble to the Universal Declaration of Human Rights begins with the following statement: "*Whereas* recognition of the inherent dignity and of the equal and inalienable rights of all members of the human family is the foundation of freedom, justice and peace in the world." See "Universal Declaration of Human Rights," Office of the High Commissioner for Human Rights, United Nations, http://daccess-dds-ny.un.org/doc/RESOLUTION/GEN/NR0/043/88/IMG/NR004388.pdf?OpenElement. Accessed 10 February 2016.

We should note, too, that almost all contemporary theorists committed to the ideal of equality are keen to point out that the ideal also demands an acknowledgement of and a respect for difference. For example, the "politics of difference" theorists suggest that we should begin with concerns about domination and oppression and follow more relational conceptualizations when theorizing about justice for social groups. Iris Marion Young argues, therefore, that "a denial of difference contributes to social group oppression" and that "basic equality in life situation for all persons is a moral value" and necessary for groups to have full participation in political life.[45] In keeping with the shift towards the politics of difference in the 70s, 80s, and 90s, egalitarians are increasingly careful to remind their readers that treating people equally does not preclude differential treatment (e.g. various degrees of legal, political, social, and economic rights or recognitions). Or, to put the emphasis on difference another way, Dworkin suggests that we need to clearly distinguish between "equal treatment" and "treatment as an equal." Thus, for Dworkin, treatment as an equal is a foundational principle that is essential to political morality (i.e. the right "to be treated with the same respect and concern as anyone else"), but equal treatment is a manifestation of this principle that may or may not be appropriate given our particular set of circumstances (i.e. "the right to an equal distribution of some opportunity or resource or burden").[46] However, despite this heartening shift toward emphasizing difference and an increasing sensitivity to systemic violence against social groups that remain outside the mainstream power flows of society, it is important to note that a commitment to equality as an ideal continues to entail a commitment to equal moral worth at some abstract level of theoretical analysis. Indeed, egalitarianism means precisely that one believes that at a certain theoretical level all persons possess essentially the same moral worth. In other words, "treatment as an equal" – if it is to be meaningful – necessarily means "equal treatment" at some level.[47]

Given our discussion of standardization and protocolic control above, warning bells should be ringing as soon as we begin talking about equality. For, affording all persons "equal concern and respect" simply makes no sense if it is to be a *personal* normative ideal. It only makes sense as a principle for developing and shaping the actions of something totalizing

45   Young, *Justice and the Politics of Difference*, 10, 14.

46   Dworkin, *Taking Rights Seriously*, 227.

47   Indeed, if this were not the case, if our ideal of equality did not at least include some notion of valuing persons the same way, we should be happy with simply using language such as "non-domination," "justice," "reciprocity," etc. rather than "equality."

like a singular, bureaucratic state institution. Equality as a normative ideal relies upon a universal normative metric such that each and every person is individuated and included within the same fundamental framework that shapes and bounds the articulation of normative consideration. However, a universal normative metric such as this must, by definition, be abstracted beyond the lived relations of one person, his family, friends, neighbours, clan, tribe, nation, etc. In order to be an egalitarian, one must try to think like a state and, in so doing, maintain a wide gulf between thought and practice (because no one can live as a state).[48] As we saw above in our discussion of freedom as self-determination, the administrative bureaucracy of the modern welfare state represents a hierarchical "abstract regularity" that sweeps the self up into a system of political interactions that transcend the personal relations of the self with others.[49] Indeed, it is only in this transcendent realm of abstract regularity that equality can be meaningful as a normative ideal. Equality is at best quasi-normative ideal and only truly meaningful as a policy within the framework of a unitary state institution because commitment to the ideal involves conceiving of moral worth as an abstract ideal rather than an assessment that takes place within the actual relations people have with the world around them.[50] In other words, one views moral worth as if it were something that is independent of the one who is doing the recognizing (i.e. the one who posits the moral worth drops out of the picture) and also disembodies and decontextualizes the person(s) to which one

48 Theoretically one could, in a sense, hold equality as a personal aspirational goal – e.g. "I hope to treat everyone I encounter with the same concern and respect" – but this goal can never become more than metaphorical. Indeed, treating everyone in one's life with equal concern and respect in any literal sense is clearly undesirable and unhealthy behaviour – i.e. the one who endeavours to live this way will be seen as inhuman and anti-social. Cf. the example of the missing child and the comparison between the response of the police, the father, and the villager in Miller, "Cosmopolitanism," 81–2. If it is not unhealthy behaviour, then, as Miller points out, there is "a gap between our moral assessments of states of affairs and the reasons we have for acting in relation to those states of affairs." Ibid., 81. So I am suggesting that if there is no gap then one will be acting dramatically out of sync with what has been normal ethical behaviour for thousands of years and will therefore be understood as engaging in deviant behaviour.

49 Weber, *Economy and Society*, 983. As Lasch writes, "the capacity for loyalty is stretched too thin when it tries to attach itself to the hypothetical solidarity of the human race. It needs to attach itself to specific people and specific places, not to an abstract ideal of universal human rights. We love particular men and women, not humanity in general." Lasch, *The True and Only Heaven*, 36.

50 By "quasi-normative ideal" I mean that equality as an ideal – even if it is understood as equality with regards to a certain particular kind of concern (e.g. equality in voting for representatives in a legislative body) – appears to us as a normative ideal, but it is not arising from a localized relationality and is not, therefore, a genuine *normative* ideal.

refers (i.e. the one who is said to have the moral worth drops out of the picture).[51] In this manner, not only does the normative ideal of equality have within it a logic of idealization and abstraction away from the real, asymmetrical world of persons and interpersonal relations, but this "retreat from the real" facilitates a totalization of norms to accord with a totalized subject – i.e. the state – and an individuation of individual subjects living as beings-in-common.[52]

The normative totalization of liberalism may be seen in the logic of liberal moral theory outlined already in Adam Smith's *The Theory of Moral Sentiments*. It is here that Smith argues for a vision of the perfection of human nature rooted in social interaction but also, importantly, a kind of interaction governed by a universal or totalized perspective called the "impartial spectator." As we go through the thought of Smith, we should be struck by the dramatic similarities between the "impartial spectator" in Smith and the person behind the "veil of ignorance" in Rawls. Both Smith and Rawls depend upon the use of the individual's imagination to extract them out of their lived, embodied situation and into the fictional perspective of an abstract, universal person who can judge based upon the certainty of a singular normative metric. This fictional person possessing the singular view of the universal normative metric and holding no interest in one side or another is judged, because of his universality, by no one but God himself.[53] But, how does Smith come to rest his moral theory upon a fiction.

---

51   It is not correct to say that the theorist and the subjects of the theory do not drop out because the differences of persons are still acknowledged (e.g. various natural talents, etc.). It is true that when theorists use the term "equal" they seem to mean "different, but the same." However, the "different" element seems to simply "attach" to the descriptive assumptions behind the phrase (i.e. the assumed actual differences between men and women) and the "the same" element "attaches" to the normative aspiration (i.e. the intention to ensure men and women are treated the same in some sense). And, it is precisely this strict separation between the descriptive and the prescriptive that is of concern here.

52   This tendency toward universalization can be seen within the abstraction and idealization of both John Rawls' employment of the veil of ignorance as well as Habermas' critical approach rooted in a teleology of rational consensus. For example, see Rawls, *A Theory of Justice* and Habermas, *Communicative Action*, Vol. I. This attraction to universalization can be most clearly traced back to Kant and seems to be the reason why Rawls (following Kant) finds it necessary to grossly limit the knowledge of moral actors and thereby hem in the alternatives available to them. Rawls and Kant seek a unanimous (i.e. objective) conception of justice and are therefore lured into the painful processes of rational reductionism. See Rawls, *A Theory of Justice*, 140–1, and Kant, *Foundations of the Metaphysic of Morals*, 46.

53   Robbins, *A History of Economic Thought*, 134.

Smith begins with a statement that "how selfish soever man may be supposed, there are evidently some principles in his nature, which interest him in the fortune of others, and render their happiness necessary to him, though he derive nothing from it except the pleasure of seeing it."[54] The propensity to feelings of sympathy is inherent within human nature and, therefore, gives us the starting point for understanding moral behaviour. But how do we sympathize? We come to sympathize through our imagination, which copies our own impressions of our senses and projects them onto others (or projects us into the other's situation). Sympathy, therefore, arises in and through social interactions – i.e. as one becomes a spectator of others who are themselves directly affected in their senses (e.g. feelings of pain). But, sympathy itself is not enough – for we surely discriminate between proper and improper feelings of sympathy. On the one hand, to approve of others is to say that we sympathize with them and to not approve is to say that we do not sympathize with them. On the other hand, being the object of resentment or gratitude only means something to us to the extent that we judge these feelings to be appropriate in others. How do we know if feelings of sympathy are appropriate or not? Simply put, if we can say that the feelings would be approved of by an impartial and indifferent spectator, then we can say they are natural or appropriate.[55]

Importantly, Smith argues that people are not only naturally selfish and inclined towards their own feelings (either direct or sympathetic) but also naturally inclined to seek the perspective of an impartial spectator as the judge between moral and immoral feelings. We are inclined to seek the perspective of an impartial spectator because, he suggests, everyone understands one's own happiness to be of the greatest importance but no one can hold to this as a moral position when facing mankind as a whole. So, in order to develop the rationale for the morality of an action, one must take the perspective of an impartial spectator; one must place oneself in in the position of an imaginary singular, abstract representative of the whole of humanity.[56] It is posited, in this way, that it is natural (and the only way to really justify normative judgment) for each individual to project themselves outside themselves by imagining what humanity as a universal collective might think of a particular behaviour.

54 Smith, *The Theory of Moral Sentiments*, 1.
55 Ibid., 2–4, 7, 114.
56 Ibid., 140–1. Smith presents a similar argument in *The Wealth of Nations* when he suggests that cooperation and mutual aid are best obtained through mutually beneficial contracts. See Smith, *Wealth of Nations*, 19.

Further, equality (e.g. in terms of citizenship) means the individual stands in a direct and immediate relation to the state (or, in more socialist terms, to society as a whole). I say direct and immediate relation to the state because if all persons (citizens) are to be considered equal, then no single person or group of persons short of the whole of the society may function as the "object" that stands in relation to us as the person-subjects. It is the totality of the state that subjectivizes us, we are subjects-in-common. However, our identity is actually relational rather than free-standing; we live out moral lives precisely because we have the kind of interconnections and relations denied by the totalization. The condition of existence of every identity, therefore, also depends upon the affirmation of a difference, the determination of an "other" that gives us our outside. The egalitarian identity allows the state (or society as a whole) to overshadow the individual as a distinct being – it puts the individual in a dualistic existential relation to the seemingly benevolent Leviathan that is the state institution.

The ideal of equality hands down a judgment upon the other in an effort to overcome their otherness – i.e. they are just like everyone else deep down in their essence and it is this essence that should determine (at least to some relevant degree) others' moral relations with them (whomever these others might be). The ideal of equality leads us to seek consensus (i.e. to achieve agreement) or reconciliation (i.e. to restore harmony) but we know that this involves a reductionism that essentializes persons and commits them to a telos of unified patterns of living. This kind of homogenizing impulse should therefore be understood as the illegitimate use of power (i.e. domination) insofar as it is an overcoming of the other – a destruction of reciprocal identity in political relations (as we saw in our discussion of Levinas and the transcendent other above). This impulse issues forth from the ideal of equality and is made manifest as the domination present within the drive to singularity that characterizes a universal metric of moral worth. The universal metric denoted by the language of equality as an ideal does violence to the other insofar as it promulgates a myth of containment and definement in the name of justice and thereby inspires policy measures designed to create a common citizenry (as we saw in the discussion of protocolic domination in chapter 3). That is, the ideal of equality represents an illegitimate use of power that, rather than providing us with an ideal of democracy, actually does violence to the diversity that is at the theoretical core of democracy. The deep pluralism at the heart of democracy demands the recognition of the other as that which is other and, in this sense, provides us with a critical approach that undermines the current domineering processes of protocolic control. The standardization is born in the lack of reciprocity – i.e. the talk of equality involves a one-way or unidimensional positing of moral worth without the negotiation process of relation. The dynamic interplay of dialogical relations is something that cannot take place between a bureaucracy (the institutionalization of abstract regularity) and real, flesh and blood persons. It should not be surprising, therefore, that the underlying theoretical moves assumed in the egalitarian ideal inevitably lead to a problematization of difference both theoretically and practically.

In conclusion, although there is much more to be said about the ideals of liberalism, we are beginning to see the basic shape of a logic at work within the liberal tradition. Just as proceduralism possesses a dualistic logic that eclipses normative and political relations, so too do the central ideals of liberalism – self-determination and equality – deny the possibility of localized political community and the normative relations of which they are composed. And, insofar as these ideals demand a universal political community, they disallow a multilogical approach to diversity in the world. We have roughly sketched an outline of dualistic logic and suggested that it is the defining feature of liberalism, but its nature and manifestations should become much clearer in our analysis of the third mode of liberalism.

C. THE FREE MARKET, SCIENCE, AND COSMOPOLITANISM

The third mode of liberalism – seen most clearly in the political economy of the free market and the modern scientific method – is perhaps the most powerful and disturbing. Although there is much to be said regarding the structural violence that takes place within the markets of liberal economies and the relentless advancement of science, in what follows we will remain quite focussed on the cosmopolitan social theory underlying both a market-based political economy and the modern scientific method. And, the cosmopolitanism of liberalism is driven forward by a logic which says that the best way to achieve material prosperity, accurate knowledge, and moral perfection is through interaction and exchange with others – i.e. that intercourse between the multiplicity will lead to a common or singular advancement. This interactionist logic forms the foundation of liberal capitalist economics (the free market) and the modern scientific method (universalizable hypothesis testing) as well as, importantly, liberalism's commitment to a common public sphere of political interaction. Although this logic can be traced throughout the liberal tradition, we can perhaps see it best in the works of: the founder of modern economics (Adam Smith), a key pioneer of experimentalism (Robert Boyle), and the foremost contemporary theorist on the public sphere (Jürgen Habermas). We can see the dualistic logic of liberalism running through the centre of their work and activating their understanding that economic, moral, and political progress is to be achieved through the material and social interaction of individual subjects.

The theme of progress through material and social interaction can be traced through both Smith's theorizing regarding political economy as well as his work on moral sentiments. In his discussions of the economy and morality, Smith depends upon some important conclusions regarding human nature and the human situation and, therefore, the telos that arises from this nature and the condition within which it finds itself. For example, in *The Wealth of Nations*, he writes that there is "a certain propensity in human nature ... the propensity to truck, barter, and exchange one thing for another" and this propensity seems to be "the necessary consequence of the faculties of reason and speech."[57] Both the propensity to contractual exchange and to feelings of sympathy are inherent within human nature and, therefore, give us the starting point for understanding economic prosperity and moral behaviour.

However, we cannot understand the relevance of these propensities within humans until we understand the situation within which humans find themselves. Interestingly, Smith suggests that the propensity for exchange is driven by the fact that an individual human is vulnerable and "stands at all times in need of the co-operation and assistance of great multitudes" for, whereas mature animals are almost entirely independent, "man has almost constant occasion for the help of his brethren."[58] Or, in *Moral Sentiments*, he writes that "all the members of human society stand in need of each others [sic] assistance, and are likewise exposed to mutual injuries."[59] So, given the fact that we are vulnerable and dependent beings who are in need of interactions to subsist and prosper, we possess a nature that propels us toward material and social exchange. Both material and moral progress, in this way, are understood to be achieved through a process of exchange and, consequently, any hindrance to this exchange is a hindrance to progress and the forward drive toward the perfection of human nature. Adam Smith who, as the Karl Polanyi says, developed the "paradigm of the bartering savage" and founded modern economics by treating material wealth as a distinct field of study, established not only a vision of humans as beings which engage in exchange in order to survive but humans as beings that seek

57 Ibid., 18.
58 Ibid., 19.
59 Smith, *The Theory of Moral Sentiments*, 146.

the perfection of their nature as exchanging beings.[60] With his vision of humans as the exchanging animal, he was able to separate financial from cultural relations (i.e. insofar as cultural ties threaten the free exchange of the market). The political and economic implications of this progress-through-exchange vision are tremendous and have dramatic reverberations throughout the theorizing of the liberal tradition to this day. But, before we turn to its implications for contemporary theorizing regarding the public sphere, let us briefly consider the pioneering work of Robert Boyle and how its focus on progress-through-interaction forms the background for Smith's interactionalism.

One hundred years before Smith published his *Moral Sentiments*, Boyle published his *New Experiments Physico-Mechanical* as a set of forty-three experiments with a new machine to be used in the generation of scientific facts – an air pump.[61] Boyle, of course, not only developed a technique of mechanized experimentation but, in the process, developed a parallel technique of social interaction to verify experimental results and thereby transform experimental results into scientific facts. Differing philosophical forms of life necessarily entail differing political organizations as the boundaries guiding and shaping knowledge generation, verification, and propagation determine the nature of political life. Hence, as Steven Shapin and Simon Schaffer write, solutions to the problem of knowledge acquisition are, in an important way, solutions to the problem of social order.[62] The means of establishing matters of scientific fact necessarily also served as means of establishing the rules of social interaction. For matters of scientific fact are not simply mirror images of nature but are, rather, *socially determined ways of imaging nature*. Therefore, as Shapin and Schaffer explain, assumptions regarding matters of fact bring with them assumptions of social interaction. They write, "an experience, even of a rigidly controlled experimental performance, that one man alone witnessed was not adequate to make a matter of fact. If that experience could be extended to many, and in principle to all men, then the result could be constituted as a matter of fact. In this way, the matter of fact is to be seen as both an epistemological and a social category."[63] Accompanied by a social theory of interactionalism, therefore, Boyle's mechanized experimentation became nothing less than scientific fact-production. Let us consider this social theory of interactionalism a little

60 Polanyi, *The Great Transformation*, 46, 116.
61 Boyle, "New Experiments Physico-Mechanical," 117.
62 See Shapin and Schaffer, *Leviathan and the Air-Pump*, 332.
63 Ibid., 25.

further for it is here that we see the key to Smith's moral and economic theory as well as the liberal notion of the public sphere more generally.

Put simply, progress in knowledge production came to be seen as residing in the objectification of phenomena. That is, the establishment of scientific facts depends upon a coming to recognize certain phenomena as given to humans rather than created by them. And, as Shapin and Schaffer point out, Boyle's innovations and influence throughout the past 400 years rests upon a bringing together of a material and a social technology in order to achieve this goal of objectifying phenomena.[64]

First, his material technology was found in his air pump or a "new pneumatical engine" which was a brand new design constructed specifically for the conducting of his experiments. Like the microscope and the telescope, the air pump (a) allowed human senses to go beyond their natural reach (cf. the imaginary projection of the senses in Smith) and, simultaneously, (b) placed certain boundaries upon the process of fact production. Perhaps most obviously, the use of the machine disciplined the interaction associated with the production of facts insofar as it limited access to the experimentation process. For example, not only could very few people make use of the machine, but only certain people were allowed access to witness the experimentation process itself within the laboratory. Additionally, the use of the machine facilitated a sharp delineation between "physical" and "metaphysical" questions by allowing Boyle to focus on the idea of a vacuum as "not a space, wherein there is no body at all, but such as is either altogether, or almost totally devoid of air."[65] In this manner, he was able to shift the debate away from the plenist idea in which a container devoid of air would be replenished by some ethereal matter to a simply experimental question regarding the precise nature and effects of a "natural" vacuum as produced by the pneumatical engine.[66] The advancement of the senses and the governance of the interaction by the dependence upon the machine, however, would have been of limited historical significance if not for its coupling with a social technology that would ensure the objectification of phenomena.

Thus, second, and more importantly for our discussion here, he advanced a *social technology* rooted in a theory of interactionalism whereby experiments with a machine (i.e. the production of phenomena) could be witnessed and reproduced by others wherever they might be in

64 They actually discuss three technologies – a material, a literary, and a social technology – but for our purposes here the literary and social may be combined into one social theory of interactionalism. Ibid., 25 and 76ff.

65 Boyle, "New Experiments Physico-Mechanical," 10.

66 Ibid., 37–8, and Shapin and Schaffer, *Leviathan and the Air-Pump*, 38–40, 45–6.

time / space. Collective witnessing of phenomena facilitated objectification but only in a limited or localized fashion. The writings of Boyle were therefore essential in allowing the universalization – and thereby objectification – of the experimental phenomena. As Shapin and Schaffer write, "the literary technology of virtual witnessing extended the public space of the laboratory in offering a valid witnessing experience to all readers of the text."[67] Of course, this technique of experimental learning depended upon the technology of publishing and disseminating literary works and Boyle makes it very clear that he is writing so that others might replicate the experiments in their own time and space in order to thereby advance the "commonwealth of learning."[68] What he was calling "experimental learning" was, therefore, accomplished in the process of objectifying phenomena for all people in all places at all times.[69]

Immediately, however, a problem arises – if we are relying upon the witnessing of phenomena as a means of objectifying it, then how do we translate each individual and diverse witness report into one single and coherent account of the phenomena? Or, as Shapin and Schaffer note, "the problem with eye witnessing as a criterion for assurance was one of *discipline.* How did one police the reports of witnesses so as to avoid radical individualism?"[70] In order to be able to advance the objectivity of the phenomena, Boyle insisted that the witnesses must be multiplied in such a manner so as to transform their individual acts of testimony into a collective act of certain verification.[71] Of course, the means of policing the process of translating multiple witness accounts into one universal account were numerous. From the initial limitations placed upon access to the machine and the experimental practices themselves to the development of an experimental community that would govern and shape the story of the phenomena in and through history, the creation of universal account of the phenomena was a social and political affair. But, because the establishment of scientific facts depends upon a coming to recognize certain phenomena as *given* to humans rather than *created* by them, the second key problem arises – is the process of creating scientific facts reaching its final end precisely when the process of fact-creation is itself obscured?

This finality would not be problematic if, for example, a fact simply meant "a temporarily agreed-upon understanding of a certain phenomena." For, if this was all that was meant by a scientific fact, then it would

67 Ibid., 77.
68 Boyle, "New Experiments Physico-Mechanical," 6, 10, 117.
69 Ibid., 6.
70 Shapin and Schaffer, *Leviathan and the Air-Pump,* 56.
71 Ibid., 56ff.

be entirely understandable that the process of creating scientific facts reaching its end precisely when the process of fact-creation was no longer taking place. Or, in other words, if a scientific fact was simply defined as a unity of thought then, by definition, a scientific fact would exist precisely at the point where we cease disagreeing. However, I would argue that something more is meant by "fact" in modern science for, as we noted above, a scientific fact was understood as being something that was objective in the sense that it was *given to* rather than *created by* humans. It is problematic and somewhat deceptive, therefore, to deny the policing of interaction between witnesses simply because the policing is effective enough to generate relative consensus. It is deceptive in the sense that the denial at the point of consensus inevitably projects backwards in history to conduct an erasure of the entire policing process. In this sense, then, the interaction process is constantly being re-interpreted as singular progressive movement that encompasses and unifies the multiplicity active within the diversity of interaction. This is, of course, the kind of erasure of politics that I am suggesting the dualistic logic within liberalism is guilty – i.e. the activity of the multiplicity is abstracted away into a common procedure of interaction that eclipses the persistence of the diversity. And Habermas' social theory is a key example of this logic of progress-through-interaction.

In a sense, Habermas' work can be seen as an attempt to bring material and social interaction together into one unified theory of communicative action that will produce economic, moral, and political progress. Or, put somewhat more precisely, his project is to develop a normative foundation for the critique of ideology (understood as power's systematic distortion of communication) through the reconstruction of the universal conditions of possible mutual understanding between individuals.[72] As a post-war German intellectual, Habermas was concerned that the post-Hegelian (e.g. Nietzschean), postmodern (e.g. Foucauldian, Derridean, Lyotardian, Rortian, etc.), and hermeneutical (e.g. Heideggerian, Gadamerian) lines of thought were unable to resist the rise of harmful ideologies. He turned, therefore, to the Enlightenment project of building a just society: a project in which the development of philosophical theory is understood to be the emancipatory tool for the liberation of reason from the corruptions and distortions of mythological superstition and parochial ideology.

72 Habermas, "What Is Universal Pragmatics?," 21, and Habermas, *Communicative Action*, Vol. I, 1–3.

In his attempt to develop what he understands to be a genuinely liberal social theory, Habermas sets out to rework the notion of rationality because it is the internal functioning of rational exchange that operates as his reference point for human progress. He begins by suggesting that every consensus rests on an intersubjective[73] recognition of criticizable validity claims and we can therefore presuppose that those acting communicatively are capable of mutual criticism. The rationality of communication lies not in any correspondence with an absolute ideal, but in the fulfillment of expectations regarding communication; rationality itself must be understood in a socio-pragmatic sense – i.e. it must be rooted in the lifeworlds of the society.[74]

In the development of his theory of communicative action, Habermas focuses upon creating a thoroughly critical social theory by bringing together the theoretical and critical rigour of philosophy and the empiricism of the social sciences.[75] This pragmatic synthesis of philosophy and the social sciences, for Habermas, allows the philosophy of history – as a project of historical materialism or social evolution – to be more genuinely post-metaphysical and critical instead of transcendental and dogmatic.[76] His critical theory is designed to allow philosophers to actively resist the commodification and bureaucratization of social relations. In other words, the pathological inclinations of modernity that displace communicative forms of solidarity can be resisted through an understanding of the processes of discourse and the relationship between the plurality of value spheres and the universality of validity claims. Habermasian critical theory, therefore, represents an attempt to develop a dialectical method of formulating the necessary – albeit hypothetical and fallible – conditions of societal evolution.

Unlike the empiricists and the rationalists of the Enlightenment, Habermas asserts that rationality has little to do with knowledge of, or correspondence with, the object-world. He argues instead that rationality means that an action or statement can be criticized or defended such that the persons involved are able to justify them through the exchange

---

73 The term "intersubjective" is technically insufficient because it denotes a number of subjects coming together. Habermas' emphasis is more upon radical intersubjectivity or dialogical being-in-the-world.

74 Habermas, *Communicative Action*, Vol. I, 302.

75 McCarthy, "Translator's Introduction," vii, and Bernstein, "Fred Dallmayr's Critique of Habermas," 581–3.

76 Habermas, "Questions and Counterquestions," 407. Also see McCarthy, *The Critical Theory of Jürgen Habermas*, 75–91.

of argumentation.[77] In this sense, rationality itself assumes the interaction of communication insofar as something is rational only if it meets the necessary conditions of generating understanding in common with others.[78] Importantly, validity claims necessarily engage would-be interpreters of speech and require their response as participants within the dialogical process. "An interpreter cannot," he writes, "interpret expressions connected through criticizable validity claims with a potential of reasons (and thus represent knowledge) without taking a position on them."[79] Reasons can always be expanded into arguments that are understood only when they are evaluated against some standard of rationality (at least intuitively). And, from the evaluative perspective – i.e. the perspective of the participant – "rationality standards must always claim general validity."[80] Therefore, validity claims are internally linked to reasons and "a speaker owes the binding (or bonding: bindende) force of his illocutionary act not to the validity of what is said, but to the coordinating effect of the warranty that he offers: namely, to redeem, if necessary, the validity claim raised with his speech act."[81] This coordinating effect goes out to all would-be participants and therefore necessitates a warranty that is offered as good against the whole world. By this he means that, if argumentations continued long enough and in an open enough manner, the disagreement would be resolved and consensus achieved.[82]

In order to develop his concept of reason as the normative grounding for critical theory Habermas turns to the notion of an ideal speech situation.[83] His ideal speech situation is one in which every possible perspective or interpretation is heard without coercion – the place where the only goal of the participants is pure communication unbiased by power relations. That is, reason, rather than power, is what directs actors to come to mutual understanding within the ideal speech situation. Importantly, this ideal is "neither an empirical phenomenon nor a mere

77   Habermas denies that the pragmatic dimension of language must be left to exclusively empirical analysis. See Habermas, *On the Pragmatics of Communication*, 26.

78   Giddens, "Reason Without Revolution?," 99.

79   Habermas, *Communicative Action*, Vol. I, 116.

80   Habermas, "Questions and Counterquestions," 204.

81   Habermas, *Communicative Action*, Vol. I, 302, emphasis removed.

82   He explains that "unity of rationality in the multiplicity of value spheres rationalized according to their inner logics is secured precisely at the formal level of the argumentative redemption of validity claims. Validity claims differ from empirical claims through the presupposition that they can be made good by means of arguments." Habermas, *Communicative Action*, Vol. I, 249.

83   It should be noted that, according to Habermas, "one should not imagine the ideal speech situation as a utopian model for an emancipated society. I use it only to reconstruct the concept of reason, that is, a concept of communicative reason." Habermas, *Autonomy and Solidarity*, 90.

construct, but rather an unavoidable supposition reciprocally made in discourse. This supposition can, but need not be, counterfactual; but even if it is made counterfactually, it is a fiction that is operatively effective in the process of communication."[84] Therefore it is neither a mere regulative principle against which we could measure our discourse nor an existing concept in our world – it is in fact the "constitutive condition of rational speech."[85]

Habermas is consistent in his search for a theoretical framework that will provide a robust and ongoing critique of ideology through reason. However, due to the dualistic logic at work within his notion of communicative action, he has an unfortunate tendency to eclipse the politics of his own power use and ideology in the process of developing his social theory. The more Habermas develops a theory of law and politics, the more he needs to account for the present reality of the modern state power structures (if he continues in keeping with his goals of developing a dialectical theory that includes both philosophy and the empirical sciences). So, for example, he seeks to develop a concept of the ideal connection between communicative action and the production of law – i.e. democratic decision-making – in order to talk of the legitimacy of law. However, there is good reason to be suspicious of the notion that decision-making through democratic deliberation can be the ideal that will ground legal legitimacy and protect it from the corruptions of ideology. For, as we saw above, the corruptions of ideology required reason's ability to transcend the immediacy of history and the relativism of contextualism to provide a robust critical impulse that could move beyond systematically distorted communication. Reason, as conceived by Habermas, could only accomplish this opposition to ideological distortion by means of its singularity – its ability to transcend the multiplicity of history-bound life of reasoning persons and identify the universal conditions of rationality itself. Singularity, however, is not appropriate when considering democratic deliberation or legal legitimacy. Indeed, consensus absolutized (i.e. singularity that can transcend the corruptions of ideology) cannot function as the normative ideal of democracy – or, by extension, of legal legitimacy. Again, despite Habermas' valiant attempts to develop a dialectical theory that moves between philosophy and the empirical sciences, we are seeing a failure to truly recognize multiplicity – an inability to deeply acknowledge and theorize regarding pluralism – within liberal social theory.

---

84 Habermas, "Wahrheitstheorien," 258–9, quoted in McCarthy, *The Critical Theory of Jürgen Habermas*, 310.

85 Ibid.

Why is this so? As we have seen above, Habermas' project involves the development of a normative foundation for the critique of ideology through the reconstruction of the universal conditions of possible mutual understanding. His understanding of the universal conditions, however, was developed within an idealized speech situation that was devoid of any coercion. This idealized communicative world grants the social theorist the perspective needed to critique systemic distortions of communication within history. However this idealized speech situation does not give an outside perspective from which to evaluate the distortions within democratic processes; absolute consensus is itself a distortion of democracy. Indeed, power imbalances represented in social and material inequalities are a necessary foundation for democratic decision-making. There is good reason to contend, therefore, that the idealization and universalization underlying Habermas' critical social theory fails to provide a theoretical foundation for democracy or legal legitimacy unless his notion of rationality is dramatically reinterpreted as multiple and embodied. That is, if it is understood as a process in which world-embedded communicative actors make context-transcending validity claims and reciprocally acknowledge (or not) their co-communicators' validity claims from within their own context. This process, however, does not allow for an ideal of society as a whole – the ideal itself must be multiple because it, or rather they, exist in relation to beings-in-time throughout history and, in this sense, allow for normative orientations that are politically efficacious – i.e. they neither absolutize singularity nor reify present communicative processes. To do this would be to deny the dualistic logic within the proceduralist turn of liberalism and seek to become more attune to what might be called the natural ordering of our world and ourselves. Indeed, it would be an abandonment of liberalism.

By turning to this third mode of liberalism, we were able to trace out in very broad strokes another area in which we can see dualistic logic at work within the connections between knowledge generation and sociopolitical coordination. Comparing modern economics, the scientific method, and the cosmopolitan ideal, offers us a glimpse into the totalizing impulse within dualistic logic. We are able to see more clearly how liberalism's inability to localize translates into a drive to moral and material progress as well as an inability to develop politics that are accepting of a deep pluralism. We were able to begin seeing some of the rationale behind liberalism's perpetual problematization of difference.

CONCLUSION

In conclusion, I have moved very quickly through dramatic historical shifts in thought and practice that are complex and multifaceted. My claim, once again, is not that this brief discussion captures the liberal tradition in all its multiple manifestations, but that we can see some of the commonality that allowed liberals to engage in a conversation with each other over the past 400 years. And, further, we are able to begin seeing how the gains achieved in the development of the liberal tradition have been accompanied by a corresponding intolerance toward diversity. I have argued that the "problematization of difference" so prevalent among democratic theorists indicates that there is something fundamentally wrong with the way we are theorizing within the liberal tradition. That is, if we feel that differences within society are a problem that needs to be dealt with in our political theorizing, then we are on the wrong track. This chapter, therefore, represents an invitation to begin a deproblematization of difference. It is my hope that we can instead begin problematizing dualistic logic and resisting its totalizing impulse by fostering resilience in localized political communities that are rooted in nature, family, and tradition.

We began the third section of this chapter with a brief look at Adam Smith's role in the development of modern economics and traced out the connection between his theories of political economy and moral sentiments. We noted that, in both areas, a unified progress would be achieved through the interaction of a multiplicity of individuals. Both the market economy and cosmopolitanism relies upon a sweeping away of certain barriers to interaction between individual actors while, at the same time, seeking to determine the nature of the interactions from within the actors themselves. And, earlier in this chapter, we discussed the dualistic logic underlying the proceduralist turn and how this logic governed the normative reasoning one used in approaching the idea of the public sphere. We looked at how Rawls was unable to escape from the slippery slope to universalism inherent within a substitution of the right for the good and, further, the limits he was forced to put upon the interaction between individual actors that would lead to something he could accept as progress of the whole. And, of course, we see the same thing in Habermas insofar as he is forced to develop an otherworldly notion of power that is categorically distinct from violence in order to explain how the discreet interactions of communicative action could lead to legitimate power use within the institutions of the totalized state. Indeed, the proceduralist turn, the ideals of self-determination and equality, as well as the free economic and cultural exchange of the free market and cosmopolitanism each in complementary ways serve to govern the removal of barriers to interaction while simultaneously shaping the interaction process itself in hopes of a certain, transcendent or universal outcome. This governing and shaping is achieved through dualistic logic insofar as simultaneous individuation and totalization disintegrate the barriers to interaction (i.e. in the push to individuation) while requiring a kind of universal scoping within the structures and processes of interaction (i.e. in the push to totalization). Further, as we saw above in our discussion of protocolic control and acceleration, we are now in a place to begin seeing how the dualistic logic of liberalism not only feeds on acceleration (i.e. in order to disintegrate barriers to interaction between individuated subjects), but fuels acceleration through the facilitation of interaction scoped as widely as possible (or at least always scoping wider and wider as relevant opportunities arise).

Our project here is to root out and understand the effectiveness of the logic underlying liberalism and begin developing the capacity to recognize the violence at work within this logic. Part of this project means, therefore, a rethinking of liberal normative ideals and the hope in turning to interaction itself (or a story of rationality as a certain kind of nonviolent interaction) as a means of achieving some progress in reaching ideals. And, if we are to go further toward a reconceptualization of interaction as a means to progress, and a recognition of the violent implications of this proceduralist turnaround, more will need to be discussed regarding rationality, interaction, and progress than what has been sketched out above. We will need to begin groping toward a conception of rationality that will legitimize violence without advancing the protocolic domination of dualistic logic. And, therefore, it is to a reconceptualization of rationality, democratic legitimization, and transcendence that we now turn in chapter 5.

5

Legitimizing Violence

A. REASON AND THE VIOLENCE OF TRANSCENDENCE
Reason is a process of making connections beyond oneself (transcendence) which could be either stabilizing or destabilizing and, therefore, can contribute to freedom or domination.

B. FREEDOM AS RESISTANCE
Freedom is an engagement in the process of political resistance – the creation of political space and time through the development of resilient networks that resist standardization.

C. REDEMPTIVE POLITICS AND THE LEGITIMATION OF VIOLENCE
Legitimacy is an ongoing positive normative judgment regarding one's participation in the power at work within processes of reconfiguring patternings.

INTRODUCTION

In the last chapter, we sought to deproblematize difference and instead problematize dualistic logic with a view to begin fostering network patternings that resist standardization. The liberal market, science, and cosmopolitanism rooted in liberal ideals of independence and equality were therefore understood as bringing with them a logic that undermines resilient natural, familial, and traditional patternings. We saw how asymmetrical relations of dependence and the vulnerability of specificity – relations between persons, places, and things that simply cannot be substituted for other persons, places, and things – made up deep differences that were denied by the oscillation between atomism and universalism. In its dogged search for procedures that will effectively transcend dependence and vulnerability, liberalism's pursuit of progress has fuelled acceleration and disrupted and displaced the patternings of our world. Now, the question remains, how are we to begin

theorizing regarding the norms of democratic politics in a positive manner? How, for example, are we to avoid domination within nature, family, and traditions? Or, more generally, how are we to understand the
legitimization of violence? What role does reason and freedom play in
the processes of legitimization?

As we have seen above in the discussion of politicization in chapter 1,
politics is all about the interconnections and interactions of embodied
people in history and their localized place within their material and social environment. Hence, the deep pluralism at the heart of democracy
must be acknowledged and embraced. Abstractionism should be resisted
and idealizations avoided. However, a kind of Habermasian question remains: is it not still important to abstract away from real life in order to
develop a critical impulse that can be applied as a reforming principle
that will not be corrupted by the domineering power dynamics of life? I
began with a quote from Wittgenstein's *Philosophical Investigations* in
which he speaks of the danger of a rationalism that is not rooted in the
actual practices of people, but instead leads us into believing that we
need to "repair a torn spider's web with our fingers" through abstractions away from everyday life.[1] In response to rationalism's presuppositions of uniformity and universalism that distort our thinking through
formalistic constraints, Wittgenstein's call challenges us to return to the
rough ground for it is only upon the rough ground that we find the friction we need to walk. Yet if the ideals of independence and equality are
understood to be antidemocratic insofar as they are driving forces within
an empire of uniformity, then where do we turn for a check upon the
evils of domination that have so often been rooted in the hierarchies of
tyrannical regimes or the violence of nature, family, and tradition? If we
do not hold fast to the ideals of independence and equality, from where
do we obtain a critical approach? Are we simply left with the injustice of
domination within the status quo?

Before going on to suggest some ways in which we might theorize regarding the normative "rough ground" of politics, it is worthwhile to
briefly consider what we are looking for in a critical approach that takes
the real lives of people seriously. James Tully, following the lead of
Wittgenstein and Foucault, has also emphasized the centrality of practice
and, consequently, the need for multi-logical critical approaches. For example, he has argued that we would do well to free ourselves from the
idea that political life is free and rational only if it is grounded in some
ideal form of critical reflection.[2] Tully seeks to temper the hegemonic

---

1 Wittgenstein, *Philosophical Investigations*, 46e.
2 See Tully, *Democracy and Civic Freedom*, 39ff, and Tully, "Wittgenstein and Political
Philosophy."

aspirations of certain practices of critical reflection – specifically the justificational form (e.g. Habermas) and the interpretational form (e.g. Taylor) – and bring each one back down into the messy back and forth of political life as a practice of reflection among many different practices. He writes that "no type of critical reflection can play the mythical role of founding patriarch of our political life presumed of it in the debate, because any practice of critical reflection is itself already founded in the popular sovereignty of our multiplicity of humdrum ways of acting with words."[3] It is Tully's approach to critical reflection that provides the starting point for our discussion of reason and the legitimization of violence that we will discuss in this chapter – rationality is rooted in embodied practice rather than ideal singular processes of disembodied thought and is therefore multi-logical and supportive of a plurality of critical approaches. In the discussion that follows, then, I will proceed in a Tullian manner and suggest a few different (but interrelated) ways in which we might ensure that our concerns regarding the dualistic logic of liberalism manifest in the ideals of independence and equality do not lead to a bare acceptance of the status quo.

First, I will challenge the idea that reason is the foundation of freedom. Instead, I will show how reason is best understood as a process of making connections beyond oneself, of transcending one's immediate patterning. This process of transcending, however, can contribute to domination or freedom because it can either create greater instability and fragility or it can build stability and resilience within patterning relations.

Next, we will look at what we mean by freedom. Rather than viewing freedom as a kind of independence or ability to disconnect from material and social relations, I will outline a conservative approach to understanding freedom. For a conservative, freedom is an engagement in the process of developing political resistance; it is the creation of political space and time through the development of resilient network patternings that resist standardization and the disruptions of acceleration that it brings with it.

Finally, I will suggest that we consider our response to violence. As we discussed in chapter 2, violence is best viewed as a violation of patternings and, as a pervasive flux within the patternings that make up our world, neither morally repugnant nor acceptable in itself. However, when violence becomes excessive (as determined democratically by our diverse and inescapably varied normative judgments) we understand it to be domination or illegitimate violence. These normative judgments are made in a primarily reflexive manner – i.e. they make a connection between the one making the judgment and the violation about which

3 Ibid., 199.

the judgment is made – and are not therefore objective or universal judgments that can be made for all persons in all places. The fundamental reflexivity of legitimizing violence means that justice is to be found not in a reversal of power relations in order to promote the victim to the status of perpetrator or to elevate the oppressed to the position of oppressor, but in the restraint and self-sacrifice of redemptive politics. Denying the symmetry and interchangeability hidden within egalitarianism, redemptive politics represents a more effective approach to resisting domination. As a striving for justice in embodied reciprocity and reflexivity rather than abstract and universalizable impartiality, it is a relational process of legitimation in which the relations between the self, the other, and the world are transformed to build resilience and foster the deep diversity of a genuine democracy.

A. REASON AND THE VIOLENCE OF TRANSCENDENCE

The ontology of res ecologia outlined in chapter 2 above highlights the fact that we are connected to our ecological, social, and spiritual environment as well as (importantly) dependent upon this connectedness and vulnerable to changes and disturbances in this larger network. Indeed, the concern regarding the threat of protocolic domination that runs through this discussion is built upon the idea of political subjects as res ecologia. The notion of legitimizing violence – the central notion in political morality and the topic of this chapter – is motivated by an acute awareness of persistent vulnerability and fragility. So, as we begin to consider the legitimation of violence and, more specifically, the role of reason in legitimation processes, let us consider the degree to which res ecologia differs from the modern conceptions of the independent, self-determining political subject. And, further, let us remember that, if we have a different ontology, we will develop a different morality in seeking to understand the legitimization of violence.

We will do well to avoid the mistakes of the classic moral philosophers who have typically avoided discussion of human dependence and weakness and, consequently, have misunderstood its importance in understanding reason and the legitimation of violence.[4] The depth of our dependence means, as we discussed in the previous chapter, that we do not simply create or posit moral judgments. Rather, normativity in actions

---

4 As MacIntyre notes, "when the ill, the injured and the otherwise disabled are presented in pages of moral philosophy books, it is almost always exclusively as possible subjects of benevolence by moral agents who are themselves presented as though they were continuously rational, healthy and untroubled." MacIntyre, *Dependent Rational Animals*, 2.

and thought is by definition dialogical and diachronic such that we are born into allegiances and responsibilities and can only alter these based upon patternings that come from beyond ourselves. Not only do we inherit numerous responsibilities as a result of our embeddedness in ecological, familial, and social relations, we unavoidably create a multiplicity of responsibilities for others as we go through life.[5] As Alasdair MacIntyre rightly notes, "it is most often to others that we owe our survival, let alone our flourishing, as we encounter bodily illness and injury, inadequate nutrition, mental defect and disturbance, and human aggression and neglect."[6] Therefore, given this pervasive dependence as well as the persistent vulnerability and ignorance that accompany it, it is appropriate that we begin a consideration of reason and freedom with a certain degree of skepticism.

Importantly, we should also note up front that this emphasis upon the dependency of the political subject is not to deny the agency of the self as a being that projects its will, it is simply to recognize that the agency of the self is of a certain kind – namely, an agency that is dependent upon its nature as an embodied, vulnerable, and dependent being-in-the-world. Or, to put it another way, as we saw above in chapter 2, we possess two fundamental drives – one towards autonomy (multiplicity) and one towards solidarity (unity). The first drive is the self's push to establish itself as the focal point for understanding and relating to the world. The second drive is the self's push to move beyond and become other than itself. These two drives produce a forward-moving impulse insofar as they are intolerable as a resting place; the network self contains within it a tension between independence and dependence that works itself out (dialogically and diachronically) in history. An appropriate conception of reason, legitimation, and freedom will be rooted in this understanding of the irreducibly complex nature of the political subject.

This understanding of the dynamic nature of the political subject shapes the problem we seek to overcome in our appeal to reason when talking about legitimizing violence. As we have seen above, Habermas appeals to reason in order to find some escape from what he sees as the deep-seated violence of ideology. However, it was also made clear above that Habermas has fundamentally misunderstood the nature of the problem of violence and has therefore advanced a legal and political philosophy that obscures some very real excesses of violence taking place in the world (i.e. tends to justify some illegitimate uses of power and

---

5 Sandel, *Liberalism and the Limits of Justice*, 179.
6 MacIntyre, *Dependent Rational Animals*, 1.

structural violence) while at the same time overplays the dangers of some other uses of power. We might ask, then, for what kind of problem are we seeking a solution? Or, perhaps more accurately, what is the trap within the human condition from which we seek to escape?

In chapter 3, I outlined the problem of protocolic control that formed the background for the turn to a network approach to democracy. It was made clear that protocolic control has a logic of universalization or a homogenizing impulse present and active within its dualistic logic. Given the dualistic logic and its universalization or homogenizing impulse within protocolic control, the problem is not how best to assert the independence of the self – e.g. to disagree with, or transcend, traditions and collective ideologies – but how to avoid an excess of structural violence. As we saw above, dependence, unlike the liberalized notion of domination within republicanism, is not inherently problematic and domineering. In fact, in a network approach to democracy dependence is essential. The question is: what kind of dependence? For, again, as we saw above, there can be great security and stability in relations of dependence such that dependence can serve as protection against the danger of domineering power relations. As we will discuss below, dependence itself allows for a kind of transcendence beyond the self and, if it is a healthy kind of dependence, it is a transcendence that never uproots (i.e. excessively disrupts) the self. The network self is nested within a larger network that reinvigorates and reinforces the patternings of the self-network. Dependence (e.g. grounding in the particularity of a specific tradition) may thereby provide some much needed protection from the danger of excessive disruption and displacement. The goal, therefore, is to avoid domination by legitimizing violence through structures and processes of governance that encourage self-transcendence *through immanence*. What then do we mean by "legitimation," "transcendence," and "immanence"?

As noted, an appropriate conception of reason, legitimation, and freedom will be rooted in an understanding of the tension within the very nature of the political subject. If we understand the network self (our political subject) as persistently dependent and vulnerable while at the same time striving to overcome itself and transcend its own particularities to unite with the other, then we are faced with the challenge of a balancing act. How can we stay true to the immanent specificity of the embodied network self while at the same time recognizing its struggle for transcendence? What's more, how can we walk this line between immanence and transcendence in a way that promotes structures and processes of governance that resist excessive violence? Indeed, what do we mean by "excessive" if the self contains within its own nature a drive to transcend its own immanent specificity?

First, how might we understand this fundamental drive to transcendence within the political subject given the pervasive immanence of persons as res ecologia? What do we mean by "transcendence" in both socio-phenomenological as well as structural terms? How might we understand transcendence and immanence in terms of the developmental processes of network patterning?

Phenomenologically, transcendence includes the workings of an imaginative will – i.e. a projection from one's life patterning in two dimensions (1) temporally – projecting into the future and into the indeterminacy of this future, and (2) existentially – projecting outside oneself and the limits of one's direct control as well as outside the limits of one's dependence. Transcendence, by definition, is therefore violent in its disruption of the self through the creation of a kind of independence. As the self projects beyond itself, it becomes unsettled and, to some degree, uncontrolled or unstable in its projection; it is in an unsettled state of being-beyond-itself. Of course, a network approach to democracy means that persons are understood as beings who live and move and have their being as distributive network patternings nested within broader network patterns. Therefore, transcendence within this network ontology means a making or a reinforcing of connections to network patternings outside (or larger than) the immediate network pattern of the self. Transcendence through immanence, then, involves the creation or reinforcing of connections in the patternings most local to the immediate patterning. Transcendence through immanence, therefore, means more than a bare transcendence of the self; it means *transcendence in and through dependence*. Instead of transcendence coming through a bare communicative connection with the other (i.e. as the cosmopolitanism of liberal rationalism suggests), transcendence through immanence means a return or a greater exploration of the self as well as the resulting communicative relationship with the other that develops out of this actualization process of self-realization. Transcendence without immanence involves connections that do not support the immediate network pattern; this process of ungrounded transcendence represents the creation of instable fragility and opens the self up to uprooting and displacement – i.e. domination. And because – given the realities of embodied existence – there is a finite number of connections that can be made, there is a dynamic within these nested patternings such that connections to patternings near the immediate patterning can necessitate disconnections from patternings farther from the immediate patterning. Likewise, disconnections from the distant patternings can precipitate connections with the more local patternings. What this means, therefore, is that sequential connection-making is highly significant if the dangers of transcendence without immanence are to be avoided. We should also note that, this process of creating and reinforcing connections could be originating from within the immediate pattern or from patterns outside the self; it could be originating at any level of the nesting. The level of origination is not of importance so much as the nature of the connection-making that is taking place. Connection-making that does not build in the resilience of sequential patterns – i.e. making connections from one level of nesting to the next – threatens the self and leads to domination in its instability.

The original drive toward transcendence can be seen, perhaps most clearly, in the use of reason. Given our understanding of network selves as dependent and vulnerable beings, though, we will do well to approach reason with a significant degree of caution and skepticism. Certainly, the significance of reason lies in its role within processes of self-transcendence; reason is powerful and politically relevant precisely because it is a process of the self making connections beyond itself. Reason is a process of making connections beyond oneself but these connections have the potential to develop either more fragile or more resilient interrelational structures and processes. And, in this way, reason holds the promise of freedom in one hand and the potential for domination in the other.[7]

In its promise of freedom, reason offers what is not to be thought of as independence or autonomy in the realm of action (i.e. an isolation that is nothing more than false or distorted notion of genuine freedom). Rather, the freedom that reason offers is found in stable and secure relational dependence upon the environment of the self. That is, reason can lead to a freedom in transcendence through immanence that is quite different from the contractual transcendence that is said to lie in the ability to calculate what is in one's own best interest in the rationalist's creation of a demos (e.g. Rousseau, Habermas, etc.). But, it is also quite distinct from the meta-traditional transcendence as suggested by feminists like Virginia Held and multiculturalists like Kymlicka. The freedom sought within the ethics of care as advanced by Held is similar to what

---

7 It may be said, therefore, that independence (which is, really, a kind of disconnect between the immediate pattern and the next pattern) is more prone to domination than dependence because it is inherently unstable and prone to disruption. And, as we saw above, the development of grid-like patterns around the immediate pattern represents the facilitation of connections that are not sequential, not in keeping with the nesting of distributive networks. As such, not only does the grid represent a distortion of the immediate pattern, it develops connective patterns that are lacking resilience and stability insofar as connections and disconnections can be (and are) made far from the immediate pattern, but nonetheless isolate the immediate pattern. This is, of course, what takes place in the development of protocolic control.

Kymlicka advances insofar as in both freedom is seen as a kind of autonomy in which a person develops or exercises "a capacity to reshape and cultivate new relations, not to ever more closely resemble the unencumbered abstract rational self of liberal political and moral theories."[8] However, although the freedom sought within a network approach to democracy shares this strong rejection of the liberal rationalist approach to radical, individualistic autonomy, the concept of freedom within the ethics of care and multiculturalism is still missing the problem of protocolic control and the disruptive power of domination. We have already considered the notion of freedom in Kymlicka's multiculturalism in chapter 1, but we see a similar problematic at work in the ethics of care theorists' reluctance to leave liberal ideals of self-determination and equality behind. For example, Held understands the "ethics of justice" and the "ethics of care" to be two conceptually distinct, but nonetheless necessary, approaches to moral theory. She suggests that in the ethics of justice, "the values of equality, impartiality, fair distribution, and noninterference have priority; in practices of justice, individual rights are protected, impartial judgments are arrived at, punishments are deserved, and equal treatment is sought."[9] However, the ethics of care involves "the values of trust, solidarity, mutual concern, and empathetic responsiveness ... [and,] in practices of care, relationships are cultivated, needs are responded to, and sensitivity is demonstrated."[10] Or, to put it simply, "whereas justice protects equality and freedom, care fosters social bonds and cooperation."[11] By clinging to this conception of justice as rooted in persons as "free and equal," the ethics of care approach as well as the multicultural approach problematize dependency in a way that the network approach does not. And, further, by problematizing dependency, the use of reason as a means of transcendence is embraced with a dangerous enthusiasm.

For liberal rationalists like Habermas (as well as Rawls and Kymlicka), reason offers the freedom of transcendence beyond the pervasive parochialism of one's traditions and ideologies – i.e. a kind of independence. Habermas puts forward a socio-psychological model within his conception of rationality and suggests that the transcendence of idealization achieved through reason is best understood as therapeutic.[12] He sees the ideal speech situation as anticipated and presupposed in

8 Held, *The Ethics of Care*, 14.
9 Ibid., 15.
10 Ibid., 15–16.
11 Ibid., 15.
12 See Habermas, *Knowledge and Human Interests*, 274–300, 310.

every act of communication but, importantly, the unity of reason within the ideal speech situation also provides a kind of mirror or therapeutic perspective from which one can come to recognize systemic distortions in communication. If we explore this therapeutic perspective and its underlying assumptions concerning reason a little further, however, we will come to realize that the transcendence of reason sought by liberal rationalists holds the promise of freedom, but actually undergirds the standardized modulations of protocolic control and, therefore, causes protocolic domination.

Viewing the transcendence of reason in the ideal speech situation in therapeutic terms, we can imagine a therapist that will simultaneously communicate two messages to us:

1 we should be ourselves, and
2 we should, at least in some way, be different than we presently are.

The first message is needed because a therapist will do no good if they simply tell you that you should be as they are (or someone else is). What this means is that it is quite obviously not therapeutic to be given a uniform message that everyone receives despite their unique personal characteristics and social situation.[13] The second message is needed because the therapist must have some prescriptive weight and not simply say "everybody is different and that is just fine." Indeed, without this normative element, we are back into the absurdity, inactivity, and narcissism of the relativist – i.e. the kind of thing we set out to overcome with a turn to reason. If we accept the necessity of both of these messages, then a problem remains – how do we reconcile the multiplicity of relativism with the singularity of a universal normativity? In other words, how do we reconceptualize the use of reason such that we maintain a robust normative impulse without absolutizing its singularity? Or, again, how do we then develop a normative foundation for critically evaluating power uses – i.e. how do we identify and avoid "excessive" violence given our fundamental dependence as network selves?

Habermas, like so many rationalists before him, understands the transcendent power of reason lying in its unity (i.e. the coordinating effect of warranty offered in speech is good against the whole world).[14] He further contends that the unity of reason assumes an ideal speech situation in which there is a complete absence of coercion through power and,

13 This normative essentialism is the problem with cosmopolitanism. And, indeed, it is the problem with Habermas' theoretical framework if taken as pure transcendentalism.

14 See, for example, Habermas, *Communicative Action*, Vol. I, 302.

therefore, complete and total consensus is theoretically achievable.[15] The critical impulse cherished by Habermas – the ability of the self to realize and manifest its drive towards transcendence – relies upon this pure or absolute unity of reason. However, there are two key problems with this conception of transcendence through reason. First, this notion of reason as a metaphysical unity existing in the nether realm and waiting for us to abstract away from our real lives enough to access its transcendent glory is dramatically out of step with our lived experiences with ourselves and others as embodied, reasoning beings (as Gadamer has so convincingly argued).[16] But more on this abstractionism below. Second, and more importantly for our discussion of reason, transcendence, and the legitimation of power use, reason conceived in this universalized, power-free way cannot serve as a theoretical foundation for freedom, democracy, and the legitimation of power use.

The ideal speech situation and its underlying assumption regarding the unity of reason cannot provide a perspective from which to recognize and avoid excessive violence because what is excessive must be determined diachronically from the bottom up rather than from an imagined singularity existing outside space / time. In other words, the excesses of power use must be multiple insofar as the power flows within network patternings are multiple in both their particular structures and processes as well as in their different flux-patterns through time – i.e. different networks can absorb and maintain different degrees of adaptation and reconfiguration. The degrees of power (i.e. change acting against resistance) at work within network patternings, therefore, are inherently relative to the relevant networks' background rates of change. Our judgements concerning power use, therefore, must also be multiple; our understanding of "excessive" must develop in and through the connections between ourselves as res ecologia and our world. In terms of legitimizing democratic governance, the unity of reason simply cannot serve as a critical or therapeutic perspective from which to gain an understanding of systemic power distortions of democratic processes because, as will be made explicit below, democracy has the multiplicity of power imbalances

---

15 The singularity of the ideal speech situation could be compared to John Rawls' idea of an original position behind the "veil of ignorance." Here, Rawls says, "it is clear that since the differences among the parties are unknown to them, and everyone is equally rational and similarly situated, each is convinced by the same arguments." Rawls, *A Theory of Justice*, 139. Of course, Rawls' notion of justice is monological (there is nothing that requires intersubjective communication in his thought experiment) whereas Habermas' ideal speech situation is inherently dialogical.

16 Gadamer, "The Historicity of Understanding," 260.

at its theoretical core. In other words, deep or complete consensus represents the vanishing point of democracy.[17]

Put another way, interests cannot be generalized completely or they will cease to be meaningful in any political sense – i.e. there must be opposition or limitations pushing up against the interest for it to be politically efficacious.[18] Consensus cannot provide an operative ideal for democracy because democracy, by definition, remains a process of dealing with conflicting values and norms. That is, inequality of difference should be understood as a structural necessity rather than an ideological contingency that is to be overcome through a critical theory.[19] Or, to put this same point in more Habermasian terms, democracy – even in the ideal – includes a lack of confidence in validity claims and argumentative discourse. Habermas suggests that communicative action may be consensual (where speech takes place within an already present consensus) or dialogical (where speech takes place based upon common recognition of validity claims and with the goal of agreement).[20] But, due to their reliance upon the singularity of consensus, neither consensual nor dialogical communicative action can point us toward the ideal of democracy.

17 Richard Bernstein has pointed out that, although there is nothing wrong in principle with a counterfactual in a scientific theory, it is not at all obvious what kind of "evidence would even be relevant to supporting or refuting such a claim ... What evidence or arguments would even be relevant to refute the counterfactual claim that despite all signs to the contrary every speaker who engages in communicative action is committed to the presupposition of the discursive redemption of universal normative validity claims?" Bernstein, *Beyond Objectivism and Relativism*, 193. I would like to suggest that my approach to his ideal speech situation – i.e. arguing that it does not achieve the intended outcome of democratic governance – is an example of a kind of refutation of Habermas' counterfactual. That is, Habermas is engaged in positing hypothetical universals that are necessary conditions. However, these conditions are not only subject to empirical justification and therefore fallible, but they are developed in order to provide a normative foundation for law and politics. His dialectic synthetic project involves a redefinition of scientific endeavours (it is, for Habermas, rooted in moral-political concerns) and so the simple Popperian call for falsifiability must also be redefined. If it can be shown that Habermas' counterfactual does not provide an adequate normative foundation in the ideal, then there is good reason to question the counterfactual itself as a necessary condition for practical thought. That is, if the counterfactual involves a situation in which democracy has been dissolved, to what degree can it serve as the foundation for a critical impulse?

18 Or, as Derrida says, there is no politics without *différance*. See McCarthy, "The Politics of the Ineffable," 161. Of course, this notion of *différance* has implications beyond an ideal of democracy and challenges the very notion of a rational consensus. Also see Mouffe, *Deconstruction and Democracy*, 8, and Misak, *Truth, Politics, Morality*, 131, 144–5.

19 See Dryzek, *Deliberative Democracy and Beyond*, 20. Note that Dryzek makes this distinction, but does not – as I do – argue that inequality is a structural necessity.

20 See McCarthy, *The Critical Theory of Jürgen Habermas*, 290, and Habermas, *Communicative Action*, Vol. II, 121.

Quite simply, democracy involves the questioning of validity claims not the redemption of validity claims. Some questions remain: If there is no transcendent unity of reason from which to gain a critical perspective, what then do we have to say regarding reason and its potential for contributing to freedom and limiting systemic violence? Or, more specifically, how do we avoid excessive violence when violence is systemic within ourselves and our very processes of self-transcendence through reason?

Reason, as outlined above, can be understood as manifesting the drive toward transcendence in the political subject in two primary ways: (a) a bare transcendence that reaffirms an independent self or detaches and isolates a self from its social and material environment or (b) a transcendence that rejuvenates the connections that make up the self and works outward in a sequential manner from the most immediate patterns of the self. Put very simply, the former manifestation of reason leads to domination and the latter to freedom. That is, reason working in the service of freedom allows a self to better realize its place within ecological, social, and spiritual environments that are not of its own making; reason in the service of freedom grounds and reinforces the self as a kind of rationally dependent being. Developing immanence means a struggle to ground the self through a process of deepening the patterning of the self in its relation to the world around it (i.e. stabilizes and embeds it). Reason is the self-reinforcement and replication or the projection of the self outward after a stage of moving inward.[21] It is this rejuvenating process of both deepening and reconfiguring that allows the self to resist domination by patterning after a larger pattern, a transcendent self of a certain kind. Reason operating in the service of freedom, then, should be understood as inherently and fundamentally relational.

For Hegel, what is rational is real and what is real is rational. In other words, history is the self-realization of reason. As such, he was correct to understand the rational as what exists in the world and what the world is becoming, but he was wrong to take such an objectivist perspective. That is, he speaks of the rational and the world as if from a perspective outside it. But a more subjectivist approach is needed. The point of the rational is to develop a grounding of sorts for appropriate political behaviour – i.e. to avoid the whimsical emotivism of romanticism. However, it is too rationalistic to consider the world-in-itself. Rather, we should consider the rational as that which exists in the world from our perspective as embodied beings-in-the-world. What this means, then, is

---

21 Compare with Hegel's notion of Spirit as absolute freedom – i.e. self-consciousness as pure being. See Taylor, *Hegel*, 403.

that rationality is a way of expressing our striving for a kind of network formation that is coordinating with that within which we are embedded – i.e. it is a becoming one with the world. It is a self-actualization driven by a thirst for transcendence but guided by the structures and processes of network patterns beyond oneself. Reason, therefore, is neither within oneself nor within "the world" as if it were a thing-in-itself. Reason exists (i.e. is made manifest) within the relationship between the self and the world.[22] Phenomenologically, it may be seen as the process of coming to acknowledge, understand, and embrace one's vulnerability as a dependent being (i.e. as piety). Structurally, it may be seen as the process of creating, reinforcing, and rebuilding the connections of dependence that make up, support, and enhance the self.

Although we cannot avoid violence insofar as it is within our nature to strive for transcendence, we can legitimize violence and thereby avoid the excessive violence that is domination. And, further, we can come to recognize excessive violence to the degree that we can come to an understanding of the limits of our legitimization of violent power use (that which is not legitimate is excessive by definition). How then do we legitimize the power use of violence?

Put simply, legitimation is a process of coming to recognize and embrace the violence that leads to greater resilience. Legitimacy, then, is a recognition that one's participation in the power at work within patternings is contributing to greater freedom rather than greater domination. It is (a) a dialectical process of self-other legitimation and (b) a diachronic process – i.e. an ongoing, embodied process of relational development that takes place through time. However, at this point, it may be helpful to once again consider how we might best understand legitimation in terms of transcendence through dependence. And, in order to begin recognizing the dialectical activity of legitimation, we need to begin seeing democratic legitimation as:

(a) a dialogical process of self-realization and self-determination – a reflexive process of self-legitimation, and
(b) not simply a theoretical process, but a practical, embodied process of social and material relations taking place in and through history – a diachronic process.

Legitimacy is an ongoing recognition and positive normative judgment regarding one's participation in the power at work within processes of

---

22 Hegel, *Philosophy of Right*, xix, and Taylor, *Hegel*, 422.

reconfiguring network patternings – i.e. a judgment that one is helping create freedom rather than domination. This dialogical and diachronic approach is founded upon the fact that, to put it very simply, we ourselves – and our understanding of ourselves – are determined within and through history. I say "are determined" because ourselves and our understanding of ourselves should be understood not as two fundamentally distinct things or processes, but as one reflexive process of actualization. As Gadamer explains, "we stand always within tradition, and this is no objectifying process, i.e. we do not conceive of what tradition says as something other, something alien. It is always part of us, a model or exemplar."[23] Put another way, the authority of tradition comes from within and, at the same time, the degree to which we recognize the authority of tradition (or even notice traditions) is motivated by our present interests and concerns.[24] Thus, recognizing our inherent prejudices and the depth of their role within our understanding helps us to gain a more appropriate conception of ourselves as historically situated, interdependent beings and, therefore, a better awareness of our epistemological situation.

The interplay between the authority of tradition and our present interests and concerns, if it is to guide us in avoiding excessive violence, may be understood in terms of legitimate and illegitimate power use. As we saw above in chapter 2, illegitimate power use may be best understood as being excessively violent or domineering. The liberal rationalist tradition has come to elevate deliberation and public reason as the sole means of legitimation because it continues to be fixated on a concept of freedom as self-determined action that is attuned to universal reason. This obsession with deliberation and public reason as the only means of legitimation has led to imperialistic standardizations in order to facilitate communication across radically different cultures and societies. Because, for the liberal, there can be no legitimation without sufficient commonality, standardization in the face of deep difference is itself understood to be legitimate. For one concerned with the domination that is manifest in and through the modulations of protocolic control, however, this continued obsession with deliberation and public reason represents an

23 See Gadamer, "The Historicity of Understanding," 265. This inner historicity of experience makes objective interpretation impossible. See Rosen, *Hermeneutics as Politics*, 165.

24 See Gadamer, "The Historicity of Understanding," 267. For Gadamer, "our self-understanding is tradition bound. If it criticizes aspects of that tradition, it does so only in the tradition's own terms." Warnke, "Social Identity as Interpretation," 317.

unfortunate and unsuccessful attempt to justify what should be understood as excessive systemic violence.

Finally, in addition to sociological terms, legitimation may be understood in psychological terms. In this sense, legitimation takes place as one gains hope or optimism regarding what kind of relationship one may develop with the other. Legitimacy is not only best understood diachronically, but also as primarily future-oriented. It may be seen in the willingness to suspend some negative judgments for a time in hope of a future in which one will be free.

The problem of legitimacy is indeed highly problematic if it includes an ideal requirement that the violence of, say, state law encapsulate fundamental or finalized norms and procedures at any given point in time as a fully legitimate standard of behaviour. Understanding a body of laws as having not only its content, but also its source (e.g. the state), caught up in a continuing political process of reform and correction that (fallibly) develops restraint as an educative and interpretive process tempers this problematic somewhat. As Jack Balkin writes, "legitimacy is a gamble about what the future will bring. This faith cannot be reduced to the existing content of the laws or of the system of government at the present, because those laws and that system may change. Rather, the faith that legitimacy requires is faith despite uncertainty about how things will turn out."[25] It is appropriate, therefore, to conceive of a legitimate legal system as an ongoing process in which those who do not agree with the law nevertheless put up with it in the sense that they presume that the dominant power flow is temporarily legitimate even if it is illegitimate according to their ideal notion of justice and will one day become recognized as illegitimate.[26] This does not depend upon meaningful legitimacy at the time of authorship (e.g. for a law or constitution) or the Rousseauian notion of a homogenous and/or super-virtuous citizenry but, instead, requires some sort of minimal degree of internal acceptance regarding the future potential of the law. There is, then, somewhat of a parallel here between democratic legitimacy and the future orientation of the warranty given in rational discourse as outlined by Habermas. Specifically, (as mentioned above) he suggests that although a speaker owes the binding force of his illocutionary act to the coordinating effect of the warranty he offers – i.e. to redeem, if necessary, the validity claim raised with his speech act – it should be understood that this redemption will *always* be compromised and partial. The rationality of the

25 Balkin, "Respect-Worthy," 495.
26 Habermas, *Between Facts and Norms*, 474–5.

communication lies not in any correspondence with an absolute ideal, but in the fulfillment of *expectations* regarding communication that will take place in the future.[27]

Not only is it helpful to understand legitimation as taking place in the development of hope for the future development of resilient network connections, but it is appropriate to conceive of political legitimation taking place through two central strategic processes – deliberation and resistance. The former, quite understandably, holds more potential for those close to the power flow rather than those more outside the power-flow of their society.

Deliberation, understood strategically, is something political theorists know all too well – it is a process of reinforcing communicative connections, it is a kind of agreement or agreement-reaching process. What we tend to focus too little on, though, are the broader, structural changes that need to take place to facilitate (and even encourage) this process of communicative connections. And, of course, some of these changes have already been outlined above in terms of the standardization of protocolic control. Deliberation, therefore, represents a process of developing dependence as communicative connections (ecological, social, and spiritual) are created and reinforced. This dependence may be understood as developing in a twofold relationship – first, dependence upon the other with whom one is deliberating and, second, dependence upon the means of communication itself. Because legitimation is fundamentally a process of self-legitimation (as should become clear in what follows), the processes of deliberation (in terms of both its end and its means) are taken up into, and begin to alter the trajectory of, the network self. Deliberation, therefore, can represent a certain kind of dependence-building, but also will look differently depending upon the other with whom communicative connections are made. That is, depending upon the other and the means of communication with the other, the trajectory of the network self will be altered in very different ways. In this sense deliberation itself (like reason) can be legitimizing or

27 Habermas, *Communicative Action*, Vol. I, 302. Indeed, there is some indication that Habermas himself actually does understand reason in a dialectical manner not terribly unlike what I have roughly sketched out above. He suggests that the singularity of reason (in its inherent universalization) is actually a *condition* of the multiplicity of value-spheres. For example, he argues that "the transitory unity that is generated in the porous and refracted intersubjectivity of a linguistically mediated consensus not only supports but furthers and accelerates the pluralization of forms of life and the individualization of life-styles. More discourse means more contradiction and difference. The more abstract the agreements become, the more diverse the disagreements with which we can *nonviolently* live." Habermas, "The Unity of Reason in the Diversity of Its Voices," 140.

delegitimizing depending upon the kind of dependence that is developed in and through the processes of building communicative connections. Deliberation, therefore, is not enough to legitimize all violence (especially if dramatic power imbalances are at work) and we must turn to another concept – resistance.

B. FREEDOM AS RESISTANCE

As we have seen above, Habermas seeks to develop a concept of the ideal connection between communicative action and the production of law in order to talk of the legitimacy of state-centred law.[28] However, there is good reason to be suspect of the notion that decision-making through democratic deliberation can be *the* ideal that will ground legal legitimacy and protect it from the power at work within ideology. For as he argued in his debates with Gadamer, the corruptions of ideology could only be pushed back through reason's ability to provide a robust critical impulse that could overcome systematically distorted communication by transcending the immediacy of history and the relativism of contextualism.[29] The systematic distortion of communication, then, can only be recognized and understood in contrast to the ideal speech situation in which every possible interpretation can be heard without the influence of power relations – i.e. the distortion can only be recognized from without. Reason for Habermas, as we noted, could only accomplish this opposition to ideological distortion by means of its singularity in the ideal – its ability to transcend the multiplicity of history-bound life of reasoning persons and identify the universal conditions of rationality itself.

28 Habermas' critical theory is an attempt to outline the conditions for emancipation in undistorted communication and therefore set out the possibilities of protecting the symbolic reproduction of the lifeworld from the material reproduction of the system. But, as some critics have noted, this analysis is too simplistic in that it does not differentiate between various forms of power and diverse methods of lifeworld protection. See, for example, Shabani, *Democracy, Power, and Legitimacy*, 122. Indeed if lifeworld colonization and the distortion of power are everywhere then there is no clear critical analysis that allows for meaningful political action and reform on the ground. In order to rectify this lack of specificity and applicability in his theory of communicative action, Habermas, therefore, turned to an analysis of law and democracy in *Between Facts and Norms*. It is here that he outlines the legitimacy of law's position between system and lifeworld. Indeed, Habermas writes that "the modern legal order can draw its legitimacy only from the idea of self-determination: citizens should be able to understand themselves as authors of the law to which they are subject as addressees." Habermas, *Between Facts and Norms*, 449.

29 See, for example, Habermas' conception of the ideal speech situation in Habermas, *Communicative Action*, Vol. I, 294. Also see Gadamer, "The Historicity of Understanding," 260.

We also took note of the fact that the idealization and universalization underlying Habermas' critical social theory – his telos of consensus – fails to provide an adequate theoretical foundation for democratic legitimacy. The problem is that singularity is not appropriate when considering democratic deliberation or legal legitimacy; consensus absolutized (i.e. singularity that can transcend the corruptions of ideology) cannot function as the normative ideal of democracy or, by extension, legal legitimacy. In other words, the ideal speech situation does not provide a perspective from which to critique the social power imbalances that may be distorting the democratic processes because democracy has the multiplicity of power imbalances at its theoretical core and deep or complete consensus means the dissolution of democracy. Therefore, consensus cannot provide the operative ideal for democracy because democracy, by definition, remains a process of dealing with opposing or conflicting values and norms – indeed, a way of dealing with conflicting ways of life. There is, therefore, a deep conflict within the theoretical work of Habermas that stems from his simultaneous commitment to democracy and opposition to the power imbalances present within a deep pluralism.[30]

This notion that inequality is a structural necessity within democracy runs contrary to Habermas' liberal cosmopolitan bent. Instead it picks up conservatism's emphasis upon difference and situated oppositionalism that we can see in, say, the political philosophy of Carl Schmitt. For example, his *The Concept of the Political* is an attempt to achieve state unity by defining the content of politics as opposition to the "other" – i.e. an enemy, a stranger, someone or thing that presents an existential threat.[31] He does not understand this friend / enemy distinction as a metaphor or moral dilemma, but as a concrete antagonistic opposition.[32] The political is "only the intensity of an association or dissociation of human beings whose motives can be religious, national (in the ethnic or cultural sense), economic, or of another kind and can effect at different times different coalitions and separations."[33] Further, the enemy is not to be

---

30 "Deep pluralism" is a recognition and embrace of "deep diversity." And, by "deep diversity" I refer to what Anthony Laden has described as "human diversity that is not thought to stop at some common core of human nature. It is diversity that goes all the way down." See Laden, *Reasonably Radical*, 1. It should be noted that Laden himself takes this idea from Charles Taylor. See Taylor, "Shared and Divergent Values," and Taylor et. al., *Multiculturalism and the Politics of Recognition*.

31 See Schmitt, *The Concept of the Political*, 27.

32 He suggests that liberalism has erred in attempting to "transform the enemy from the viewpoint of economics into a competitor and from the intellectual point into a debating adversary." Ibid., 28.

33 Ibid., 38.

understood as a personal or private adversary, but as a public enemy – an enemy of the state. As a right-wing German scholar in the interwar period, Schmitt was concerned with the shameful treatment of Germany by the victors of the First World War and sought to develop a justification for a highly unified German state. His conception of the "other," therefore, quite quickly becomes understood as external to a unified nation-state rather than internal to the state or society as a pluralist might suggest. In other words, for Schmitt, the state is the exclusive bearer of politics and the enemy is an oppositional force to the state's existence as an organized political entity.[34] Although the universalism underlying the liberal cosmopolitanism of Habermas is drastically inappropriate, the state-centric oppositionalism of Schmitt is also inappropriate. Where, then, do we find the road between Habermas' ideal of egalitarian consensus and Schmitt's ideal of violent opposition to the enemy?

This middle road is to be found in an understanding of freedom and political resistance. As we saw above, legitimation is a process of coming to recognize and embrace the violence that leads to greater resilience. And political resistance is the creation of political space and time through the development of resilient networks that resist standardization. Freedom, then, is an engagement in the process of political resistance – and democracy is the logic of political resistance at work in the world. Power use comes to be legitimized to the degree that it is understood to be developing resilience or, in other words, creating freedom.

As we noted earlier in this chapter, we not only have reason to be cautious regarding reason and the appeal to reason in our understanding of freedom and transcendence, we have reason to understand freedom as a process of network development that stabilizes and embeds the immediate patterning of the self. In contrast, the creation of instability within the patterning of the self and its nesting within larger patternings opens up the greater possibility of domination. Resistance to domination, therefore, lies in the development of resilience within the nested network patterns. This resilience is developed as certain kinds of connections are made; namely, connections that are in keeping with the nesting of the patternings. Sequential connections, therefore, that either develop one "level" of networks or join one "level" of networks to the next "level" are connections that build resilience by preventing the universalization of certain connections. In terms more common to political theory, we might say that local community building develops the kind of resilience that allows for resistance to domination; the development of asymmetrical

34 Ibid., 32.

nestings of network patterns prevents the standardization needed for protocolic control. That is, patterns of connections that are inherently limited or local have built-in circuit breakers that prevent the violence of power use that disrupts and displaces through standardization.

Resistance is the development of resilience and a refusal to be contained; it is the development of a kind of specificity or particularity that cannot be smoothed over and shifted through the layerings of uniformity within the modulations of protocolic control. Political resistance takes place in a dialectical process that begins with political subjects as dependent beings (immanence), and pushes outward to disrupt and displace (transcendence), only to develop greater selves (transcendence-through-immanence). For example, resistance to the modulations of protocolic control can take place through a fixing upon a single mode – e.g. a re-traditionalizing of the self to become more rooted. Resistance, understood in this dialectical manner is not only in keeping with the contradictory nature of the political subject that was discussed above, but is focused upon the development of resilient network systems that prevent standardization and, therefore, prevent rapid change within patternings of the self and the world.

Resistance as a process of legitimation, because it is in opposition to the homogenizing impulse within liberalism, is much less understood, but no less important than deliberation. Resistance is a process of preventing or unmaking communicative connections, say, because they are excessively violent or have the real potential for excessive violence. This kind of uncommunicative action is important when there is a dramatic power imbalance between two communities such that deliberation will be inherently and unavoidably dominating (i.e. delegitimizing) or, indeed, in cases where there is a pervasive structural violence at work such as protocolic control. In this sense, then, resistance is a way of disengaging or disagreeing that is stronger than toleration. It can be engaged in by either the powerful or the powerless; the powerful restrict or remove themselves in order to preserve and protect the vulnerable other whereas the powerless withdraw or remove themselves in order to preserve and protect themselves. The powerless may also understand that a relation of domination is destructive toward not only themselves but also the dominator, and distance themselves in order to prevent that destruction of the other. For example, as we will see in our discussion below, in a relationship of power imbalance such as colonial relations, the domineering relations do great harm to not only the colonized, but the colonizer as well. However, an act of resistance can be motivated, in the most immediate sense, by an attempt to help others. Resistance, therefore, represents legitimation as transcendence through immanence in the sense that dependence is developed through a process of disconnection from the other and the world. That is, the dependence is developed as the structures and processes of the network self are reinforced in opposition to structures and processes of the network other and the world.

Of course, it is important to also remember that there is a sense in which both deliberation and resistance will be taking place and will be mutually reinforcing. For example, deliberation within a community will strengthen the community's self-understanding as a "we" and, in so doing, strengthen the community's understanding of the other as a "they." In a similar fashion, the resistance of one community against another will involve the strengthening of the community's understanding of the other as a "they" and, in so doing, strengthen the community's self-understanding as a "we."

Rather than understanding freedom as some abstract or essential quality of human beings as has been typical in the liberal tradition, we do best to see freedom as an engagement in the dialectical process of resistance. As Foucault noted, "rather than speaking of an essential freedom, it would be better to speak of an 'agonism' – of a relationship which is at the same time reciprocal incitation and struggle; less face-to-face confrontation which paralyzes both sides than a permanent provocation."[35] Freedom, then, should not be conceived of as pure self-determination because, just as one's political identity has its being in opposition to the other, so too does freedom exist in opposition to resistance – i.e. there is no freedom without freedom from. In this way, we should understand positive and negative freedom as two sides of the same coin. Positive and negative freedom come together when we realize that capacity (e.g. positive freedom) only exists in and through the overcoming of obstacles (e.g. negative freedom) and vice versa. In other words, freedom is not the *absence* of obstacles (be they internal or external), but an *overcoming* of obstacles (albeit only to a limited degree). Freedom, then, is best understood as a close kin to power. The self exists in opposition to the other – i.e. in overcoming the other (to a limited degree) – so a realization of

---

35 Foucault, "Afterword," 222. Or, as Charles Taylor observed regarding the difference between liberals and conservatives: "with his belief in man's essential freedom, the liberal regards the landscape as something to be subdued and exploited in the name of progress. There is neither reverence nor any sense of roots: nature is something to be used. To the conservative, on the other hand, man and his world are part of an organic whole – a unity which includes other races, other species and the land itself. His view is always touched with awe: the landscape is important not only for what it can provide, but also for what it has meant to earlier generations, for how it feeds our imaginations, and for the place it holds in some larger natural order of which man is only one component. Taylor, *Radical Tories*, 79–80.

the self's capacity (positive freedom) is only possible in an overcoming of obstacles (negative freedom). This is so because it makes little sense to speak of freedom in terms of exercising capacity if these capacities are not limited in some manner – e.g. self-control, moral discrimination, self-awareness, etc.[36] But how could there be this kind of reflexivity without the opposition of the other against the self – i.e. something beyond the pure self-positing of the self as if it were a *Ding an sich?*

If we understand freedom as an engagement in resistance, then deliberation and negotiation between communities that are marked by deep differences must remain perpetually open to resistance if violence is to be legitimized. A simple, unidirectional movement from antagonism to agonism as Mouffe suggests is insufficient and even inappropriate in some instances. As we saw briefly above, Mouffe's notion of transformation from antagonism to agonism holds, like the deliberative democrats' notion of transformation, the danger of domination through the homogenizing impulse of standardization and its resulting vulnerability to rapid modulations. This danger exists because Mouffe's transformative process is fuelled by a recognition of the legitimacy of one's opponents. However, legitimation of power relations takes place primarily in a process of self-legitimation rather than a process of legitimizing the other. And if the notion of transformation is rooted in a process of legitimation of the other, the transformative process is unidirectional and perpetually holds the threat of the stronger community transforming the weaker community rather than a transformation of the we-them relationship itself. That is, without adequate room made for resistance as a means of legitimation, Mouffe puts forward a transformative process that begins to look quite like a process of liberalization and its accompanying modulations. One of the reasons for this is the fact that the transformation from antagonism to agonism as Mouffe conceives it is somewhat unrealistic when communities possess dramatically asymmetrical power relations and exist side by side in ongoing conflicted relationships. Instead of legitimizing violence, it is a recipe for domination.

In order to avoid domination as much as possible, both the powerful community (e.g. the state) and the powerless community (e.g. a small indigenous nation) must remain open to periods of resistance within their relationship if domination at the hands of the state is to be avoided as much as possible. Further, not only is this kind of openness needed, but the communities must engage (at least periodically) in actual practices of resistance. Mouffe argues that a relational conception of identity

36 See Taylor, "What's Wrong with Negative Liberty," 215.

"does not mean of course that such a relation is necessarily one of friend / enemy, i.e. an antagonistic one. But we should acknowledge that, in certain conditions, there is always the possibility that this we / they relation can *become* antagonistic, i.e. that it can turn into a relation of friend / enemy. This happens when the 'they' is perceived as putting into question the identity of the 'we' and as threatening its existence."[37] The violence of "overcoming the other" in a process of deliberation is precisely a putting into question the identity of the other such that his / her / their existence is threatened. This threat can come from a relation in which there is no dialogical dynamism that allows for an ongoing redefinition of the relations of power. Finality represents a threat because self-other (master-slave / colonizer-colonized) relations are "constitutive of subjectivity: one becomes an individual subject only in virtue of recognizing, and being recognized by another subject."[38] This relational ontology of identity, of course, is rooted in Hegel's notion that "self-consciousness exists in and for itself when, and by the fact that, it so exists for another; that is, it exists only in being acknowledged."[39] Importantly, though, the master-slave relation of Hegel's *Phenomenology* embodies a dialectical tension that seeks resolution in transcendence beyond the relation itself. And an existential threat develops when the relationality of the self-other is totalized – i.e. the other is unable to hold an internal dynamic of relationality within himself. If the other is excessively transformed by the relation between the self and the other (i.e. when the self has dramatically more power), then the existence of the other begins to be threatened.[40] And without the periodic assertions of power stemming from the internal dynamism of the other, the powerless other begins to be standardized in and through the self-other relations. Therefore, the possibility of becoming antagonistic must at least be periodically realized or the relationship between the powerful and the powerless will develop into a process of standardizing the powerless community's ecological, social, and spiritual relations – i.e. an overcoming of the other. For example, this overcoming of the other may be seen (from the perspective of the colonized rather than the colonizer) in the subjection that takes place through the internalization of colonized relations. As Glen Coulthard writes, "without transformative struggle constituting an integral aspect of decolonization the Indigenous population

---

37 Mouffe, *On the Political,* 15–16, emphasis in original.

38 Fraser and Honneth, *Redistribution or Recognition?,* 11.

39 Hegel, *The Phenomenology of Spirit,* 178.

40 Identity is purposive in this sense. It is not something that is simply self-made, but it is a way of talking about a dynamism or aliveness within the network of the self.

will not only remain subjects of imperial rule insofar as they have not gone through a process of purging the psycho-existential complexes battered into them over the course of the colonial experience – a process of strategic desubjectification – but they will also remain so in that the Indigenous society will tend to come to see the forms of structurally limited and constrained recognition conferred to them by their colonial 'masters' as their own."[41] In other words, "in contexts where recognition is conferred without struggle or conflict, this fundamental self-transformation ... cannot occur, thus foreclosing the realization of authentic freedom."[42] The need for (at least) periodic resistance is applicable to, for example, co-management regimes (whether there are, say, extended land claims negotiations between the state and indigenous peoples, systems of governmental regulation, etc.).[43] That is, it is essential that there is a dialectical process in which the relationship is best characterized as co-management and then moves into conflict, back to co-management, again into conflict, etc. Depending upon the communities involved, the conflict could take place inside (e.g. legal action, lobbying politicians, filing official complaints, etc.) or outside (e.g. blockades, protests, direct action, etc.) the state institutions; the important thing, of course, is that the conflict manifests and reaffirms a "we" in opposition to the "they" of the state.

In the past, centralized governmental structures have exerted control over commonly held property resources and this exertion of control has generated a significant degree of conflict between state and non-state actors.[44] As Joseph Spaeder and Harvey Feit explain,

In efforts to either mitigate these conflicts, or work around them and provide for sustainable resource management, a plethora of new co-management regimes has evolved over the past decade and a half in contexts where neither strictly local resource control nor state resource control is possible or effective. In practice, different kinds of co-management exist from informal consultation to full and equal sharing of authority ... Uses of co-management have thus ranged from serving as a means of enlisting uncontrolled social groups and movements in the conservation of resources, while simultaneously and covertly co-opting them into compliance with nation state regimes,

41 Couthard, "Subjects of Empire," 449–50.

42 Ibid., 449.

43 As Spaeder explains, "co-management refers to decentralized institutional arrangements involving the sharing of management responsibilities between community-level and state-level actors." Spaeder, "Co-management in a Landscape of Resistance," 165.

44 See Spaeder and Feit, "Co-management and Indigenous Communities," 148.

to being a means of empowerment of disenfranchised rights claimants, to serving as a vehicle for continuing socio-political struggles.[45]

In other words, powerful and centralized bureaucratic structures of governance hold within them an inherent exertion of protocolic control when engaged with more traditionalist communities. The unidirectional process of deliberation alone, therefore, will not allow for the minimization of domineering power relations because it will totalize the self-other relation by locking the relations into a binary oppositionalism that possesses only one possible future – an identity formed through opposition to the other of the state. It is only through a dynamic back-and-forth dialectical process of moving between deliberation and resistance that we come to understand the dynamic nature of legitimation as truly dialogical and diachronic.

Resistance, if we are to dig a little deeper into its exercise in relation to state law, may take place through two primary strategies: avoidance and confrontation. In the strategy of avoidance, the powerless act so as to disregard the state law and govern themselves while avoiding the state-imposed sanctions for illegal activity. For example, as Joseph Spaeder recently wrote concerning state-indigenous relations in Alaska, "in Western Alaska indigenous hunters practice a broad array of such anonymous and unorganized strategies of resistance including widespread disregard for most game laws, stealth in harvesting, avoidance of agency personnel in the field and nearly total non-compliance with mandatory paperwork, such as game permits and harvest reporting."[46] This kind of resistance is typically neither organized nor focused on the transformation of legal regimes directly and is instead dedicated to the minimization of risk for those within the powerless community. Confrontation, on the other hand, represents an overt, antagonistic engagement with the state's power use. Further, in order to deepen the resistance, the subaltern community needs to not only assert its own power against the state's assertion of power, but also do so in a way that disengages itself from the administrative and judicial structures of the state. That is, the subaltern community may need to assert its radical differences in opposition to the standardizing institutions of the state; it may need to enter a process of explicitly legitimizing itself in the face of delegitimizing state processes.

45　Ibid., 149.
46　Spaeder, "Co-management in a Landscape of Resistance," 167.

This twofold kind of resistance may be understood as a kind of distancing or a non-exclusionary differentiation. Differentiation, as explained by Miroslav Volf, is "the creative activity of 'separating-and-binding' that results in patterns of interdependence."[47] It is not, therefore, a bare separation but a simultaneous separation *and* binding. Separation by itself would lead to self-enclosed, self-identical, and autonomous beings.[48] And indeed, the radical distancing of a bare separation represents an exclusionary attempt to construct an autonomous self and therefore leads inevitably to domineering relations. Both the need for separation and the dangers of separation depend upon the context. In a situation of radical power imbalance, more separation may be essential to the development of resilience. However, this kind of separation must remain related to binding in a kind of balance between the two. Radicalized separation – i.e. separation taken to its farthest extreme – will lead to domineering relations just as radicalized binding will. Again, as Volf writes, "exclusion can entail cutting of the bonds that connect, taking oneself out of the pattern of interdependence and placing oneself in a position of sovereign independence. The other then emerges either as an enemy that must be pushed away from the self and driven out of its space or as a nonentity – a superfluous being – that can be disregarded and abandoned."[49] Resistance as non-exclusionary differentiation, in contrast, is most often thought of as a legitimation strategy of political communities on the weak side of asymmetrical power relations. The question is: in the face of resistance from a weak community against power use, how should a strong community respond if it is to ensure its power use is legitimized? Put simply, resistance to the state from a subaltern community has the effect of delegitimizing the state's power use. In response, those within the state need to engage in processes of relegitimation regarding their uses of power in relation to the subaltern community. This process of relegitimation in the face of delegitimation through resistance needs to involve the distancing or withdrawal of the strong community – i.e. a process of self-legitimation by means of self-restraint or, again, a process of transcendence through immanence. As noted above, the mere engagement of a dramatically more powerful community has domineering effects as power-flows become aligned with those internal to the powerful community.

The following question regarding legitimation remains: how are we to develop stability and security while we are advancing patterns of resistance

47 Volf, *Exclusion and Embrace*, 65.
48 Ibid.
49 Ibid., 67.

to homogenizing forces? That is, is there not something inherently or inevitably unsettling and disruptive in resistance to domineering forces? The
short answer is that if we are to develop stability and security we need to
advance patterns of resistance that are enacted in and through grounding
processes (i.e. transcendence through immanence). Of course, though,
resistance itself is not necessarily a grounding process, but it will only be
effective resistance in the long-term if it is a strategic process of grounding;
both avoidance and conflict must be of a certain nature if resistance is to
be successful in the long-term.

In order to understand the requisite nature of effective resistance, we
may benefit from a consideration of the dialectical processes at work
within political communities. A community – not unlike an ecosystem –
possesses an internal logic of development and, therefore, a telos or a
teleological impulse within its structural causation. However, a community cannot realize or actualize itself without relations of resistance with
the other. It is, therefore, fundamentally and simultaneously complete
and incomplete in a manner not unlike the contradiction that begins
Hegel's ontological dialectics. As Charles Taylor explains, in Hegel's *Phenomenology of Spirit* both the historical and the ontological dialectics begin with the recognition of a dialectical contradiction. That is, "we start
off with something which is intrinsically characterized by the purpose it
is bent on realizing or the standard it must meet. We then show of this
thing that it cannot effectively fulfill this purpose or meet the standard
(and the 'cannot' here is one of conceptual necessity). We are up against
a contradiction."[50] There is, likewise, a contradiction of independence
and dependence that needs to be worked out dialogically and diachronically. Hence, there is a need for a back-and-forth between deliberation
and resistance if communities are to be realized. We should remember,
as Hegel also points out to us, that all forms of life are destined to be
replaced by others. The goal is not, therefore, to halt this process entirely, but to understand and mitigate against rapid change and the inevitable harms of excessive violence that come with it.[51]

In situations of significant power differentials between differing political communities, not only is deliberation doomed to descend into

50 Taylor, *Hegel and Modern Society*, 57.
51 Finally, our inadequate (or simply partial) understanding of our purpose is part of
the reason why we fail to achieve our purpose. When I say "reason why," I do not mean
simply in a psychological-behavioural way, but in an historical-ontological way. We so fail to
achieve our purpose – i.e. living in relative harmony with the earth and each other –
because we misconceive our purpose as being the achievement of greater independence
and invulnerability.

domination of the weaker community if it is unaccompanied by resistance, but resistance alone will also inevitably result in excessive violence. As we saw above, powerful structures of governance hold within them an inherent exertion of structural violence when engaged in relations of either deliberation or resistance. The unidirectional process of deliberation alone (i.e. moving toward greater and greater standardizations of social, material, and spiritual relations), therefore, will not allow for the minimization of domineering power relations – communities with less power will be forced to change rapidly in ways that excessively disrupt and displace. Resistance, likewise, without being accompanied by deliberative relations (at least periodically), will inevitably lead to relations of domination. Resistance by itself has the tendency to develop into antagonistic relations that are unstable and prone to replications of domineering power imbalances. For example, as Gandhi rightly pointed out, subaltern communities that do not undermine the oppressive regimes with the development of moral authority are destined to imitate the violence of their oppressors. The singularity of a unidirectional push towards the antagonism of resistance will be prone to the development of illegitimacy whether you are viewing it from the perspective of the powerful or the powerless. Further, as we will see below, non-domination as redemptive politics means that non-domination is an ongoing transformative process rather than a finalized, abstract ideal to be obtained. Indeed, non-domination is the relational process of legitimation outlined above – i.e. both the self and the other are redeemed in their ecological, social, and spiritual relations. The redemption happens in the legitimation of the other; the other is redeemed through a process of self-legitimation as they enter into ways of life that give hope and optimism regarding their future being-in-the-world. When it comes down to it, this kind of transformation is a process of network formation that is violent, but is violent primarily towards oneself rather than towards the other. Resistance without deliberation, however, is a projection of violence toward the other without the reflexivity – i.e. the self-legitimation – needed to legitimize the power use of the other.

It is also important to keep in mind that, although this notion of dialectical relations between deliberation and resistance has been worked out in bilateral terms (i.e. as if there was one single powerful community and one single powerless community involved), the same approach should be taken when there are (as is almost inevitably the case) multilateral relationships between multi-layered political communities. In fact, it should be noted that consideration of the multilateral power relations that so often exist allows us to recognize the importance of focusing upon legitimation of power use as a process characterized primarily as self-legitimation.[52] Legitimation, therefore, must be understood as a process that is *primarily* reflexive.

C. REDEMPTIVE POLITICS
AND THE LEGITIMATION OF VIOLENCE

Legitimate violence and, conversely, excessive violence are determined through an ongoing normative judgment that is primarily reflexive. That is: "Am I contributing to increased fragility in network structures and processes and, therefore, making them more susceptible to rapid change or am I developing resilience within network patternings?" The classical approach to understanding the legitimacy of power use involved a two-step process for justifying one's own participation in systemic violence: (a) describe the self's actions as "power use" and the other's actions as "violence," and (b) take up a position from which one assumes one can judge from afar the other's actions as legitimate or illegitimate violence. However, there are a couple key reasons why a judgment between legitimate and illegitimate is primarily reflexive: (a) because of the fundamentally interdependent nature of political subjects and the world within which they live, and (b) because a normative judgment is only relevant to the degree that one is involved in processes of building more fragile or more resilient network patternings. Further, the importance of reflexivity in this normative judgment becomes clear when one considers a situation in which one has the greater power in a relation with dramatic power imbalance. Mouffe's transformative process from antagonism to agonism is driven forward by a recognition of the legitimacy of the other (i.e. one's opponents). And, to the degree that the judgment regarding legitimacy is outward-looking, such recognition is therefore a projection of the self in an overcoming of the other (i.e. rather than a transformation of the self-other/we-them relationship itself).[53] If, on the other hand, one is in the powerless position in a relation of dramatic power imbalance, one has no viable option but reflexive legitimation. That is, from the victim's perspective, the oppressive or domineering actions of the other can only be legitimized through a removal of oneself from the position of the victim. The focus of legitimation must always be

52 As Volf notes, domination is not something apart from us – it is a kind of barbarity within civilization, an evil among the good, a crime against the other within the self. See Volf, *Exclusion and Embrace*, 60.

53 As we saw, this overcoming was the result of a totalization of the self-other relation rather than a transformation of the self-other relation in relation to the patterning process of the self.

upon the we-them relationship from the perspective of the "we" rather than simply upon the "them."

A central question underlying this discussion concerning the legitimation of violence and the we-them (or self-other) relationship I take to be the following: what is the nature of agreement and disagreement? And, more specifically, in what sense does our fostering of structures and processes of agreement and/or disagreement relate to the realities of our life-situation? We come to this question for two key reasons. First, there is a sense in which deliberation may be understood as a kind of agreement and resistance as a kind of disagreement and we have yet to fully examine these processes in terms of democratic normative ideals lived within embodied beings. Second, we come to this question because the goal of our discussion is to understand how the differences of inequality are at the root of democratic disagreement as well as to point toward some ways in which we might foster the appropriate – i.e. non-domineering – kind of political disagreement.

In order to gain a clearer picture of what is meant by political disagreement (or, indeed agreement), I would like to once again emphasize that our existence as res ecologia means we are embedded beings-in-the-world. That is, all knowledge is situated knowledge that is embodied in time and space and, as we have seen, our reason takes places within certain embodied life-narratives. Two things follow from this shift away from reason as an abstract process of disconnecting and reconnecting some ghostly symbols of a formal language: (1) a reinterpretation of rationality and (2) a reinterpretation of moral worth.

To this end, Wittgenstein provides us with a helpful perspective from which to begin understanding communication and the process of coming together in agreement. As he writes in *On Certainty*, "giving grounds, however, justifying the evidence, comes to an end; – but the end is not certain propositions striking us immediately as true, i.e. it is not a kind of *seeing* on our part; it is our *acting*, which lies at the bottom of the language-game."[54] In other words, because the meaning of our language lies in its use, agreement takes place not simply through a connection of signs and significations, but through a coming together of forms of life – a kind of co-configuring of patterns in human existence.[55] A chorus of voices takes place in common forms of life rather than in certain abstract

---

54 Wittgenstein, *On Certainty*, 28e, emphasis in original.

55 Wittgenstein demonstrated how the meaning of words resides not in any correspondence with particular objects in the world. Rather, the meaning of words is the way in which they are used in social interactions. For example, see *Philosophical Investigations*, 20e.

connections made in the recesses of a disembodied mind.[56] The "retreat
from the real" that runs through the liberal rationalist tradition(s) – e.g.
in the normative idealization of equality – reveals a significant misunderstanding of the nature of rationality and, by extension, political agreement.[57] For, as Schmitt writes in *The Crisis of Parliamentary Democracy*: "In
the domain of the political, people do not face each other as abstractions, but as politically interested and politically determined persons, as
citizens, governors or governed, politically allied or opponents – in any
case, therefore, in political categories. In the sphere of the political, one
cannot abstract out what is political, leaving only universal human equality; the same applies in the realm of economics, where people are not
conceived as such, but as producers, consumers, and so forth, that is, in
specifically economic categories."[58] Political agreement and disagreement, then, should not be understood as a matter of some abstract
thought or connections made in the heavenly places, but as a coming together in real-life practices that exist in time and space.

What is needed is an awareness that our forms and processes of argumentation are rooted in and determined by our practices, our being-in-
the-world. To be sure, our ideas and conceptions of the self are not to be
understood in a bare, deterministic manner as if they were nothing more
than a simple projection of the patterns of life. Rationality should be understood as both structure and agency because persons are simultaneously both subject and object, instrument and agent in their contemplative
processes.[59] We need not abandon argumentation or a commitment to
the importance of creative thought within this approach, we simply need
to recognize the embeddedness and embodied nature of our thought.

Understanding agreement as a coming together of forms of life means
that political disagreement is correspondingly rooted in divergent ways
of life. Therefore, because forms of life are all different (i.e. our bodies
and histories are all unique) there can actually be no complete or absolute agreement on any matter.[60] The result being, as Webber writes,

56 Mouffe, "Deliberative Democracy or Agonistic Pluralism," 12.

57 It represents a misunderstanding of politics in potentially two ways: first, regarding
the oppositional nature of politics and second, regarding the pervasive nature of politics
– i.e. it is a mistake to believe that one can step outside the realm of the political in order
to develop a conception of justice that is beyond the rough-and-tumble power relations of
human interaction.

58 Schmitt, *The Crisis of Parliamentary Democracy*, 11.

59 Barnard, *Herder on Nationality, Humanity, and History*, 93.

60 Indeed, this seems to be the reason why Rawls (following Kant) finds it necessary
to grossly limit the knowledge of moral actors and thereby hem in the alternatives available
to them. Rawls and Kant seek a unanimous (i.e. objective) conception of justice and are

"people of good faith disagree. In part this is the result of the fact that each person necessarily formulates their position on the basis of their inevitably partial experience. As a result, we can have no confidence that a more perfect reason will produce concord. Disagreement is endemic."[61] In the same sense, then, because we are all alike (i.e. our bodies and histories are all shared to some degree as we are all humans living on earth) there can be no complete or absolute disagreement. When we encounter the other, we do so from a certain contextual perspective – a human perspective that is not simply meted and bounded by presuppositions but, more accurately, lived in and through patterns of life. When we do come to agreement, what we are doing is developing a way of living with some enhanced degrees of commonality and interdependency. Likewise, when we disagree, we take up or continue in differing ways of life and relative independence.

One may dwell on this further. Given this understanding of agreement and disagreement, it makes little sense to speak of political disagreement taking place if two or more persons share the same life situation (i.e. if they were to be thoroughly equal). In actuality, of course, it makes little sense to speak of persons sharing the same life situation or being thoroughly equal precisely because they are *different persons*. Even if we are to speak of equality in rough terms, however, it makes little sense to speak of two persons disagreeing regarding anything of political significance if they share the same intellectual abilities, have the same emotional dispositions, share the same economic and social background, etc. These are the processes and patterns of life within which our language lives and breathes and has its being and it should make no significant difference whether it is fundamental and abstract conceptions of justice, or simply particular and local policy questions that are the subject of the disagreement. In a sense, then, the point here is quite simple – if disagreement is a different way of life it cannot be found in the same way of life.

This understanding of agreement and disagreement in democratic terms also leads us to consider effective means of agreeing and disagreeing in seeking to avoid excessive violence. For example, we will do well to consider Gandhi's clear arguments against the notion that the struggle for justice is understood to be a direct confrontation with the other in an attempt to reverse the power relations. Instead, he suggested that the relationship between the self and the other needed to be transformed if

---

therefore lured into the painful processes of rational reductionism. See Rawls, *A Theory of Justice*, 140–1.

61 Webber, "The Hobbesian Premise," 6.

genuine progress was to be made in the struggle for justice. In this "non-violent" paradigm, the oppressed could not simply attack the oppressor in order to create a new, peaceable relation; the oppressed needed to manifest the new relation by fostering the development of the other's true self as a peaceable being. Gandhi believed there was an underlying unity to reality and it could only be realized through an undermining of oppressive power relations, a changing of the rules of the oppressor-oppressed game by clinging to a notion of this underlying reality regardless of the suffering and self-sacrifice that may be required.

Although I would certainly question Gandhi's notion of the underlying unity of all, his asymmetrical approach to transforming the oppressor-oppressed relation is entirely in keeping with the network approach to democracy. His approach is asymmetrical because it is the self that is to take action to transform the relationship rather than to transform the other (i.e. as we discussed in the reflexivity of legitimation); the self's duty to open itself up to the other is absolute. If one is seeking equality, however, the motivation is not found in changing the rules of the game or in transforming the self-other relationship through self-sacrifice. Instead, pursuing equality leads one to seek a direct or binary reversal of power relations and, therefore, a continuance of violence (i.e. the dominated become the new dominators).[62] This reversal is justified because of the posited equality (which hides notions of equivalence or interchangeability). This kind of reasoning seems to come out in Todd May's writings on Jacques Rancière where he argues that the active equality (politics) of Rancière can take place in and through dramatically high levels of violence. For example he writes:

> There seems no bar to placing side by side the claims that one's adversary is one's equal and that, because of the adversary's refusal to recognize one's own equality, one must injure or kill her. To defend oneself against another does not require a denial of that other's equality. It requires instead an embrace of one's own. The emergence of violence in such a struggle [i.e. a democratic struggle] arises on the basis of a persistence in one's own equality, of the effort to maintain the expression of the presupposition of equality

---

62 Frantz Fanon's notion of decolonization – at least in his later, more political-economic work – is quite a clear example of this notion of inverting the power structures. For example, in *The Wretched of the Earth*, he suggests that decolonization is the putting into practice of Jesus' saying "the last shall be first and the first shall be last." He continues to write that "if the last shall be first, this will only come to pass after a murderous and decisive struggle between the two protagonists [i.e. the colonizers and the colonized]." Fanon, *The Wretched of the Earth*, 37.

in the face of steadfast refusal to allow that expression. Seen in these terms, although the effect of violence may be a denial of the other, it is not because of the attempt to deny the other but to preserve one's own democratic expression that violence can be resorted to without violating the ethical strictures of a democratic politics.[63]

Rancière's notion that democratic politics is the process of actively struggling towards egalitarianism allows one to justify one's violent actions as being simply an act of political self-defence. There is, in this egalitarian notion of justified violence, a temporal collapse of the means and end insofar as violence (the means) may be justified to the extent that it is simultaneously an act of democratic expression (the end). This collapse, however, is sustained only to the extent that one feels justified in limiting the concept of democratic expression to be nothing more or less than the struggle for egalitarian power relations. And, as we have seen above, there is no good reason to cling to such an odd, narrow conception of democratic expression.

Furthermore, there are at least three things to note in Rancière's notion of politics as active egalitarianism. First, the idea that politics is a disruption of the harmony of distinctive bodies that were previously understood as having a telos is problematic. As Rancière writes, "political activity is whatever shifts a body from the place assigned to it or changes a place's destination."[64] As such, his notion of politics as active equality seems to be an unavoidable step down the path toward excessive violence due to its inherent disruptive impulse (i.e. in its contrast to policing as the project of creating and maintaining order and harmony).[65] Second, the idea that politics is the creation of a single, common world is dangerous. Again, as he writes, "politics exists because those who have no right to be counted as speaking beings make themselves of some account, setting up a community by the fact of placing in common a wrong that is nothing more than this very confrontation, the contradiction of two worlds in a single world."[66] As we know from our discussion of agreement and disagreement above, however, the notion of a coming together in a common world – i.e. as if all were to be considered equal in the abstract – is an inappropriate and undemocratic conception of democratic politics. Third, the idea that there is a heavy burden placed upon the powerless insofar as their struggle is understood to be a process of

---

63 May, *The Political Thought of Jacques Rancière*, 138.
64 Rancière, *Disagreement*, 30.
65 May, *The Political Thought of Jacques Rancière*, 43.
66 Rancière, *Disagreement*, 27.

inverting power structures to pull power down from the powerful to be used by the relatively powerless is highly questionable. For him, the burden is on the powerless (or at least weighs most heavily upon the powerless) to make citizenship happen.[67] In this sense, then, those who are relatively powerless are drawn into a struggle in which they are understood to be on even terms with the powerful (if not in a practical sense, then at least in an ideal-being-manifest sense).

However, a very different struggle faces the one engaged in the asymmetrical power relations of redemptive politics. In redemptive politics, the symmetry of equality never serves as a normative ideal; asymmetry rather than symmetry serves as the guide all the way through the struggle (i.e. in conceptualizing the struggle, to understanding one's place within the struggle, to understanding the strategies and tactics to be used in resisting domination, etc.). Therefore, the goal is to change the nature of the relations between the self and the other by changing the self rather than seeking to change the other or even by seeking to change the relationship directly. In this way, redemptive politics involves a more thorough and convincing collapse of means and ends and, consequently, a more effective approach to resisting domination. As we will see below, redemptive politics involves a striving for justice in embodied reciprocity and reflexivity rather than abstract and universalizable impartiality; it is a relational process of legitimation in which the self, the other, and the world are redeemed in and through the transformation of the relations between the self, the other, and the world. This deep-seated reflexivity ensures that the disruptive domination in the modulations of protocolic control are resisted. The self-referential nature of redemptive politics simply does not allow for the excessive violence of the dualistic logic at work within protocolic control.

What might a transformation of the self-other relationship look like in patterns of deep disagreement and dependence? Unfortunately, examples of the self-sacrifice of redemptive politics do not abound within Canadian politics. And, indeed, we can point to examples of the opposite of what this kind of sacrifice might look like. For example, in *Delgamuukw v. British Columbia* the Supreme Court of Canada decided that Aboriginal rights could be infringed if the infringement is (a) "in furtherance of a legislative objective that is compelling and substantial" and (b) "consistent with the special fiduciary relationship between the Crown and aboriginal peoples."[68] And, as Chief Justice Lamer writes, a

---

67 Ibid., 31.

68 *Delgamuukw v. British Columbia*, [1997] 3 SCR 1010, paras. 161–2. Also see Tully, "Aboriginal Peoples," 413.

compelling and substantial legislative objective can include nearly any economic activity. For example "the development of agriculture, forestry, mining, and hydroelectric power, the general economic development of the interior of British Columbia, protection of the environment or endangered species, the building of infrastructure and the settlement of foreign populations to support those aims, are the kinds of objectives that are consistent with this purpose and, in principle, can justify the infringement of aboriginal title."[69] The Supreme Court of Canada, therefore, decides that the collective rights of indigenous peoples, although formally recognized, will be overridden if an upholding of these rights might hamper the power of the Canadian state – i.e. the rights of indigenous peoples will only be recognized in practical terms "insofar as this recognition does not throw into question the background legal, political and economic framework of the colonial relationship itself."[70] The self-sacrifice of redemptive politics, therefore, could be understood as a reversal of the logic displayed by the Supreme Court of Canada in *Delgamuukw*.

Instead of justifying infringements upon the rights of indigenous peoples if settlers have any interests in the economic development of the land, the logic of self-sacrifice will mean a denial of settler interests if these interests might cause harm to indigenous peoples. And, of course, there is sacrifice in terms of limits placed upon the economic development of the settlers and the restraint upon the Canadian state's legal, political, and economic power use.

CONCLUSION

We began this chapter with questions concerning how we might begin theorizing in a positive way regarding democratic norms given our central concern regarding acceleration fuelled by the standardizations of dualistic logic. Specifically, we sought to understand the roles reason and freedom play in the process of legitimizing violence. Freedom was seen as an engagement in the process of political resistance – the creation of political space and time through the development of resilient networks that resist standardization. Reason, therefore, is a process of making connections beyond oneself (i.e. transcendence) which could be either stabilizing or destabilizing and, therefore, could contribute to freedom or domination. The democratic question, therefore, is an assessment of

---

69 *Delgamuukw v. British Columbia*, [1997] 3 SCR. 1010, para. 165.
70 Coulthard, "Subjects of Empire," 452.

whether or not the processes at work in the patternings of oneself and one's environment are leading to freedom or domination. If the judgment tends toward viewing the patternings as developing greater freedom, then the violence of the patterning changes is being legitimized. That is, as we saw above, legitimacy is an ongoing recognition and positive normative judgment regarding one's participation in the power and violence at work within processes of patterning reconfiguration. The judgment of legitimization is democratic because it must be made within the dialectical movement of transcendence through immanence and, therefore, is both a dialogical and diachronic process.

This more thoroughly democratic approach to normativity, it is hoped, will give us a greater ability to build resilience and resistance into our systems of social and economic governance. Put another way, in response to the homogenizing process of standardization underlying protocolic control, this kind of network democracy is an attempt to not only provide support for traditionalists resisting a common citizenry, but support for intentional resistance through desynchronization and deceleration. The normative ideals of democracy, therefore, must be such that they support and promote resistance to the domination of the homogenizing impulse that comes through standardization; the normative ideals of democracy must foster asymmetry, particularity, and specificity rather than symmetry, commonality, and universality. Resistance to the modulations of protocolic control, therefore, will be found in the development of these normative ideals of democracy. In the next chapter we will discuss the challenges facing attempts to translate these democratic norms into patterns of life in the modern, liberal world and how we might begin to democratize our lives and our communities.

6

Conservative Democracy

A. JUSTICE AS RESTORATION
The most effective counter-action the normative eclipse within the dualistic logic of liberalism is the cultivation of an ethic of mutual support and restraint that invests society with stability and resilience.

B. TOWARDS RESILIENCE
A resilient society requires intermediate structures and civil enterprises to develop tradition and reciprocal responsibilities in familial, social, political, and economic life.

INTRODUCTION

T.S. Eliot's 1934 poem "The Rock," about the troubles of modernity, lamented the emptiness of so many of our actions in an accelerating world. The poem also contains an astute phrase that derides the foolishness of those who would seek to build an ideal political system. He describes them as constantly trying to "escape from the darkness outside and within by dreaming of systems so perfect that no one will need to be good."[1] Inspired by the dualistic logic of liberalism, the modern market state described in the opening chapter is perhaps the premier example of this same kind of idealist attempt to build a just society for all that transcends all. As the form of the state that is superseding the nation state of the twentieth century, the market state holds the promise of optimizing opportunities for its individual members to access global markets unhindered by parochial market restraints. Inspired and shaped by the dualistic logic of liberalism, the push to open globalized marketplaces is understood to be violent, but a violence that is legitimized by the opportunities it offers the members active within the marketplace. Indeed, it is only

---

1 T.S. Eliot, "The Rock," 1934.

here when individual citizen-consumers participating in the global market that justice is said to be found. As we have seen above, however, there is good reason to believe that the opposite is true. Due to the severity of the violence taking place, it is not at all clear that the violations of localized patternings (material, social, and spiritual) taking place in this push for a universally individualized citizen within a globally universalized marketplace are capable of being legitimized. The abstraction away from the lives of real, embodied people – people bounded by the localized struggles to find the good through family, tradition, and community – is a violent process of simultaneous assimilation and exclusion fuelled by the dualistic logic of liberalism.

The violence of liberalism is reiterated and reinforced when we retain and continue to promulgate, even if unwittingly, the core liberal ideals that undergird and inspire the institutions of the market state. When we participate in upholding the institutions of the market state, we foster the ideal of a global system in which we will no longer fear the darkness, the stranger, and the wilderness. This ideal, however, is built upon the normative eclipse at work within the dualistic logic of liberalism and is increasingly illegitimate. We know that the globalized market state is disintegrating civil society, decapitalizing the poor, and destroying ecosystems at a phenomenal speed. And it is becoming increasingly difficult to legitimize this violence because of not only the speed at which it is taking place, but also the fact that the ethics of mutual support and restraint upon which we depend for our ability to legitimize violence are being undermined as the in-between worlds of mutual support between families and communities, along with our interdependence with the natural world, are being destroyed. The stability and resilience of the family, tradition, and community are being supplanted by the rapid modulations of protocolic control.

The violence of the liberal age is fragmenting the patternings of our world and can best be resisted through the cultivation of an ethic of mutual support and restraint that invests society with stability and resilience. As discussed in previous chapters, the legitimization of violence is a process of coming to recognize and embrace the violence that leads to greater resilience. That is, legitimation is a dialectical process of self-other legitimation; it is an embodied process of relational development that takes place through the revealing of a contestation between ourselves and the world as the broader significance of things are articulated. We depend upon this democratic politicization and its making of res publica, the making of oneself public in relation to a thing, if we are to begin legitimizing the violence of high-speed global markets. Our ability to engage in democratic politicization, however, is undermined by the

modulations of protocolic control and the dualistic logic of liberalism
that fuels them.

Therefore, the legitimization of violence through democratic politicization must be worked out piecemeal in the rough and tumble of embodied and localized lives; it cannot be done in advance for all people
in all times and all places because normative judgment itself depends
upon the extension of an embodied trajectory that is dialogical and
diachronic. Democratic freedom itself depends upon an ethic of non-
domination enlivened and worked out within the complex interrelations of a healthy civil society and local economy. Whereas the dualistic
logic of liberalism debases democratic governance and the capacity for
politicization, the interconnections of the institutions of civil society
and a civil economy build resistance to standardization. Or, in other
words, the most effective counter-action to the normative eclipse within
the dualistic logic of liberalism is to cultivate an ethic of mutual support
and restraint that builds upon and reinforces stability and resilience
within society. A resilient society requires intermediate structures and
civil enterprises to instil tradition and reciprocal responsibilities in social, political, and economic life.

A. JUSTICE AS RESTORATION

The liberal state and the liberal market – insofar as they are governed by
a shared dualistic logic – destroy res ecologia and prevent the politicization process. As such, they foster the advancement of protocolic control
and its rapid modulations by undermining the capacity for living in a way
that is governed by moral judgment and mutual support within communities. We have seen this destruction of community take place with unpre-
cedented speed in recent years. As Blond writes, "under the auspices of
both the state and the market, a vast body of disenfranchised and disengaged citizens has been constituted. They have been stripped of their
culture by the left and their capital by the right, and in such nakedness
they enter the trading floor of life with only their labour to sell."[2] Insofar
as our ability to live a moral life is undermined, we lose our capacity for
engaging in politics. As we saw above in our discussion of the self as res
ecologia, politicization is best understood as a revealing (an apocalypse)
of a contestation between ourselves and the world that takes place
through a movement from the local to the global and back again. It is, in
this sense, an articulation of the broader significance of things – the

2 Blond, *Red Tory*, 281. Also see Hacker and Pierson, *Winner-Take-All Politics*.

process of making things res publica. I say "contestation" between ourselves and the world because in the process of making a public thing one
makes *oneself* public as a thing-in-relation-to-a-thing. That is, in order to
make a thing public, we cannot simply recognize this thing in some internal sense, but must demonstrate in a communicative manner the significance this thing has for ourselves as res ecologia. And this entails a
contestation between oneself and the world because the significance one
gives this thing is necessarily relative to the *in*significance that others
communicate regarding this same kind of thing. Consequently, a destabilization and delocalization of the self diminishes the self's ability to
engage in the politicization process because, to the degree that it is unable to locate itself, the self will be unable to articulate its relation to a
thing and, indeed, will be unable to articulate the significance of the relation itself.

It should be clear at this point in the discussion that the liberal state
and the liberal market (and, especially, the collusion between the two)
delocalize the self by means of their dualistic logic of simultaneous individuation and totalization. The self as res ecologia exists only in the in-
between world of localized relations. The absolute polarization of subject
and object operating within liberalism's market state creates an erasure
of the self as a relational being-in-the-world that is always ready to politicize. That is, the self is either radically subjectified as an isolated individual existing in opposition to the world or radically objectified as a
universalized self existing in opposition to the parochialism of specificity.
The moral and political subject exists only in the in-between world of
interconnected and incarnate relations that are neither absolute nor final in their contestations.

Therefore the only way to effectively counter the normative eclipse
within the dualistic logic of liberalism is to cultivate an ethic of mutual
support and restraint that invests society with stability and resilience. As
Blond writes in *Red Tory*, mere procedural reforms are not enough. An
ethic of mutual support that can inspire and guide us in our search for
just and democratic governance is needed. He writes, "there is no point
in changing the institutions or their rules if the values we enthrone within them are the same values that have corroded us in the first place.
Projects for constitutional reform, no matter how worthy they might be,
do not get to the heart of the matter."[3] Or, as E.F. Schumacher writes,
the deepest problems of our age "cannot be solved by organization, administration, or the expenditure of money, even though the importance

3 Blond, *Red Tory*, 167–8.

of all these is not denied. We are suffering from a metaphysical disease, and the cure must therefore be metaphysical."[4] We need to recreate and restore a genuine ethos of mutual support and civil engagement – an ethic of non-domination – that will manifest in renewed and resilient social, political, and economic communities that are able to resist the totalizing impulse of protocolic control.

The ethic of non-domination I am speaking of here involves a notion of justice that is neither utilitarian nor deontological because it is not centred around the universalizing normative ideals of liberalism and, hence, not beholden to the totalizing impulse within liberalism's dualistic logic. At the same time, it is not entirely accurate to describe this ethic of non-domination as Aristotelian because it also resists a fixed hierarchicalism. In order to move beyond the current injustice of domination taking place within the modulations of protocolic control, we need a vision of justice that will more directly apply the democratic concern for non-domination to everyday political life. That is, we need "an account of the common good that is cultivated organically from within" in such a way as to instil restraint and stability in societies through the development of "intermediate structures and the politics of community and reciprocity."[5] We need a conception of justice as restoration. Only in this way can we begin to understand justice as a conservative vision of society that resists the protocolic modulations outlined above.

Justice is best conceived of as a process of restoration that takes place within network patternings in response to violence.[6] There is, therefore, a very close connection between political resistance, freedom, and justice. Whereas political resistance is the *development* of resilience within network patternings to resist standardization, justice may be understood as the *manifestation* of a network's resilience in response to violations of the network's structures and processes. There is, then, an even closer connection between freedom and justice such that whereas freedom is an engagement in the process of political resistance that involves a dialectical process from immanence to transcendence-through-immanence, justice is simply part of the third step (i.e. the "through-immanence" part) in the dialectical process. In other words, justice is more conservative than freedom in that it is simply a response to violence rather than a process that is driven forward by a drive to

4 Schumacher, *Small Is Beautiful*, 80.
5 Blond, *Red Tory*, 153, 171.
6 Structural justice, then, is a diffuse process of restoration in response to structural violence. Also, whether redistribution or some kind of retribution, justice is always reactive as a response to some problem or injustice.

transcendence. This understanding of justice is rooted in conceptions of interconnected or networked identities and therefore does not point to inherent rights (which are rooted in a concept of identity as either originating entirely from within or as existing in relation to a divine being), but instead serves as the inspiration for relational rights and duties within social and economic networks. This shift toward notions of interrelational selves and networked identities as well as a commitment to non-domination provides the foundation for new normative ideals of justice – reciprocity and resilience – that can only be found in the specificity of embodied, localized relations of mutual dependence.

It should be noted that I am not arguing that just relations are somehow captured in reciprocity – i.e. in reciprocal relations of dependence. Rather, I am arguing that reciprocity is one central element in just relations whereas impartiality – due to its underlying dualistic logic – is not. Admittedly, the dominant theory of justice in modern political philosophy, almost without exception, is centred upon the notion of impartiality.[7] The issue of impartiality has loomed large in modern legal theory. In fact, a great number of debates in jurisprudence revolve around questions of impartiality and various thinkers' underlying assumptions regarding partiality and impartiality. Further, not only have jurisprudential debates been coloured by the distinction between partiality and impartiality but the ethic of impartiality has become the dominant characteristic of what is understood to be good governance and a kind of "natural justice" in the administration of the modern welfare state. The centrality of impartiality in the modern conception of justice has been made manifest in an ethic of impartiality (along with accompanying degrees of functional differentiation) that has become a key characteristic of modern bureaucratic governance.[8]

Impartiality has been most prominent within liberal contractarian schools of thought. For example, Rawls uses the notion of a veil of ignorance to get at his contractarian concept of justice as fairness and, in so doing, seeks to develop a universalist justification for a conception of justice as impartiality. This project is, of course, following in the footsteps of Kant and his search for a pure, a priori moral philosophy. For example, as Kant writes in his *Groundwork of the Metaphysic of Morals*: "a pure moral philosophy, completely cleansed of everything that may be only empirical

---

7 Although one can certainly get specific regarding various kinds of impartiality or the distinction between "first order impartiality" and "second order impartiality," I am content with a very general definition at this stage. So by "impartiality" I simply mean a lack of regard for particular characteristics or one's particular relationship to an other when making normative judgments.

8 Weber, *Economy and Society*, 225.

and that belongs to anthropology ... that there must be such a philosophy is clear of itself from the common idea of duty and of moral laws. Everyone must grant that a law, if it is to hold morally, that is, as a ground of obligation, must carry with it absolute necessity ... [it must be] a priori simply in concepts of pure reason."[9] Kant argued for the categorical imperative but by the middle of the twentieth century it was considered too explicitly metaphysical. So Rawls developed what came to be seen as a non-metaphysical strategy for attempting to abstract away from any partialities one might possess and thereby freely come to universal agreement.[10] In other words, Rawls sought to define the reasonable or free person and he did this through an appeal to an ideal – albeit hypothetical – place from which to begin reasoning. The reasonable person is one who has no consideration for its own particular characteristics or being-in-the-world and simply considers all persons alike – i.e. just like itself. The reasonable person is said to be self-interested but is unable to distinguish between itself and another and is therefore able to be fair to all. Universal agreement is sought in the darkness of a universal epistemic blindness behind the imaginary veil of ignorance.

The search for universal agreement is central to the impartialists' theoretical projects. Brian Barry's soft constructivist position is no different. Like all impartialists, he seeks to justify social and political institutions such that all persons could approve of them.[11] The problem with this approach, to put it simply, comes not in the attempt to justify social and political institutions, but in the attempt to do so for all persons. For indeed this is simply impossible. The disagreements between persons run deep because our conceptions of good and evil are tied deep down into our ways of life and the lives of our ancestors. But revealing his assumption that disagreements actually do not run deep among persons, Barry argues that any theory of justice – if it is to be a theory of justice rather than a theory of, say, hurricanes – must be acceptable to all "reasonable" persons. This is an important move. Faced with the impossible task of justifying for all persons, the impartialist seeks to limit the number of persons to which one needs to justify a theory and, in order to accomplish this, excludes those who would disagree by making a distinction between "reasonable" and "unreasonable" persons. In this manner, the "problem of partiality" is moved from the question of justification (e.g. "the good") to the question of rationalization (e.g. "the right"). So, the distinction between the good and the evil is redescribed as a distinction

9 Kant, *Groundwork of the Metaphysics of Morals*, 3.
10 Barry, *Justice as Impartiality*, 9.
11 For example, see ibid., 6.

between the right and the wrong. The distinction between the right and the wrong is then spoken of as a distinction between the rational and the irrational.

By appealing to the distinction between rational and irrational, Barry seeks a neutral way of resolving conflicts regarding various goods. But, of course, in so doing, he is revealing his own notion of "the good." Like Rawls, Barry is a constructivist, but he believes that, in the ideal hypothetical situation, the actors must be conceived of as more than merely self-interested beings – they must be reasonable beings. Barry suggests that the motivation for behaving justly – acting impartially – "is not reducible to even a sophisticated and indirect pursuit of self-interest."[12] Rather, the motivation comes from a desire to be able to justify our actions to ourselves and to others without self-reference. As he writes, "the desire to be able to justify our actions to ourselves and others on a basis capable of eliciting free agreement is, as common experience attests, widely shared and deeply grounded."[13] This notion of reasonable as free agreement has moral content and, admits Barry, it *necessarily* has moral content.[14] Indeed, Barry admits openly that "the whole idea that we should seek the agreement of everybody rests upon a fundamental commitment to the equality of all human beings."[15] Or, again: "a theory of justice which makes it turn on the terms of reasonable agreement I call a theory of justice as impartiality. Principles of justice that satisfy its conditions are impartial because they capture a certain kind of equality: all those affected have to be able to feel that they have done as well as they could reasonably hope to."[16] There is an important subplot taking place here in terms of the moral content of his appeal to reasonable agreement. That is, he speaks of reasonable agreement because he suggests that reasonable agreement is available without being exclusive because if it is reasonably agreeable it is universally agreeable by definition.[17] It is understood to be universally agreeable because it is understood to be treating all people the same in some manner. Barry admits, however, that this commitment to egalitarianism as a grounding for the appeal to universal reason is a circular argument. But – he suggests – it is not a vicious one. I tend to agree. It is not illogical, it is simply posited as a good. But as I have been arguing, we have good reason to question the "goodness" of this "good."

---

12 Barry, *Theories of Justice*, 7.
13 Ibid., 284.
14 For example, see ibid., 272.
15 Barry, *Justice as Impartiality*, 8.
16 Ibid., 7.
17 Ibid.

In keeping with the game of redefining "good" as "right," Barry seeks to redefine "reason" as "free" in order to – it seems – appeal to some moral intuitions that uncoerced agreement is an ideal to which we should strive. Therefore, he writes, "'reason' means reasoned argument, from premises that are in principle open to everyone to accept." Namely, "premises which reasonable people, seeking to reach free, uncoerced agreement with others, would accept."[18] So, now we see that the question has moved once again. No longer is it a question of reasonable and unreasonable (because "reason" is simply that which "reasonable people" agree upon), but free and unfree. Free people agree, or at least agree in theory. So, he concludes, the "principles of justice are inconsistent with claims to special privilege based on grounds that cannot be made freely acceptable to others."[19] However, this is, of course, simply a continuation of his game of redefinition. More specifically, it is a game of redefining the rules of the game and this redefinition takes place based upon the assumption that (a) reason is universal and (b) universally accessible. That is, disagreements between very different people are actually not as deep and insurmountable as they may appear and the job of the enlightened political theorist is to peal away the superficial differences to reveal the underlying commonality and thereby continue the Enlightenment project. His willingness to superficialize the deep difference and disagreement between peoples can be seen even in his confidence that he can define the central problem in theories of justice. For example, he writes, "the central issue in any theory of justice is the defensibility of unequal relations between people."[20] In other words, equality does not need to be justified, only departures from equality.

Before moving on to consider what I mean by embodied reciprocity and reflexivity in justice, it will be useful to take a step back and consider some the core theoretical commitments that Rawls (justice as reciprocity) and Barry (justice as impartiality) share. Both Rawls and Barry are moral constructivists and as such believe that moral principles arise in and through the social interactions of moral agents.[21] As Allan Gibbard explains, under this kind of constructivism the theorist "specifies an ideal, hypothetical situation in which people choose the principles that shall govern them. He then proclaims that whatever principles would be chosen in that situation are, by virtue of this very fact, valid principles of

18 Ibid.
19 Ibid., 7–8.
20 Barry, *Theories of Justice*, 3.
21 Liberal interactionalism means not that the universe is without order and meaning, but that it is entirely dependent upon the interactions of subjects constructs meaning for themselves. See Sandel, *Liberalism and the Limits of Justice*, 176. This kind of metaphysical constructivism was clearly expressed in Ackerman, *Social Justice in the Liberal State*, 368.

justice."[22] However, quite naturally, both the nature of the agents and the nature of the structure within which the agents may act are defined according to the underlying metaphysical and epistemic presuppositions regarding the nature of persons and their environment.

For Rawls and his liberal theory of justice as reciprocity, persons are discrete individuals engaged in moral relations that look much like contracts in which the contracting parties are very aware of their own desires and needs. That is, even before they are considered to be in the "original position" or behind the "veil of ignorance," the persons that are considering Rawls' approach to justice are understood by Rawls to be self-interested individuals seeking their own notion of "the good." As Barry explains, though, "the addition of the veil of ignorance means that this pursuit of advantage fails to take off, so that we finish up with a prudential calculation by one person under conditions of radical uncertainty."[23] In this sense, the idea of justice (or fairness as "the good") as a worthy goal is assumed to exist before considering the hypothetical situation and assumed to persist through the entire process. Or, as Rawls writes, a well-ordered society is one in which "everyone accepts and knows that the others accept the same principles of justice" and one whose "members have a strong and normally effective desire to act as the principles of justice require."[24] Further, there is an underlying conception of persons as independent actors that make calculations regarding their actions as if they were engaged in discreet interactions, completely disconnected but for the precise moment of the particular moral transaction. In this model, causation takes place in a linear procession from cause to effect as individual actors (the parts) interact to make up a just society (the whole). Admittedly, this general orientation toward reciprocity is attractive because reciprocity (in a general sense) is quite in keeping with our intuitions concerning justice and just action. As Allan Gibbard notes, "many of our chief moral sentiments are reciprocal overtly: a sense of fair dealing, feelings of gratitude, urges to retaliate."[25] However, a problem arises when one considers the blind spots one might have regarding the breadth of one's morally relevant community. Consequently, if one did not see how one could possibly have an interaction with an other that was beneficial for oneself, there was no reason to engage in a moral transaction. In this manner, then, those beings that are seen as having nothing to contribute are excluded from society.

---

22 Gibbard, "Constructing Justice," 265.
23 Barry, *Justice as Impartiality*, 60.
24 Rawls, *A Theory of Justice*, 454.
25 Gibbard, *Wise Choices, Apt Feelings*, 261.

Barry and his theory of justice as impartiality admits the fundamental ignorance of those making the normative judgments such that, when they are seeking the principles of justice, they are not making self-interested calculations regarding their needs and wants. Instead, he suggests that we need to simply abstract away to a general category of actors in order to include them all (and include them all equally). This notion of justice relies upon the idea that (a) persons are the same in some fundamental, yet morally relevant, manner such that we can abstract away from their real lives to some non-political, powerless realm of normative interaction, (b) the hypothetical interactions of abstract moral agents are relevant to our considerations of our social and political governance, and (c) that this abstractionism does not foster the advancement of structural domination like protocolic modulations. As we have seen above, there are some significant problems with the process of abstracting away into realms of thought that are understood to be devoid of power relations. Additionally, we simply cannot understand the relations of moral agents apart from a consideration of persons as embodied and historical beings that interact within their environment.

Therefore, my conception of justice as restoration should be distinguished not only from Barry's notion of justice as impartiality, but also from Rawls' interpretation of justice as reciprocity. Rawls understands justice as reciprocity to be a hybrid theory that combines a pursuit of mutual advantage with a sense of fairness.[26] A network approach to justice is developed with attention paid to the interconnected nature of the self and its environment. What this means, then, is that justice as reciprocity must be highly reflexive in a way that Rawls is not. Or, in other words, justice involves the way one's action will necessarily transform *oneself* as a result of transforming one's relations with the other. Reciprocity, then, means making a normative judgment to evaluate the appropriateness of an action or inaction with the purpose of improving the relation between oneself and the other. It is the relation itself rather than the self or the other as discreet beings that has priority within this conception of justice. The principle of reciprocity is one of the keys to a network conception of justice because – when it is properly conceived – it does not place an emphasis upon any known benefits (as if they were epistemically transparent), but upon the underlying relations between the self and other. Further, an emphasis upon reciprocity (a) brings out the reality that the self is created and sustained in relation to the other and (b) that normative judgments must be made with consideration to the

26 See Barry, *Justice as Impartiality*, 46.

relation between the self and the other rather than the self or the other as if they were discreet and independent moral beings.

It should be very clear by now that the notion of justice as impartiality as both Rawls and Barry have outlined it is undergirded by a corrosive individualism and universalism that disallows the reciprocity of mutual dependence. This individualism, despite its appeal to our intuitions concerning the relationality of justice, nevertheless produces relations of justice that are best conceived of as a process of radical subjectivization. This process, rather than resisting protocolic modulations through an ethic of non-domination, is nihilistic and destructive of the embodied interdependencies needed for normative judgment. The progression of this process is perhaps best characterized by Max Stirner's dialectic of liberalism. In basic terms, his dialectic proceeds as follows:

(a) "Political Liberalism" – the doctrine of equal rights reduces persons to a general, universal political identity ... citizen. In this stage, the state dominates through direct, unmediated relations with the individual.
(b) "Social Liberalism" – equality is extended to the realm of social and economic life. In this stage, the individual is alienated by, and subject to, the abstract generality of society.
(c) "Humane Liberalism" – individual differences are overcome as the drive for the essence of humanity proceeds. In this stage, the individual ego is abolished and the particular is dominated by the general.[27]

As Deleuze suggests, Stirner (like Nietzsche) thereby represents "the dialectician who reveals nihilism as the truth of the dialectic."[28] The impartiality of equality places persons in a direct citizen-state relation that develops a radical subjectification of domination. All persons that fall into the category of citizen find themselves in an unmediated relationship with the state or its market – i.e. bare subjects in relation to a pervasive state-object and naked individual actors in a competitive market. This kind of individualism, of course, can tolerate no genuine reciprocity that represents the resilience of mutual dependence and will inevitably fall into some kind of impartiality between individualized subjects.

Genuine reciprocal relations (i.e. those that are restorative) are those connections between persons and their environments – those societies

27 Newman, *Power and Politics in Poststructuralist Thought*, 16–21. Also see Stirner, *The Ego and Its Own*, 93–125.
28 Deleuze, *Nietzsche and Philosophy*, 161, emphasis removed.

– that are fostered and governed by an ethic of non-domination. They are relations that transcend the modern notion of society as a contract between self-interested individuals seeking to escape the state of nature. Instead of a universal conception of the good that finalizes an ideal set of relations, an ethic of non-domination involves a diachronic perspective in which dialogical relations with the other are engaged in with a view to the future. That is, organizing-oriented interaction with the other relies upon a relation built upon what the other may become. Indeed, identities change through time and it must be recognized that the other may become less or more antagonistic in the future. There is, therefore, never finality to agreement and disagreement and it is inappropriate to establish structures and processes that fail to reflect this indeterminacy. Further, it is essential that the ethic of interaction is coloured by a humility rooted in the recognition that there is no final arbiter in the present and that all disagreements will be judged by future generations. So, it is important to resist the domination of uniform protocol even if a reassertion of difference is not coming from an ideal alternative. Indeed, this emphasis upon indeterminacy is important in the deproblematization of difference.[29]

As we saw above in the discussion regarding the legitimization of violence, non-domination can mean increased engagement or disengagement with the other through a celebration of diversity in the restraint that exists within the localized specificity of embodied living. That is, it is important to note that part of non-domination, and hence justice as restoration, means a legitimization of violence through an undermining of violence by refusing to retaliate in retributive actions and instead forgive those who are domineering. Admittedly and understandably, talk of forgiveness is radically out of sync with current conceptions of justice. For, indeed, forgiveness is unjust if one is operating within the terms of abstract or non-relational ideals of justice rooted in universalized principles. Forgiveness is self-sacrifice or suffering in the forsaking of retribution. In a sense, the injustice of domination that destroys patterning processes needs to be countered with the creative and restorative "injustice" of forgiveness, rather than the further destructive power of revenge.[30] To the degree that forgiveness is violent in its disruption of existing relations, it is a fully legitimized violence that cannot lead to domination; it is deeply restorative.

29 For an example of this approach to resistance, see Žižek, "Holding the Place."
30 See Volf, *Exclusion and Embrace*, 120–5.

B. TOWARDS RESILIENCE

If we understand justice as restoration and we are concerned about the illegitimate violence of protocolic modulations fostered by the liberal market state, we are well placed to begin searching for practical means of developing resilient relations. It is the resilience of relational patternings that allows them to be restored in the face of violations and avoid the homogenizing impulse within protocolic domination. The problem is: if our political norms and structures of governance have been dominated by the dualistic logic of liberalism for the past approximately three hundred years, how can we move forward into practical policy in a way that does not replicate the problems from which we seek to escape?

Although we cannot expect to leave liberalism behind anytime soon, there are steps that can be taken to begin moving into a post-liberal political arrangement. The first, and most important step, we have already identified – the need for us to be committed to developing an ethic of non-domination that undermines the violent dualism of liberalism. Any structural or procedural changes must be guided by a sense of the good and the need for mutually supportive interdependencies. There can be no deep or lasting change without virtuous citizens, families, and associations guided by a search for the communal good. The second step, I would like to suggest, is the need to move beyond the hierarchies of the modern welfare state. Because it is the modern state structure that develops legal systems and maintains the infrastructure of the market, we must set out to not only fracture state monopolies, but also begin to develop the means of infusing legal systems with reflexivity and restraint such that markets are no longer stripped of their governing norms. In other words: we need to democratize the social, political, and economic systems that govern our everyday lives in order to move away from the fragility of a direct individual-to-state relation or the vulnerability of isolated individual actors within a globalized, competitive market. "Instead of the vertical sanction of the state, which citizens can only experience as an act of external coercion," writes Blond, "a good politics requires the horizontal sanction of our peers, friends and colleagues. Crucial to a revival of virtue is the restoration of a genuine liberty, which must be organically embedded in particular social formations with particular privileges and duties."[31] We need a stable and resilient civil society and civil economy governed by norms outside the state-market system.

31 Blond, *Red Tory*, 171–2.

In what follows, therefore, we will consider (a) some means of moving beyond the state's monopoly on violence in the rule of law and, then, (b) some means of remoralizing the market. The problem of the monopolizing hierarchies of the modern welfare state – or, the problem of bureaucratic domination – tends, among liberal theorists, to focus on the sluggardly nature of the modern welfare state's hierarchical administrative institutions. Most notably, new governance theorists complain that the structures and processes of the state institutions are outdated and unable to meaningfully respond to the complex and ever-changing world in the twenty-first century.[32] Indeed, new governance theory brings some important concerns and critiques of the modern state to the forefront.

There seems to be no doubt that the hierarchical model or abstract regularity of the modern welfare state's bureaucracies is clearly outdated and out of touch with the lives of many of the citizens in Canada. The technological revolution begun in the late twentieth century is changing everything. Increased global competition, capital hyper-mobility, and dramatic advancements in information sharing have created a "radical indeterminacy" in social and economic interactions that are not matched by a flexible and adaptable structure of governance.[33] As the modern life accelerates – e.g. as citizens become more mobile and instantly connected through communications technologies – it is becoming increasingly obvious that government legislation, regulation, law enforcement, adjudication, and service delivery must be more integrated and purposively interdependent if it is to be effective. Without attention to diversity and an ability to dynamically engage with the citizenry, a bureaucratic system becomes domineering in its top-down, expert-based inflexibility. But the question is: should the sluggardliness that new governance theorists have identified be the primary concern when we are faced with the spectre of domination through accelerating protocolic modulations? Is there not a very real danger that procedural reforms seeking greater flexibility and nimbleness in government will actually facilitate the dualistic logic of liberalism and thereby fuel the rapid modulations of protocol that are creating so much violence?

If we accept the political ontology of res ecologia and the dangers of acceleration fuelled by liberalism's dualistic logic, the concern regarding the cumbersome nature of hierarchical bureaucracies and their

32 See Dorf and Sabel, "A Constitution of Democratic Experimentalism." Also see Weber, *The Protestant Ethic and the Spirit of Capitalism*, and Weber, *Economy and Society*.

33 See Gerstenberg and Sabel, "Directly-Deliberative Polyarchy," 292. Also see Lobel, "The Renew Deal," 358.

inability to represent individual citizens from the bottom up should not be primary. Rather, our primary concern should be the push toward standardized uniformity that takes place within governance insofar as it represents a manifestation of protocolic control. We should be concerned about standardizing impulses that universalize within the state as well as standardizing impulses that are at work within the marketplace. And, more specifically, we should be concerned about the accelerating modulations that are fuelled by the standardization resonating between these two systems.

There should be little doubt that the hierarchical administrative model of the modern bureaucracy standardizes and, perhaps even more importantly, facilitates standardizations in and through other spheres of life. Before the rise of the modern welfare state, Max Weber already aptly described the inherent push for standardization within the structures and processes of modern bureaucratic institutions in his *Economy and Society*: "bureaucracy inevitably accompanies modern mass democracy in contrast to the democratic self-government of small homogeneous units. This results from the characteristic principle of bureaucracy: the abstract regularity of the execution of authority, which is a result of the demand for 'equality before the law' in the personal and functional sense – hence, of the horror of 'privilege' and the principled rejection of doing business 'from case to case.'"[34] Weber's notion of "the abstract regularity of the execution of authority" rooted in a quest for impartiality lays bare the nature of bureaucratic domination. The indeterminacy of real-world political communication processes are distorted in the process of abstracting into standardized processes within the hierarchical and command / control administrative model. In other words, bureaucratization is an objectification of persons and their behaviours in an attempt to maximize linear models of efficiency. He further describes this objectification process as follows: "Bureaucratization offers above all the optimum possibility for carrying through the principle of specializing administrative functions according to purely objective considerations. Individual performances are allocated to functionaries who have specialized training and who by constant practice increase their expertise. 'Objective' discharge of business primarily means a discharge of business according to *calculable rules* and 'without regard for persons.'"[35] There is a connection, therefore, between bureaucratization and the egalitarianism of the welfare state that Weber notes. "Bureaucratic organization has usually

34 Weber, *Economy and Society*, 983.
35 Ibid., 975.

come into power on the basis of a leveling of economic and social differences."[36] Again, we can see the problematization of difference fostering a monopolizing state structure that creates a worldview that can only conceive of the complex and multilateral organizations in the associations of civil society as being irrational and illegitimate.

In contrast to the abstract standardizations of bureaucratic organizational processes, a new institutional design theory – a theory that outlines structures of governance that are more dynamic and better suited to handle complex dissonance – is needed. New governance theorists or "democratic experimentalists" suggest that the traditional model of public sector structures and practices has already begun to shift into a new model that includes more participatory and collaborative practices. The state-society relationship is being redefined as multiple stakeholders are increasingly encouraged to participate in the governance project.[37] In this shift to more dynamic systems of governance, experimentalists rightly argue that power needs to be moved out and down from the centre / top and invested in the civil associations of local communities.[38]

This decentralizing impetus, however, is contrasted by centralized bodies that are understood to coordinate, facilitate, guide, and monitor performance for the policy experimentation taking place at the local level – say, to prevent local organizations from simply acting in their own, limited self-interest rather than the public good. But the administrative centre should focus upon being a provider of infrastructure, a definer of broad projects and societal goals, and a locus of information for performance evaluations. It is suggested that this process of orchestration by the central body ensures problems do not become isolated and opportunities for improvement lost. The decentralization is accomplished through an interpenetration of policy boundaries, new public / private partnerships, negotiated rulemaking, performance-based rules, decentralized problem solving, disclosure regimes, and coordinated information collection.[39]

36 Ibid., 983.
37 Lobel, "The Renew Deal," 344–5.
38 For example, see ibid. and Sabel, "A Quiet Revolution of Democratic Governance," 134.
39 Democratic experimentalists have pointed to a number of state-society relationships that are being redefined as multiple stakeholders are encouraged to participate in the governance project and have suggested that a more collective and dynamic approach is being used (and should be used) to deal with complex and diverse problems of governance. For example, see Sabel and Dorf, "Drug Treatment Courts and Emergent Experimentalist Government"; Stephens, "Lessons From the Front Lines in Canada's Restorative

There is a very real danger, however, that the information flows and methods of real-time action coordination within democratic experimentalism will be standardized such that the deep diversity of peoples and nations are eroded in and through their interactions with the state's administrative structures and processes and they are made susceptible to the destructive violence of radical change. In other words, there is a danger that the decentralization of formal governance structures, although ostensibly being less prone to standardizations that fuel acceleration, will actually bring with them a more insidious standardization in protocolic modulations that move much faster than any hierarchical administrative model of state governance. Therefore, we should view the democratic experimentalism of new governance theorists with a certain degree of skepticism. If we are to move outside the dualistic logic of liberalism, this move toward more dynamic systems of governance must actually build patterns of resistance to standardization and resilience to rapid change into structures of governance. And in order to begin doing this the state must not only be increasingly responsive to the lived diversity of citizens in its own administrative structures, but also be increasingly oriented towards empowering resistance to standardization and rapid change in familial, religious, and localized socio-economic governing structures. Put in general terms, resistance to protocolic control, therefore, will be found in the development of particularity and asymmetry not in more nimble forms of governing institutions. Admittedly, the resistance of particularity and asymmetry does not throw up a wholesale blockade against the open communication patterns of standardized information flows but, instead, helps build in a kind of circuit breaker or dampener that will simply retard the homogenizing impulse. This resistance may take the form of a broad level approach (e.g. the decolonization process from the 1960s onward) or a narrow approach (e.g. the reinforcement of local traditions and patterns of communication). Either way, this kind of piecemeal resistance in the face of an immovable flood allows for movement towards open-ended and constantly changing (i.e. indeterminate) administrative structures and processes, but can only allow small degrees of change in localized areas if it is to be resilient against the violence of protocolic modulations.

If we are successful in this approach, we will be able to focus not merely on the organizational infrastructure of governing institutions, but also on the broader processes of governance and become more attuned to

---

Justice Experiment"; Braithwaite, *Restorative Justice and Responsive Regulation*; Liebman and Sabel, "A Public Laboratory Dewey Barely Imagined"; and Sabel and Zeitlin, "Learning from Difference."

the violence of universalization. In moving beyond the state infrastructure, we need to also ensure we do our best to avoid the enclosure and standardization of diverse peoples, socio-political movements, and economic systems – i.e. avoid the destruction of society itself.[40] As Magnusson notes, the local politics of municipal institutions are designed "to provide an enclosure for popular politics, and so to render that politics safe for the state, the market, and the other forms of government to which we are subject. The state in turn encompasses these enclosures and formally centres politics upon itself."[41] This process of state enclosure, then, is accompanied by a process of standardization and an important part of this standardization process involves the development of a universal market able to facilitate the penetration of protocolic control into all areas of life. As we will see in the discussion below, it is the standardizations of the market state that operate so as to destroy the very means of resisting protocolic domination – that is, society and its market rooted in the specificity of locality.

One area where there is a potential for building resistance to state-centred and state-facilitated standardization is in our understanding and practice of citizenship. So, let us consider citizenship under the governing institutions of the modern state and trace the basic process of enclosure and standardization taking place through governance in history. Through these two primary mechanisms of enclosure and standardization, the institutional structure of the state posits, as Magnusson and Walker note, "a false opposition between identity and community within, difference and anarchy without."[42] As Tully suggests, modern citizenship has been developed in terms of the constitutional rule of law (nomos) and representational government (demos).[43] The modern citizen, in this sense, is constituted through a corralling into a space demarcated by the development of nomos and demos and, in this process of corralling, is standardized as a single unit operating in relation to the singular whole of the nomos / demos.[44] The institutional structure of the state serves to dominate political life such that the self qua citizen lives, moves, and has its being in relation to the state.

However, citizenship is best understood not as something given by an institution from above, but as a lived activity in the process of developing and engaging with community that transcends the self. Again, "citizenship

---

40 See Blond, "Rise of the Red Tories."
41 Magnusson, *The Search for Political Space*, 10.
42 Magnusson and Walker, "De-centring the State," 60.
43 Tully, *Imperialism and Civic Freedom*, 249–50.
44 Magnusson and Walker, "De-centring the State," 37.

is not a status given by the institutions of the modern constitutional state and international law," suggests Tully, "but negotiated practices in which one becomes a citizen through participation."[45] Further, he writes that "agents (individual or collective) *become* civic citizens only through actual participation in civic activities. It is only through apprenticing in citizenship practices that one comes to acquire the characteristics of a citizen: linguistic and non-linguistic abilities, modes of conduct and interaction in relationships with others, forms of awareness of self and other, use of equipment, the abilities of questioning and negotiating any of these features and of carrying on in new and creative ways."[46] Of course, though, this participation need not be participation in reiterating the nomos or reconstituting the demos in direct relation to the state or the universal market. Additionally, and importantly, participation in a universal marketplace is a key mode of being and becoming a modern citizen. As Magnusson writes, "the market is at least as important a feature of contemporary political arrangements as the state. It is a grave error to attribute politics to the state and economics to the market and to attempt to analyse the latter as a natural rather than as a political phenomenon."[47] Avoiding the excessive violence of standardization, therefore, means reimagining citizenship by moving away from a state-centric, market-based conception of citizenship and toward an understanding of citizenship as a mode of being in the world that demonstrates democratic politicization – i.e. a certain kind of engagement in the patterns and processes of one's environment such that freedom is achieved.

Further, we need to avoid a notion of citizenship that falls into the trap of counter-hegemonization that takes place when one attempts to create a monolithic counter-bloc to the state-centrism by uniting and standardizing diverse social movements in opposition. For example, as Magnusson and Walker write concerning the leftist vision of Laclau and Mouffe, "they may not want a working class party, but they do want a counter-hegemonic force to contend with capitalist hegemony. Recognizing the unity of capital and the diversity of the social movements that respond to it, they want somehow to reduce that diversity to a unity – to hegemonize it – and so create a unified force capable of overcoming capital itself."[48] However, as Magnusson and Walker continue to argue, the question is not so much whether a movement is working within or without the state's institutional apparatus, but the degree to which a movement is able to undermine the

45 Tully, *Imperialism and Civic Freedom*, 248.
46 Ibid., 271.
47 Magnusson, *The Search for Political Space*, 9.
48 Magnusson and Walker, "De-centring the State," 46.

governing processes underlying the hegemonic processes themselves. They write, "the crucial question is not where [a social movement] acts in the political space defined by states, but whether it can create for itself new political spaces that transect and disrupt the space established by bourgeois politics."[49] Or course, though, our concern is not specifically with bourgeois politics (whatever that might mean) but with the homogenizing impulse that leads to rapid protocolic modulations. We must seek, therefore, to develop social movements that disrupt the political space of the state insofar as it is facilitating the advancement of standardization through protocolic control. And, importantly, we must seek to develop diverse familial, religious, and socio-economic movements that can provide some resistance to the standardization of protocolic control that inevitably arise in and through both the state institutional structures and through processes of counter-hegemonization.

In addition to a reconceptualization of citizenship, if we are to begin moving outside the dualistic logic of the modern welfare state, we need to undermine the monopoly the state has over education and violence. Under the monopoly of the market state, the purpose of education is inevitably the well-being of the state and, more precisely, the well-being of the state via the universal market that it nurtures.[50] Mass education under the supervision of the state historically developed for two key reasons – (a) to produce enlightened, problem-solving liberals who were loyal to the modern state structure, and (b) to train a workforce that could continue working effectively despite their vulnerability as labourers divorced from their capital.[51] As Blond notes, the method of liberalism's mass education, therefore, centres upon "inscribing the blank slates of childish minds with the procedures of an information economy and a late modern technology."[52] It should also be no surprise, given our discussion of the dualistic logic of liberalism above, that the mass education of the state typically oscillates between transmitting pure facts and creating space for pure self-expression. Without a lived tradition fostered within localized communities, either the fact-giving teacher or the expressive student are absolutized. Within the particularity of these localized traditions, however, neither the teacher's nor the student's place within the education process can be absolutized; both are kept in play

49 Ibid., 67.

50 See Illich, *Deschooling Society.*

51 Lasch, *The Culture of Narcissism,* 130. For a history of mass education in Canada, see Axelrod, *The Promise of Schooling.*

52 Blond, *Red Tory,* 175. Also see Grant, "The Minds of Men in the Atomic Age," 55–6.

and dualism is resisted.[53] If dualistic logic undermines the embodiment of tradition, the curriculum of mass education is centred upon the institutions of the state and instilling confusion, indifference, and dependency upon its bureaucratic institutions. As veteran teacher John Gatto writes, "the first lesson I teach is confusion. Everything I teach is out of context. I teach the un-relating of everything. I teach disconnections. Fortunately the children have no words to define the panic and anger they feel at constant violations of natural order and sequence fobbed off on them as quality in education ... I teach students to accept confusion as their destiny."[54]

The modern liberal state is also constituted and said to be legitimized through a consolidation of violence that has been conceived of as an assertion of sovereignty. As William Cavanaugh writes, "the conceptual leap which accompanies the advent of the state in the sixteenth century is the invention of sovereignty. The doctrine of sovereignty asserts the incontestable right of the central power to make and enforce laws for those people who fall within recognized territorial borders."[55] Therefore, as Philip Bobbitt writes, "the State exists to master violence: it came into being in order to establish a monopoly on domestic violence, which is a necessary condition for law, and to protect its jurisdiction from foreign violence, which is the basis for strategy. If the State is unable to deliver on these promises, it will be changed; if the reason it cannot deliver is rooted in its constitutional form, then that form will change."[56] Further, Bobbitt points out that war is not best conceived of as a pathology of the state, but as a means of constituting healthy states. For both law and war sustain the state and provide it with the means of protecting and preserving the integrity of its sovereignty over land and a collective population.[57] We might best think of war, then, as an exertion of sovereignty over foreign violence and law as a monopoly over domestic violence. Both are the state's means of legitimating a mastery over violence. Not only is war

53   Blond, *Red Tory*, 176–7. For more on the importance of tradition in education for work that is not divorced from capital and destructive of mutual association, see Schumacher, *Good Work*, 112ff.

54   Gatto, *Dumbing Us Down*, 2, 4, emphasis removed.

55   Cavanaugh, "Killing for the Telephone Company," 250–1. Also see Philpott, *Revolutions in Sovereignty*, 16–17, and Loughlin, *The Idea of Public Law*, 73ff.

56   Bobbitt, *The Shield of Achilles*, 216.

57   See ibid., 780. Simone Weil was also aware of the domestic implications of war and its role in constituting a nation state. For example, she writes, "the great error of almost every study on war – an error into which all the socialists, especially, have fallen – is to consider war as an episode in foreign policy, when above all it constitutes a fact of domestic policy, and the most atrocious one of all." *Formative Writings*, 242.

conceived of as law by other means, therefore, but law may rightly be understood as war by other means.

The era of the nation-state was characterized by total war but the era of the market-state may be characterized by total law.[58] By definition monopolized violence, however, is domineering in its excess. For, indeed, not only does monopolized violence displace and degrade other legitimate violences, but the only way to restrain and limit (or legitimize) violence is to have multiple power-pushes acting and counteracting each other. Monopolized violence simply cannot be legitimized. The decentring of the state, therefore, requires a diversity of power centres that can govern our lives in different in ways that are in keeping with the specific locality of our being-in-the-world – i.e. a multiplicity of violences in our lives.[59] A rethinking of how governance ought to work, therefore, means not only a move to decentre the state, but an active development of alternate modes of life in areas of national security, law enforcement, correctional services, etc. in order to resist standardization. As Simone Weil wrote in 1933, "no matter what name it bears – fascism, democracy, or dictatorship of the proletariat – the principal enemy remains the administrative, police, and military apparatus; not the apparatus across the border from us, which is the enemy only to the degree that it is the enemy of our brothers, but the one that calls itself our defender and makes us its slaves."[60]

But before going into more detail regarding the means of moving beyond the state, let us consider further the ways in which the market state destroys society. I understand society as that set of patterned groupings and interactions that make up our daily lives and provide the environment within which substantive moral goals might be pursued dialogically and diachronically. By definition, as Gene Sharp notes, society is constituted by interconnected institutions that are operating independent of the state. As he writes: "The institutions of civil society are generally composed of organized groups that are neither vertically controlled by, nor integrated into, that part of political society regulated by the State. Examples of civil society groups include sports clubs, gardening associations, certain labor unions and business associations, religious institutions, organized social movements, and all classes of nongovernmental organizations. They can exist at the local, regional, or national level."[61]

---

58 For the connection between the nation-state and total war, see Bobbitt, *The Shield of Achilles*, 216–17.

59 Cf. Karkkainen, "Collaborative Ecosystem Governance," 242.

60 Weil, *Formative Writings*, 248.

61 Sharp, *Waging Nonviolent Struggle*, 477–8.

These organizations or patterns of interactions are governed by our virtues – i.e. our understanding and practice of the good life rather than a
monopolized threat of violence. The various interactions are also almost
always complex and interconnected due to their specificity and locality.
So, for example, labour associations are tied into social and recreational
associations, economic associations connected to familial or tribal, etc.
The messiness of this multiplicity of power relations frightens us because
the erasure of society and the denial of virtue has left us desperately
clinging to a posited direct relation between the state and the citizen.
The weight of this fear bears upon us and ensures that we dare not think
of any form of just relations other than egalitarianism.

The individual-state relation fuelled by the dualistic logic of the liberal
market state, however, undermines these associations by not only undermining the associations from within, but also reducing the complex connections that make up these "second-order" associations – the associations
between associations, such as the connections between economic and familial life. Social, political, and economic relations within the individual-
state model are made negotiable and superficial in a way that hollows
out the richness of complex interrelations in society. In turn these relations become dangerously fragile. As Cavanaugh writes, "the history of
the state is the creation of an increasingly direct relationship between
state and individual by the state's absorption of powers from the groups
that comprise what has come to be called 'civil society.'"[62] Many mutual
interrelations of dependence are non-negotiable in the sense that they
are non-fungible. For example, relations between a mother and child,
two lovers, a master and student, a priest and parishioner, etc. are not
contractual in nature. Each of these relations, if they are healthy in their
mutual dependence – that is, if they are based upon hope rather than
the predictability of control – involve a double asymmetry.[63] And, it is
this doubling of the asymmetry that prevents the reductionism of mon-
etization needed for negotiability. In other words an attempt to negoti-
ate, if pushed to a certain degree, will reduce the mutuality so much that
it will destroy the double asymmetry of the relations – it will destroy the
resilience of the relation.[64] Indeed, relations of double asymmetry are resilient in a way that symmetrical contractual relations are not because
their double asymmetry works to constantly refocus and re-centre the
relationship in a disallowal of ulterior motivations. The reductionism of
dualism, in contrast, decentres the relationship such that it no longer

62 Cavanaugh, "Killing for the Telephone Company," 256.
63 Illich, *Deschooling Society*, 105, and MacIntyre, *Dependent Rational Animals*, 108.
64 Illich, *Deschooling Society*, 100–1.

maintains its ability to be self-perpetuating – it becomes dependent upon ulterior motivations to continue.

There seems to be no doubt that our schools, courts, hospitals, churches, labour associations, corporations, recreational clubs, etc. – the associations that, in their interconnections, make up society – have been decentred by this dualistic logic.[65] The means of societal destruction are numerous and often subtle, but some of the key elements can be summarized into four areas: identity formation, legalization of relations, professionalization, and resource allocation.

First, society is destroyed through the market state's influence over identity formation. A large bureaucratic institution such as the state orients identity formation – political, economic, sexual, spiritual, etc. – toward an individual-state relation. Simply put, who we are becomes tied up in our status as those who can claim access to the rights afforded by the state. This can be seen even to some degree in the introduction and advancement of the Charter of Rights and Freedoms in Canada where residents begin to understand themselves as citizens in the sense that they are those subjects that possess Charter rights.

Second, society is destroyed through a legalization (and hence corruption) of relational interdependencies. The service delivery of the liberal state creates dependencies and a welfare model of understanding social and economic relations. Importantly, through its dualistic logic the market state not only problematizes healthy dependency relations but reduces genuine independence with a false sense of freedom rooted in its market logic. The false freedom of choice for the consumer-citizen isolates persons as lonely, self-interested individuals within the global marketplace.[66]

Third, society is destroyed through the professionalization and regulation of service delivery. The accreditation / certification / standardization model of the liberal state institution undermines trust in those who are not defined as professionals and formally sanctioned by the state. Consequently, front-line workers in the public sector are disempowered while citizens and communities are disengaged. And as a result this model causes the emphasis to become focused upon consumer choice, at the risk of further decapitalizing the poor, and upon procedures and due process, at the expense of substantive outcomes.[67]

65 Putnam, *Bowling Alone*; Blond, *Red Tory*; and Polanyi, *The Great Transformation*, 76.

66 See, for example, Belloc, *The Servile State*, 3. And as MacIntyre has pointed out, the key to genuine independence is an acknowledgment rather than a destruction of dependencies. See MacIntyre, *Dependent Rational Animals*, 85.

67 See Blond, *Red Tory*, 239–79. Also see Illich, *Deschooling Society*.

Fourth, society is destroyed through the (mis)allocation of resources into the state infrastructure rather than the intermediary associations of civil society. Social and material resources get funnelled into the state's bureaucracy and away from non-state associations such that, for example, economic systems begin to solidify within the state as universal service deliverer and singular sanctioner of violence. Localized service providers are not only increasingly delegitimized, but also gradually excluded from the market as their economic agency becomes undermined.

Fifth, society is destroyed through a rationalization of socio-economic patternings in the state's pursuit of broad political goals. As Oakeshott points out in "Rationalism in Politics," under this universalization of community, society loses its "rhythm and continuity" because "all sense of what Burke called the partnership between the present and the past is lost."[68] The capacity for normative reasoning – i.e. moral judgments and actions – that reinforce communal aims and the coordinations that make up society are only possible in localized environments.

The resilience of a society and a civil economy can only be fostered if these five means of destruction are undermined. However, more is needed. We must begin questioning the rule of law itself.

If we agree that the dualistic logic of the liberal market state is destroying society in at least some of the ways I have just described, how might we respond in more practical legal and political terms? For example, is it not simply the hierarchies of the modern bureaucracy but also the abstract regularity of the rule of law itself that upholds and ensures the advancing reach of the market state? We have discussed the importance of moving away from the understanding of justice as impartiality and into a search for restoration and increased capacity for restoration – namely, the resilience of a healthy civil society that is not dominated by the state's monopolization of service delivery and the legitimization of violence. However, if law is constitutive of the market state (it facilitates and legitimates its existence) insofar as it monopolizes authority over domestic violence in relation to the land and the population within its borders, how might we best approach the problem of the rule of law as a universalizing system?

The liberal market state has adopted and abstracted the sovereignty claimed by monarchies in premodern days. This advancement of sovereignty may be seen in, for example, the centrality of the rule of law in the modern state. The rule of law as the monopolization of domestic

68 Oakeshott, "Rationalism in Politics," 3, 23. Also see Devigne, *Recasting Conservatism*, 10.

violence entails an attempt to bring the entire population under the aegis of the state in a direct, individual-state and individual-marketplace relation. The monopoly is upheld and reproduced through a system of law that is designed to be as precise and clear as reasonably possible in its application to particular events and practices within the jurisdiction of the state. The monopoly is solidified in and through an isolation of specific, localized practices and ways of life and an establishment of a singular relationality between these ways of life and the logic of the state and universal market. That is, diverse local customs and practices are both partitioned out as distinct techniques of living and then these specific "techniques" are conceptualized and assessed in relation to the universalized totality of the state or the liberal marketplace. But before getting into the problem of standardization arising from the drive to precision in law as a generalized normative ordering, it is helpful to consider what we mean when we discuss "law" and its rule as a problematic.

The very nature of law has been the subject of significant jurisprudential debate and no more so than in the conflicting understandings of the state's role in the production and reproduction of law as represented by the positivists and the pluralists. For the positivist, the state's transcendent role in promulgation and enforcement is essential to the creation and maintenance of law. For the pluralist, the state is of little consequence because normative orderings immanent within the behaviour of communities are legal orders just as state-centric systems of ordering can be legal orders. The positivists, therefore, have tended to over-emphasize the importance of the state and their dependence upon the universalism of the state has exacerbated distrust and a disregard for normative orderings governing behaviour outside the state's purview.[69] The pluralists, on the other hand, have tended to over-naturalize the non-state normative orderings they seek to describe as legal orderings in order to undermine the state-centrism of the positivists.[70]

There is, however, a kind of third way between the positivist / pluralist debate that avoids both the state-centric and the anti-statist extremes. As Jeremy Webber has cogently argued, the division between positivists and pluralists has been exaggerated because both camps have tended to minimize the persistence of conflict within – or the fundamental contestability of – legal orders. This division is exaggerated because, as he writes, "non-state norms share a fundamental characteristic with state norms:

---

69 For example, see Hart, *The Concept of Law.*

70 For example, see Ehrlich, *Fundamental Principles of the Sociology of Law.* For an excellent analysis of the challenges facing positivists and pluralists along these lines, see Webber, "Naturalism and Agency in the Living Law," 201.

they all confront the fundamental problem of how to establish a common standard in the face of pervasive normative disagreement."[71] For, indeed, law – be it state law or non-state law – possesses two related dimensions: (a) an interpretive dimension in which "participants propose and deliberate about rules, justifying their solutions on the basis of the exigencies of the situation, the lessons of experience, and broader attitudes already established within society" and (b) a decisional dimension in which "a collective resolution is established from among the proposed interpretations."[72] In this sense all law is "both interpretive and, to a degree, peremptory" in its imposition of uniformity upon a multiplicity of behaviours and practices within societies; law "necessarily imposes a socially determined rule against a more complex and ambiguous background of normative assertion and counter-assertion."[73] Therefore, all law – be it understood as primarily statist or non-statist – is at least somewhat problematic.

To put it simply, law is problematic as a peremptory, universalized or standardized imposition because it is a normative ordering that is not fully legitimized. Although, as Webber has pointed out, no normative ordering is ever fully legitimized, law is best understood as being active in the world as a particular kind of violence, a particular kind of illegitimate violence (i.e. domination). There should be no doubt that law is very often legitimized to a significant degree in its violent imposition for, indeed, it must be somewhat legitimized or it will not even be recognized as law at all. Thus, we should see law as carrying with it both the blessing of moral legitimacy as well as the curse of illegitimacy.

Why do I suggest that law represents a particular kind of illegitimate violence? As we saw above, the localization of politicization is needed if violence is to be legitimized – but the peremptory nature of law, in its push to universalization and monopolization, disallows the localism needed for a thorough politicization.[74] We are unable to localize the normative ordering of law in a way that can effectively legitimize it. Law, by definition, persists as an imposition that may be recognized and interpreted as an imposition. Normative orderings, to the degree that they are localizable (and, hence, politicizable) are not capable of being recognized as such an imposition or disruptive force; they disappear from view as we draw near to them. Law presences before us as res publica and therefore cannot be written on our hearts without ceasing

71 Ibid., 203.
72 Ibid., 211.
73 Ibid., 211, 209.
74 Ibid., 221.

to be law. For example, because the state prevents the legitimization process by virtue of its monopolization, the normative orderings of the state institutions are quite clearly law in the sense I am describing it here. Understanding the difference between law and normative orderings in this manner allows us to tune ourselves in to the violence of law without falling into the pluralist trap of vilifying the state and romanticizing the non-state normative orderings while at the same time allowing us to avoid the positivist's state-centrism. With this understanding of law and violence, we are better able to concern ourselves with understanding legitimacy and illegitimacy as well as the changes taking place in the law that threaten to further prevent the legitimization brought about through of democratic politicization.

Democracy, in addition to being a process of political resistance at work in the world as described in political terms above, may be understood in more legal terms as an ordering of society that possesses the resilience needed to support a sufficient degree of legitimacy in law. Democracy should not be conceived of as an order of government. Fascism, communism, parliamentarianism, are orders of governance but democracy is a method of governance that may be at work within any of the orders. Democracy, therefore, may be seen in the relation between a certain kind of society and a certain kind of law – a society that is healthy and resilient enough in its normative orderings to provide the foundation for politicization that adequately legitimizes the violence of law. Democratic society exists as an opening or a possible future in which law is more fully legitimized. A certain richness in normative orderings (i.e. an embodied ethic of non-domination) is needed for democracy to exist and flourish and, as we discussed, to the degree that normative orderings are destroyed or undermined by dualistic logic, the legitimization of law is undermined. Thus, my central concern throughout this book has been the development of an ethic of non-domination that is able to foster relational connections that are resilient in their ability to resist the domineering dualistic modulations of protocolic control. Practically speaking, I would like to argue that the ethic of non-domination can be best realized and made manifest in search for reflexivity and restraint in the legal systems of the market state – i.e. in a democratization of modern life. Admittedly, however, given the advancement of formal law by the liberal market state (i.e. what we described earlier as the era of "total law"), the fostering of reflexivity and restraint will be no easy task.

In looking at the possibilities of moving beyond the totalizing unity within the state's monopolies on service delivery and violence above, I pointed to new governance theorists who are keen to develop more nimble and bottom-up responsive state institutions. However, we should also note that new governance theory is changing not only the traditional (post-Second World War) models of regulation and administration, but is also introducing a new model of adjudication. As Orly Lobel has suggested, in the new governance model, "lawmaking shifts from a top-down, command-and-control framework to a reflexive approach, which is process oriented and tailored to local circumstances."[75] Within the modern welfare state, emphasis was placed upon understanding law as "an instrument for purposive, goal-oriented intervention."[76] In contrast, reflexive law – according to Gunther Teubner – is characterized by a new type of legal self-restraint. Rather than simply taking over regulatory responsibility for the outcome of social processes, reflexive law will restrict itself to the establishment, correction, and refinement of democratic self-regulatory mechanisms. Reflexive law does not authoritatively determine social functions so much as provide "norms of procedure, organization, and competences that aid other social systems in achieving the democratic self-organization and self-regulation."[77] The "hard" orders within the regulatory model are thereby replaced by "softer" procedures that are intended to foster a flexible policy environment.[78] In other words, reflexive legal strategies restructure subsystems through incentives and disincentives that promote reflection regarding behaviour rather than simply prescribing substantive commands. Reflexive law limits itself to looking at the competences and capacities of social actors and institutions, considering the appropriate division of responsibilities, and the maintenance of self-regulatory processes.[79] For example, as Cristie Ford has observed, the Supreme Court of Canada in the Quebec *Secession Reference* accomplished something like the reflexive law envisioned by new governance theorists.[80] That is, instead of giving a clear judicial determination of Quebec's place inside or outside the Canadian federation, the Court "sets out only the broad normative framework within which democratic constitutional deliberation is to take place – that is, the four pillars of the Canadian constitutional tradition: democracy, federalism, constitutionalism and the rule of law, and respect for minorities

---

75 Lobel, "The Renew Deal," 345.

76 See Rheinstein, *Max Weber on Law in Economy and Society*, cited in Teubner, "Substantive and Reflexive Elements in Modern Law," 240.

77 Ibid., 275.

78 Lobel, "The Renew Deal," 388.

79 Ibid., 364, 401, 403.

80 Ford, "In Search of the Qualitative Clear Majority. Also see *Reference Re Secession of Quebec*, [1998] 2 SCR 217.

– and leaves the resolution of the details to the political process."[81] Throughout, the Court has procedural expectations that are to govern the constitutional debates going forward.

This reflexive approach to law within new governance theory is better able to deal with the traditional problem of legal indeterminacy.[82] The problem of indeterminacy, in a basic sense, can be understood as follows: "If the application of a rule requires deliberation about its meaning, then the rule cannot be a guide to action in the way that a commitment to the rule of law appears to require; similarly, if the content of a constitutional right (or other constitutional provision) can only be determined by exten-sive deliberation, then the Constitution does not entrench rights (or other principles) in the sense of providing foundational assurances."[83] If one is looking for clear rules with (at least largely) determinative applications, then indeterminacy is certainly a problem. If, on the other hand, law is conceived of largely as a process of assessing relative competencies, the need for ongoing interpretations of rules need not come as a surprise. And, more importantly, if the courts themselves are understood to be in-stitutions without a fixed or determinative societal role, then the fact that they must engage in continual reinterpretation of legal propositions is also not a surprise. And, as Michael Dorf points out, courts do not need to solidify or fill in all the constitutional norms and can initiate societal re-form through working with other institutions.[84]

In this way, the role of the courts is redefined as law becomes reflexive and the problem of indeterminacy fades into the background. The prob-lem has not been solved – in fact, some new governance theorists seem to celebrate the indeterminacy of law and suggest that "deliberation thrives on uncertainty" – but the indeterminacy has been embraced with-in a redefined role for the courts as experimental bodies.[85] Experi-mentalist courts will deliberately give open-ended rulings, incomplete answers, and normative guidelines that provide some direction without over-determining the required response with a hard, specific ruling.[86] In doing so, these redefined courts would explicitly rely upon the relevant actors to operate within the guidelines to establish workable solutions

81 Ford, "In Search of the Qualitative Clear Majority," 517. It seems the Court was ready to do something this open-ended because it was not a decision, but a reference.

82 Also, as Scheuerman has noted, reflexive law may be better suited to the high-speed world. *Liberal Democracy*, 215.

83 Dorf, "Legal Indeterminacy and Institutional Design," 877.

84 Ibid., 882–3.

85 Thomas, "Habitat Conservation Planning," 168.

86 Dorf and Sabel, "A Constitution of Democratic Experimentalism," 430.

within the political realm.[87] Although it may seem like this is not resolving the problem of indeterminacy so much as it is exacerbating the problem, experimentalist courts will not simply give less in their judgments, their judgments will be different. As Dorf writes, "experimentalist appellate courts self-consciously rely on the participation of affected actors to explore the implications of the framework rules that they create and use the record of such actors' efforts continually to refine such framework rules."[88] The jurisprudential inputs will be explicitly rooted in the practices and experiences of the relevant actors, but the outputs will also explicitly guide social deliberations rather than simply removing a question from the realm of majoritarian politics.

The more innovative feature of experimentalist courts, therefore, will be found in their interactions with other governing bodies. The adjudicative process is a process of self-explication where fundamental legal norms can be declared, but they are always to be explicitly subject to future change within the process of experimentation. Also, experimentalist courts would demand reasons from political actors – reasons which are intended to link principle and practice – and access their ability to deliberate upon their own process of experimentation. Therefore, courts would primarily be working to develop transparency and understanding – i.e. drawing out the actors' reasons and assessing the degree to which (and the process through which) these actors have considered their options within the broad framework of their constitutional limitations.[89]

Dorf and Sabel highlight the fact that the courts are currently faced with the task of making what are largely speculative determinations regarding the connection between legislative means and ends. And, given this problem of interpretability, the courts are faced with the less than ideal choice of either deference to the lawmakers (and, in doing so, inviting capriciousness into the process) or scrutinize the legislation and employ balancing tests (and thereby place limitations on the democratic processes and raise questions regarding their own institutional legitimacy within a democracy). The problem of interpretability, Dorf and Sabel point out, has not been created by the courts but by the process under review and, therefore, cannot simply be solved by a shift in judicial doctrine – the process of lawmaking itself needs to change.[90] They suggest that all movements toward experimentalism within the law-making process will help allow the courts to avoid being torn between deference and

---

87　Dorf, "Legal Indeterminacy and Institutional Design," 886–8.
88　Ibid., 881.
89　Dorf and Sabel, "A Constitution of Democratic Experimentalism," 389–90.
90　Ibid., 390–5.

intrusion. They write, "experimentalism provides the polity with the institutional means to ask the questions that courts otherwise need to, but cannot ask, in hard cases, and to ask them in the way most relevant – connecting means to ends – to practical decisions and judicial review."[91] The problem of judicial review arises when there is an appearance of finality within the traditional model of adjudication. And, it is this traditional model that is to be transformed into an open-ended process through experimentalism.

So within the traditional administrative governance model, courts are primarily concerned with the level of deference they grant to either elected legislatures or appointed administrative rule-makers. However, within the new governance approach courts provide a unique oversight role over civic self-governance.[92] Instead of destroying the Madisonian tradition of limited government through a separation of powers (i.e. to protect the people from the state), in the new governance model "the performance of local unity, the center's response to that performance, and the legislature's response to that reaction can be scrutinized by the other actors, the public and eventually the courts in a way that is currently impossible."[93] Like the internal information flows that are understood to enliven the democratic process and legitimize the governance through the very process of experimental governing, reflexive law is said to allow for court supervision that is limited within its very practice of oversight. For, courts would not simply rely upon judicial doctrine and abstract legal concepts, but would interact with other institutions of governance as a social co-educator. Or, as James Liebman and Charles Sabel put it, "this new kind of judicial review effaces familiar distinctions between public and private and between the sovereign and the citizen subjects. Because the legislative authorization is more a general framework for institutional experimentation in the elaboration of principle than the enactment of a well-defined public mandate, the court's role as constitutional guardian is not primarily to police the permissibility of the legislature's delegation of authority or the delegate's fidelity to legislative intentions. Rather, it is to collaborate via the continuing definition of standards with an emergent public in giving meaning to constitutional principle."[94] The "open-endedness" of reflexive law, therefore, cannot simply be injected at the judicial review stage – it must be there from the beginning (e.g. in rolling best-practice requirements). Within the

91 Ibid., 395.
92 Liebman and Sabel, "A Public Laboratory Dewey Barely Imagined," 279.
93 Ibid.
94 Ibid., 282.

experimentalist model, then, the courts would not set out to make judgments on, say, the actual regulatory practice (i.e. if it was in fact the best regulation to accomplish the goals of the legislation), but would look to see if the governing body actually engaged in the organization and coordination of information needed to develop rolling best-practice standards. Consequently, the experimentalists' vision of judicial review is largely procedural insofar as the court looks at the practices of the governing bodies in searching for a solution, rather than seeking to determine whether or not the solution selected was indeed appropriate.[95]

In response to Teubner's rejection of classic rule of law values such as clarity and precision, Ingeborg Maus has argued that the reflexive law model left those who were socially and economically disadvantaged open and vulnerable to the interests of the privileged. That is, those with the greater amount of de facto economic power are able (and willing) to exploit those with lesser power through interpretations of the vague or open-ended law. Therefore, although she does not retreat to a hard-line formalist solution, Maus suggests that law should at least be accompanied by very clear and precise procedural and organizational norms.[96] However, Teubner has good reason to avoid attempting to make a sharp distinction between the means and the ends of law and therefore avoid thinking that we could move beyond the problem of the rule of law if we retained clear and precise procedures. Indeed, procedural rules and organizational norms bring with them substantive outcomes; clear and precise procedures inevitably mean standardized legal norms centred upon the state institution.[97]

A more pressing critique, therefore, comes from Erhard Blankenburg who has argued that Teubner's suggestion that reflexive law is evolutionary – that it develops and changes its very nature through time – is unfounded. He suggests that reflexive forms of law simply add to current legal regulation and expand the social arenas of regulation rather than lead to deregulation.[98] Regulating by procedure rather than substantive rules has been used before by shrewd legislators when they were seeking to begin regulating in an area previously unregulated; it is not the next step in the evolution of law. So Blankenburg concludes that reflexive law is little more than "a legislative attempt to exert some control in areas

95 See Dorf and Sabel, "A Constitution of Democratic Experimentalism," 397. Also see Scheuerman, "Democratic Experimentalism or Capitalist Synchronization?," 115–16.

96 Maus, "Perspektiven reflexiven Rechts im Kontext gegenwärtiger Deregulierungstendenzen," 400–5, cited in Scheuerman, *Liberal Democracy*, 216.

97 Scheuerman, "Democratic Experimentalism or Capitalist Synchronization?," 116.

98 Blankenburg, "The Poverty of Evolutionism," 275.

where *ex ante* substantive regulation seemed particularly difficult or inappropriate. The technique is similar to that of delegating administrative discretion, for in both cases substantive regulation grows out of the process of implementation."[99] That is, there is nothing particularly responsive about regulation through procedure; it is simply regulation that is attentive to its own limitations. Blankenburg's point here may be reinforced if we understand reflexive law as still having a minimum level of regulatory rules promulgated and enforced (at least provisionally) by a central organization as William Scheuerman suggests it needs.[100]

As we have discussed, Teubner seems to understand reflexive law primarily as legal self-restraint. However, restraint cannot simply be a proceduralist self-restraint that operates within the institutional realm of the market state because, as Blankenburg points out, this will inevitably lead to regulation through procedure. Or in other words, the opposite of restraint would be achieved as the law's reach would extend further and further. If it is to be effective and meaningful, restraint must shape and guide the governing procedures as much as it alters and affects the substantive regulatory outcomes. And, if it is to be effective, this restraint must come from outside the structure and processes of the state.

Although the liberalism underlying and shaping his approach to law is quite concerning, it should be noted that Teubner is at least somewhat attune to this problem of restraint. For example, as Teubner argues, the state-centred mindset of global constitutionalists – i.e. those who continue to understand a constitution as primarily a framework for state-political activity – has led them into many problems. For example, the state-centric constitutionalism leads to an exclusion of many important actors such as non-governmental organizations and labour organizations and the denial of protection for those suffering at the hands of non-state actors. Therefore, he argues for a constitutionalism that moves beyond the state-political framework and gradually begins to embrace civil relations. He writes, "the constitution of world society comes about not exclusively in the representative institutions of international politics, nor can it take place in a unitary global constitution overlying all areas of society, but emerges incrementally in the constitutionalisation of a multiplicity of autonomous subsystems of world society."[101] A multiplicity of civil

---

99 Ibid., 287.

100 Scheuerman, "Democratic Experimentalism or Capitalist Synchronization?," 112, 115.

101 Gunther Teubner, "Societal Constitutionalism: Alternatives to State-Centred Constitutional Theory," (Storrs Lectures 2003/04 Yale Law School) 5, Social Science Research Network, http://papers.ssrn.com/sol3/papers.cfm?abstract_id=876941#PaperDownload.

constitutions is needed. He argues that, since the eighteenth century, constitutionalism has been preoccupied with the problem of forming, defining, and restraining political power in relation to the state but today's constitutional question must be focused on quite different social dynamics. Within the societal constitutionalism model, the Madisonian checks and balances within government begin to expand outward and incorporate civil society to a much greater degree. That is, instead of simply having multiple levels of government ready to limit any overstepping of boundaries or jurisdictional spheres (or, indeed, to limit the state's infringement upon citizens' personal liberties), the new governance theory allows for checks and balances between levels of government and civil society. Or, in other words, the organizational strength of associations within society – within the process of deliberation, resistance, and democratic experimentation – limit the powers and influence of government and each other and thereby protect against widespread structural corruption and domination.

We are here beginning to see some potential for genuine restraint within constitutionalism. And indeed as Teubner writes, "the historical role of the constitution is not, especially when it comes to fundamental rights, exhausted in norming state organisation and individual legal rights, but consists primarily in guaranteeing the multiplicity of social differentiation against swamping tendencies."[102] This has historically meant that the constitution would act as a break against expansionist tendencies within the political system that would threaten the social heterogeneity of the polity. For example, in this sense, a model of minority rights protection was established to ensure that the government itself did not become homogenized by one autonomous social movement within society.[103] Likewise, however, restraints must be placed upon the state itself to prevent homogenization under the totalizing standardizations of the rule of law.

So, the problem of self-restraint still persists. If it is the state's monopoly on domestic violence (i.e. law) that is problematic insofar as its totalizing effect is domineering, then self-restraint within the creation and reform of law inevitably produces a further extension of the state's

---

Accessed 11 February 2016. Not surprisingly, the driving force behind this movement beyond the state-political framework and toward a societal constitutionalism is understood to be the rise of digitization, privatization, and globalization.

102 Ibid., 9.
103 Ibid.

monopoly.[104] For example, not only is the market state responsible for standardizing and centralizing the law, but it is now responsible for reducing the ill effects of its own actions but can only do so by bringing non-state actors into circuits of power that are shaped and guided by the delocalizing standardization of its structures and processes. As I noted above while discussing Magnusson and Walker's critique of counter-hegemonization in the work of Laclau and Mouffe, the question is not so much whether or not we are working within the state's formal institutional apparatus, but the degree to which we are able or unable to undermine the governing processes underlying standardizing or totalizing processes themselves.[105] Or, as Webber writes, "it is better to think about law as driven by an aspiration towards order, by a will to live in an ordered community, but where that order has to be made and remade. The agent that makes this order need not be the state."[106] Our concern here should remain focused on the generalization and imposition of norms beyond the community within which they are developed and reinforced.[107] The market state simply acts as an important focal point in working out our concerns regarding standardization. The question, therefore, is how we can develop social, political, and economic ways of life that disrupt the political space of the market state insofar as it is facilitating the advancement of standardization through protocolic control. How can we limit the rule of law without simply reiterating and reinforcing the very problem we set out to escape?

If we are to develop an understanding of what might be truly resilient patternings in our lives and so avoid the problem of the rule of law, we will need to recognize not only that law is problematic in its standardization of norms, but also that laws depend upon something outside law to give them their authority. Indeed, the Anglo-American tradition of legal

---

104 There is a real sense in which societal constitutionalism, as outlined by Teubner, may be viewed as an attempt to drive out demons by the power of Beelzebub despite the fact that he calls for a kind of "social institutionalisation" that is not dependent upon "the formal existence of a constituent assembly, a constitutional document, norms of explicitly constitutional quality, or a court specialised in constitutional questions." Ibid., 5.

105 Magnusson and Walker, "De-centring the State," 67.

106 Webber, "Naturalism and Agency in the Living Law," 214. Webber is certainly correct here. However, I would also add that law is not driven simply by an aspiration to order, but also by a will to control by means of ordering one's community and environment – i.e. in order to deal effectively with the anxiety caused by the stranger, the darkness, and the wilderness.

107 Although my analysis parts ways with him in some important ways, for an important example of this kind of concern, see Ehrlich, *Fundamental Principles of the Sociology of Law*, 124–5.

philosophy has explored the question "What is law?" precisely because
what we understand law to be tells us what is outside the law. And it is
that which is outside the law that defines who we are. That which is outside the law constitutes us because it constitutes our law and the law
constitutes us by defining our agency. For example, in the liberal (impartialist) conception of the rule of law, the individual-state relation is outside the law. The individual-state relation is outside the law in the sense
that it is not contested and subject to legitimization; it is the assumed
undergirding framework that allows the liberal ideal of the rule of law to
have coherence and meaning. The liberal rule of law defines our agency
as individuals-in-relation-to-the-state. It therefore holds out the promise
of opening up all actions to the individual – i.e. "obedience to the law is
freedom." But, in so doing, it destroys the genuine agency of the res
ecologia in its totalization. Further, within the modern liberal conception of the rule of law, justified power use in and through various laws
is quite often understood to be the universalism of legality itself; the
mere fact that a law is binding upon all persons within a recognized
jurisdiction is seen as justification of that law's imposition of a standardized norm. Although this kind of law appears to be internally justified
(i.e. law is justified simply as a result of its legality), it actually depends
upon normative assumptions quite outside the laws and indeed outside
legality itself.

In his defense of right-wing socialism (i.e. fascism), Schmitt argued
that authority resided in the one who was able to define the state of exception to the rule of law.[108] However, it should be quite clear by now
that that which is outside must be multiple or the domineering standardizations of the rule of law will simply be replicated and, indeed, reinforced. Appeal to a dictator or even a counter-hegemonizing force such
as a coordinated and activated public cannot give law authority through
legitimacy because, as we have discussed, that which universalizes cannot
be localized adequately in a legitimization process. The democratic question – whether violence is excessive or not – must be asked and answered
outside the law but must be asked and answered dialogically and diachronically in the diverse ethical lives of res ecologia. And, in order to
foster restraint within laws promulgated and enforced by the market
state, not only must political subjects and their democratic agency be
defined and redefined – constituted – in multiple ways without direct
relation to the state and its rule of law, but the institutional design of our
state must be guided by an ethic that pre-exists and continues to be

---

108 See Schmitt, *Dictatorship*, and Schmitt, *Political Theology*.

fostered outside the state structure (e.g. in a multiplicity of familial relations and religious traditions).[109]

Practically speaking, we should not deny the fact that there is benefit in procedural circuit breakers that afford some degree of resistance to standardizations in universalizing institutions (e.g. the Supreme Court of Canada). For example, s.33 (the notwithstanding clause of the Canadian Constitution Act of 1982) and principles of subsidiarity rather than federal paramountcy within the Canadian federation are beneficial. However, there is a need to push the subsidiarity principle down below the state level – i.e. even the most localized government needs to perpetually draw moral legitimacy from outside itself from families, corporations, churches, etc. That is, we are in need of not just procedural circuit breakers, but moral / political ones – i.e. restraint requires an ongoing openness to escape the system and resist it from the outside. Say, to be able to claim a kind of moral superiority that has real bearing upon the law. There is a need for genuine reciprocity in which the relationship one has with the state institution is open to transformation (i.e. not just a transformation of the subject, but also a politicization of the relation in a revealing of resilient localized normative orderings). Guardians of tradition, therefore, become sources of authority in the politicization process – i.e. one's connectivity to a tradition will determine in large part the possibilities of politicizing the relations one has (and hence the relationship one's community has) with law. Additionally, not just guardians of tradition (i.e. social resilience), but also sustainability (i.e. ecological and economic resilience) is necessary for building resistance to the standardizations of the market state. So, in this manner we might conceive of a coupled critique that can guide the process of remoralizing or repoliticizing the law.

The remoralizing of law, therefore, will only be successful if we are able to recover the moral foundations of law and recover some degree of respect for authority that comes from beyond the formal, monolithic rules

109 The notion of one unitary society that matches up to the unitary state is, as Cavanaugh and Anthony Giddens suggest, highly exceptional. Cavanaugh, "Killing for the Telephone Company," 246, and Giddens, *The Nation-State and Violence*, 1–2, 52–3, cited in ibid. As Ernest Gellner writes, "in a traditional social order, the languages of the hunt, of harvesting, of various rituals, of the council room, of the kitchen or harem, all form autonomous systems: to conjoin statements drawn from these various disparate fields, to probe for inconsistencies between them, to try to unify them all, this would be a social solecism or worse, probably blasphemy or impiety, and the very endeavour would be unintelligible. By contrast, in our society it is assumed that all referential uses of language ultimately refer to one coherent world, and can be reduced to a unitary idiom." Gellner, *Nations and Nationalism*, 21, quoted in ibid.

of consensual law. That is, until we reinvigorate the normative orderings within which law lives and breathes in resistance to the standardized modulations of protocolic control, we are doomed to the tyranny of an illegitimate universalization of rules. For to the extent that we are unable to politicize law we are unable to be virtuous people living democratic lives in healthy community with each other and our natural environment.

This understanding of the authority that comes from beyond the law harkens back to premodern conceptions of moral and legal authority. For example, an understanding of the embeddedness of formal law may be seen in the conservative Tory loyalists as they struggle with reformist Whig republicans in the first half of the nineteenth century in Upper Canada. In June of 1826, a group of lawyers and law students destroyed a print shop owned by William Lyon Mackenzie for its contributions to undermining the authority of the legal-administrative elite.[110] This conflict reveals two strikingly different conceptions of normativity, authority, and law and provides us with a focal point for understanding how we might begin again to democratically politicize the law and move beyond the rule of law. Blaine Baker has demonstrated how understanding the rule of law as a distinct, self-regulating system – much like the modern disembedded economy outlined by Polanyi in *The Great Transformation* – is relatively new. Such things as the "abstract juridical equality of the subjects of formulaic, statist conventional law, notions of due process, and the ideal of an independent judiciary" is a recent phenomenon and should not be idealized as the only conception of just governing relations.[111] The older view of orderly governance understood that the constitution of the province "was not the set of explicit rules that defined its formal organs of government, but rather the unwritten, and often unspoken, spiritual and social premises upon which this Loyalist community was to be based."[112] Or, in other words, spiritual, social, and governmental orderings were regarded as inseparable insofar as they were representative of greater orderings that transcended human knowledge and the experience of any individual. Therefore, "abstracted statements of 'legal' rules capable of expression in a coherent form were only one among many 'codes' for the description and perpetuation of providential distributions of

110 For an historical account of this event, see, for example, Kilbourn, *The Firebrand*, 67ff, and Mackenzie, *The History of the Destruction of the Colonial Advocate Press by Officers of the Provincial Government of Upper Canada and Law Students to the Attorney & Solicitor General* (York: Colonial Advocate, 1827), http://ia600707.us.archive.org/19/items/cihm_92892/cihm_92892.pdf. Accessed 11 February 2016.

111 Baker, "So Elegant a Web," 186.

112 Ibid., 188.

responsibility and power in the great chain of being."[113] So, for example, according to the long-time treasurer of the Law Society of Upper Canada: "society is formed of so elegant a web that every violence done [its patterns of order] makes a breach which however repaired will long remain a blemish. In all [life's] rich tapestry distinction is necessary; this is nature or more properly speaking, the order of providence."[114] The monolithic, standardized rule of law did not therefore provide liberty and security. Quite the contrary. A focus upon the standardized rule of law eclipsed the multiplicity of democratic orderings and led down a destructive path to arrogant and irreverent tyranny. The only true guarantee of liberty and security is to be found in ordering the structures of society according to the preordained orderings of the world. Democratic freedom is worked out under the authoritative leadership of virtuous persons rooted within resilient communities and seeking that great ordering that transcends their own finite notions of justice.

In addition to developing reflexivity and restraint in our legal orderings through the rule of virtue, we must remoralize the marketplace. For, as Stefano Zamagni suggests, a civil society that fosters an ethical legality also requires a civil marketplace that fosters a remoralization of the market or it will be undermined at every turn.[115] When discussing the market state above, we noted that modern economics is best understood as coming about in the notion that the dynamics of generating material wealth could be isolated from the rest of life and analyzed as a separate field of study to be explored as a universe operating according to its own internal logic.[116] As Gudeman writes, "competitive trade reverberates in markets and usually cascades into new spaces leading to the expansion of the competitive arena and the increased use of calculative reason in practices and discourse. As the market realm expands, it *colonizes* and *debases* the mutual one on which it also relies."[117] The isolation and elevation of material gain within economic liberalism also inevitably results in the liberal state-sanctioned appropriation of non-profitmaking spheres of life by the market.[118] Therefore, instead of contributing to this ongoing collusion between the liberal state and the liberal market, which

113 Ibid., 193.

114 William Warren Baldwin to Richard Cartwright Robinson, 23 March 1823, *Journals of the Advocate Society* 9, 67–74, quoted in Baker, "So Elegant a Web," 193.

115 Bruni and Zamagni, *Civil Economy*, 2, and Blond, *Red Tory*, 185.

116 Polanyi, *The Great Transformation*, 43ff, 111ff.

117 Gudeman, "Necessity or Contingency," 19, emphasis in original. Also see Gudeman, *Economy's Tension*.

118 Polanyi, *The Great Transformation*, 111ff, 139; Blond, *Red Tory*, 186; and Perelman, *The Invention of Capitalism*.

leads to a socialization of risk and a privatization of wealth, we need to search for a new kind of capitalism – a popular capitalism that is undergirded, sustained, and guided by an ethic of non-domination and mutual support.[119]

It should be noted up front that the liberal market, although it is certainly true that it continues to undermine the non-market normative orderings of localized communities, does so through the development of its own set of domineering quasi-norms. Indeed, liberal markets destroy non-market norms in two ways – one, by exerting and entrenching their own set of illegitimate quasi-norms and two, by destroying the very capacity for normative ordering through their dualistic logic.[120]

As Dorf and Sabel note, "the organizing features of the ... economy play an important role in shaping our governmental institutions, and, beyond that, our ideas of what public administration and even the democratic public can do."[121] Or, as Michael Sandel points out, a market mechanism inevitably becomes entrenched as a kind of market norm "because markets don't only allocate goods; they also express and promote certain attitudes toward the goods being exchanged."[122] Market systems do not simply facilitate interaction between market actors. Through their structures and processes, market systems shape the very nature of the actors themselves because, of course, actors in a marketplace are not self-contained, autonomous beings but deeply and fundamentally interconnected and hence interdetermined. If market systems are dynamic in the sense that their nature is not only determined by the market actors, but they also determine the nature of the market actors themselves, then what is it about the liberal marketplace specifically that determines the nature of market actors in a way that destroys normative orderings?

First, what do I mean by liberal marketplace? To put it in general terms, a liberal marketplace means an economic system governed by the dualistic logic we discussed above. This means, therefore, (a) an economic system in which prices and wages are predominantly subject to supply and demand rather than what might be called non-market concerns and considerations or (b) an economic system in which the state regulates and restricts economic activity in order to satisfy political objectives based upon a model of all citizens being free, equal, and rational individuals. The first scenario is typically associated with right-wing liberalism

119 Blond, *Red Tory*, 208–9, 213.
120 Sandel, *What Money Can't Buy*, 113ff.
121 Dorf and Sabel, "A Constitution of Democratic Experimentalism," 292.
122 Sandel, *What Money Can't Buy*, 64–5.

in which the free market is idealized as the means to freedom. The second scenario is typically associated with left-wing liberalism in which the market is a means of supplying an idealized welfare state with the means to achieve greater equality. Of course, these are both caricatures and the market state represents a combination of these two approaches. Nonetheless, it is important to understand the two wings of liberalism as they pertain to economic management because as we come to see their common dependence upon dualistic logic we begin to perceive the demoralizing nature of our modern economic system. So to the degree that economic actors are treated as if they were interchangeable (either as freely interacting economic actors or as equal citizens under a common regime of state regulation), it is helpful to understand the marketplace as being "liberal" and therefore demoralizing.

Second, what do I mean when I suggest that liberal marketplaces destroy normative orderings? To put it briefly, they undermine the capacity for normative judgment and action by disrupting and displacing such that the specificity of locality is quite literally rendered meaningless. As we will remember from our discussion above, dualistic logic is a process of simultaneously individuating and totalizing (e.g. an economic actor) such that it eclipses multiplicity and denies history by totalizing the relationality between an isolated unit and a whole. In the context of our modern market state in which the market is undergirded and sustained by the liberal state, there is a logic at work that destroys res ecologia and prevents the politicization process. This prevention of the politicization process takes place for one simple reason – the universalizability of the marketplace – say, in the fungibility of its currency – washes over and through the economic actor in a way that disallows the localization needed to politicize. Conversely, as we will see below, in a localized market the market will not have such an effect because the market processes will themselves be invested with politicization processes.[123]

This phenomenon of politicization prevention may be seen in what has been dubbed the "the commercialization effect" as outlined in Fred Hirsch's 1976 work *The Social Limits to Growth*. Here, Hirsch writes that commercialization is "the effect on the characteristics of a product or activity of supplying it exclusively or predominantly on commercial terms rather than on some other basis – such as informal exchange, mutual obligation, altruism or love, or feelings of service or obligation."[124] Practically speaking, the commodification within a liberal marketplace depoliticizes

---

123 Ibid., 9.
124 Hirsch, *The Social Limits to Growth*, 87. Also see Sandel, *What Money Can't Buy*, 120ff.

through, say, the undermining or crowding out of civic duty. For example, in the case where citizens are motivated by civic duty to engage in self-sacrificial activity for the sake of the communal good but, when offered financial compensation for their activity, no longer understand themselves to be engaged in benevolent behaviour. Once persons are given financial compensation for their behaviour, they are suddenly operating within a very different metric of value calculations – say, individual time or risk for a common currency rather than a voluntary effort embedded within a community working for their common good.[125]

Finally, then, how might we begin to not only counteract the negative effects of the liberal market, but to resist and undermine this demoralizing system itself? Just as we could not expect a procedural solution to the destruction of civil society in our discussion above, so too should we not expect anything less than a revival of ethical living to bring about a genuine remoralizing of the market and a restoration of a civil economy. Not only is it the case that, as Blond and others have noted, moral relations based upon trust and mutual support are the precondition for a healthy economy, but it is futile to try and limit the market simply by increasing the power and reach of the state.[126] For the reasons outlined above in our discussion regarding moving beyond the state and the problem of the rule of law, an appeal to an increase in state power will only compound the problem of a demoralizing market. Instead, put in as general terms as possible, a remoralizing of the market means ensures that actions pertaining to supply and demand within the market are governed by non-market norms arising from the interdependencies of a healthy civil society – i.e. the responsibilities arising from relations within family, church, community associations, etc.[127]

In our analysis of liberalism above, we noted that the false freedom of self-determination becomes manifest in the space between individualized subjects and a subject that has been totalized. We also pointed to the objective state operating under the rule of law as a primary example of this false freedom at work in modern society. The falsity of this freedom is found in the denial of our deeply dependent and persistently vulnerable nature and in the erasure of the in-between worlds that are eclipsed by the polarizations within dualistic logic. Genuine freedom, in contrast, is realized in an engagement in the process of political

125 Sandel, *What Money Can't Buy*, 116, and Heyman and Ariely, "Effort for Payment," 787–93, cited in ibid., 121.

126 Blond, *Red Tory*, 185. Also see Gudeman, "Necessity or Contingency," 20, Gudeman, *Economy's Tension*, and Hollis, *Trust Within Reason*.

127 Blond, *Red Tory*, 187.

resistance; freedom exists in the creation of political space and time through the development of resilient networks that resist standardization. Freedom is, therefore, a process of network development that stabilizes and embeds the immediate patterning of the self. The institutions of the market state have the unfortunate effect of creating unhealthy dependence upon a centralized bureaucracy and an impersonal, delocalized market such that, instead of fostering freedom, they tend to trap people in a state of unfreedom by undermining their ability to develop resilient political and economic networks.[128] The ties of dependency and mutualism are severed and replaced by a domineering dependency operating with bureaucratic rationality to isolate individuals as little more than welfare consumers.[129] In short, the centralized bureaucracies of the market state (i.e. the market state's extreme collectivism) undermine the capacity for moral behaviour and moral activity within the market. Therefore, if we are to effectively remoralize the market, we will need to take steps to simultaneously bring together labour and capital as well as production and consumption. Without a broad-based uniting of these market elements, the capacity for politicization will not be realized.

First, the bringing together of labour and capital ... in short, the problem with capitalism operating under the aegis of the market state is that there are not enough capitalists.[130] As Blond writes: "The state-market relationship is symbiotic. As the role of the state grows, it becomes more reliant on the stability of the market – and the tax receipts that provides – and the market then has to be managed primarily for maximised profit. These interests are not wholly economic, however, but also encompass the social agenda of the state, and its maximal delivery. For big business is best able to absorb the cost of the bureaucratic burdens and social aspirations of the state – of health and safety regulation, of every complex tax returns, of holiday pay, of sickness pay, of pension contributions and of national insurance contributions. Big business is the friend of the state, because it both funds it and is capable of delivering its agenda."[131] The harsh effect of this nefarious collusion between the state and big business has been a dramatic decapitalization of those families and

---

128 Belloc, *The Servile State*, 3. Note that the market exists and thrives because of the state. See Restakis, *Humanizing the Economy*, 10, and Polanyi, *The Great Transformation*.

129 See Christopher Lasch's writing regarding a state-supported capitalism. Lasch, *The Culture of Narcissism*, 218.

130 As Hilaire Belloc made clear at the beginning of the twentieth century, insignificant amounts of capital simply bolsters a problematic capitalism. See Belloc, *The Servile State*, viii. Also see Blond, *Red Tory*, 205ff.

131 Ibid., 286.

communities that previously held small amounts of capital assets as well as a fostering of enslavement to wage labour. As Schumacher points out in *Small Is Beautiful*, it is essential that private property be an aid to creative, cooperative work rather than a substitution for it. And, in order for this to be the case, capital ownership must be widely distributed rather than centralized and monopolized. For as he writes, "in this matter of private ownership the question of scale is decisive. When we move from small-scale to medium scale, the connection between ownership and work already becomes attenuated; private enterprise tends to become impersonal."[132] When capital and labour become separated through scale and geography, the capacity for governance through norms is undermined. Indeed, the ability to work collectively in a way that reinforces mutualism and community – i.e. working with others in a localized way such that one is building upon capital assets owned by oneself and others – is central to remoralizing the market and creating widespread, distributive prosperity.

In addition to bringing together labour and capital, we need to relocalize the economy by bringing together production and consumption. This means bringing demand and supply closer together so that the non-market norms guiding these two elements might begin to reinforce each other and develop symbiotically. For example, if we are geographically and temporally removed from witnessing the negative effects associated with supplying products and services to meet our demands, we have little inspiration or context for adapting our demands based upon considerations other than the bare financial costs associated with satisfying them. In more practical governance terms, then, this localization of the economy means moving away from goods and services provided by professionals certified and guaranteed by the state. For example, to quote Blond again: "In a new model of public-sector delivery, services could be provided by social enterprises. These would be led by front-line workers, owned by them and the communities they serve. These new social businesses would exchange (often illusory) economies of scale for the real economies that derive from empowered workers and an engaged public."[133]

---

132 Schumacher, *Small Is Beautiful*, 223. The work not only becomes impersonal, but labour divorced from capital is no longer able to fulfill the three central purposes of labour as outlined by Schumacher in *Good Work*: (a) "to provide necessary and useful goods and services," (b) "to enable every one of us to use and thereby perfect our gifts like good stewards," and (c) "to do so in service to, and in cooperation with, others, so as to liberate ourselves from our inborn egocentricity." Schumacher, *Good Work*, 3–4. Also see Berdyaev, *The End of Our Time*, 94ff.

133 Blond, *Red Tory*, 241.

Finally, it should be clear now that it is somewhat misleading to say that the market itself is the problem or that economies are either embedded or dis-embedded. Rather, it is more accurate to say that the liberalism of the market or an excessive dis-embeddedness is the problem. So, as Blond astutely writes: "Through civil enterprises, a new type of market regulation becomes possible via shared ethos rather than state imposition. An ethical attitude towards salaries, prices and product quality is actually allied with sustaining market competition, whereas a total refusal of this logic tends to abolish the market in favour of oligarchic corporate control, which tends to become quickly allied to, or synonymous with, the bureaucratic operations of the state."[134] In short, a remoralized market will mean contracting understood as the building of a common horizon or a collective enterprise with substantive moral content rather than simply a functionalized technique for pursuing naked self-interest devoid of any common morality. This means, therefore, movement away from the idea that the market is simply a realm of activity for individual actors and recognizing the importance of cooperative trust within interdependent corporations and between businesses and their patrons.

CONCLUSION

We began chapter 1 by noting that something has gone very wrong with liberal capitalism and its modern market state. The collusion between the state and the market systems that seems so recalcitrant is increasingly illegitimate in the excessive violence of their destruction of civil society, localized economies, and the natural environment. The collusion is fuelling a destruction of the in-between worlds of mutual support between families and communities as well as distorting our interdependence with the natural world. We also noted that attempts to move outside the framework of the liberalism undergirding the destructive capacity of the state and the market are strikingly few. In the discussions of the chapters above, we have attempted to halt the replication of these modern systems in our theorizing regarding political normativity and propose a way of thinking about democracy that harkens back to premodern conceptions of moral judgment and the patternings upon which they depend.

In this chapter, I have suggested that the only way to effectively counter the normative eclipse within the dualistic logic of liberalism is to cultivate an ethic of mutual support and restraint that invests society with

134 Ibid., 190–1.

socio-economic stability and resilience. Further, I have argued that the only way to avoid undermining the stability and resilience of a healthy society and economy is to cultivate intermediate structures and civil enterprises that instil tradition and reciprocal responsibilities in social, political, and economic life. The integrity of ecological, social, and spiritual patternings in the world depends upon nothing less than a widespread struggle to avoid falling into the trap of a dualistic logic and to instead find places and times, increasingly, where these patternings might align ourselves to their structures and processes.

Conclusion

THERE IS INDEED A GROWING SENSE that something is very wrong with the collusion between the liberal state and market. This collusion is rapidly disintegrating civil society, decapitalizing the poor, and destroying ecosystems in a process of acceleration through standardization. The acceleration of modern industrial society is pushing forward and causing legal, economic, and political interactions to take place with ever-increasing rapidity. Everything in the world is speeding up. The flux of the network patternings of the world are speeding up and this acceleration, by threatening the stability and interdependencies of the networks, is changing the nature of these patternings. Most importantly, as a result of this acceleration, it is becoming increasingly impossible to legitimize the violence that is produced in and through the state-market collusion of liberalism. Liberalism is producing what I am calling a normative eclipse.

As we have discussed, the legitimization of violence requires resilient normative orderings that can withstand the disruptive force of violations to their patternings. However, the dualistic logic of liberalism undermines normative patternings by simultaneously individuating and totalizing. In order to understand the violation of patternings, I proposed that we need to re-imagine our political ontology in order to begin seeing how things (and ourselves) come to us from beyond ourselves. This approach brought us into a discussion of how we might best conceive of the nature of a thing and the nature of ourselves as res ecologia. The patternings of res ecologia are vulnerable to disruptions that distort their nature or their fundamental integrity. Rejecting a radical immanentism that decries all talk of structures or patternings that come from beyond ourselves, I encouraged us to become attentive to natural ordering processes in the world. Therefore, our politicization of things as well as our political identities are best conceived of as processes in which we participate rather than create. Importantly, normativity and the capacity to make normative judgments regarding disruptions to relations within and between things and ourselves comes from the integrity of these larger processes. Liberalism, insofar as it promulgates a dualistic logic, undermines these processes as well as our ability to recognize and legitimize violations of these processes because liberalism advances the standardizations that cause an acceleration that destroys society.

As should be clear by now, the goal in all of this is to uncover and make explicit the logic underlying and motivating liberalism so that we might begin developing a greater capacity for recognizing previously unseen violence at work in the modern world. This project involves a re-thinking of liberal normative ideals of freedom, equality, and rationality as well as a consideration of the standardizing nature of interaction idealized by liberal thinkers in their attempt to see some progress in reaching these ideals. We have, therefore, considered some of the dangers lurking within the idea that a certain kind of interaction will give us ever-increasing progress in society. We began groping toward a conception of rationality that will legitimize violence without advancing the protocolic domination manifest in and through dualistic logic.

Although much more work needs to be done, it is my hope that we are beginning to recognize that we need to rework our political ontology and begin seeking an understanding of transcendent authority if we are to develop a language of legal and political normativity that does not reproduce the violence at work within liberalism. Liberalism arose in response to the domineering totalizations of premodern authoritarian regimes and represents a truly innovative philosophical and political approach to understanding the nature of just relations between humans. However, the violence that is destroying the in-between worlds of mutual support between families and communities as well as distorting our interdependence with the natural world is fuelled by this same liberalism. And, proposed responses to contain and cope with the systemic violence of liberalism's market state are disturbingly few. Liberalism's economic, social, and political systems are most often reproduced in and through these seemingly critical responses. For, insofar as we remain committed to the underlying logic of our modern liberal institutions, we continue to reiterate and re-enforce the violence. Despite our best intentions to avoid or even undermine its causes, the violence will continue unabated unless we are able to counter the normative eclipse within the dualistic logic of liberalism by cultivating an ethic of restraint and mutual support that invests society with stability and resilience. A stable and resilient society requires intermediate structures and civil enterprises to instil tradition and reciprocal responsibilities in interdependent familial, socio-economic, and religious life.

Instead of perpetuating the long-standing debates between liberal constructionists and liberal positivists or between rationalists and agonists, I have suggested that we begin to rediscover and revive conservative legal and political theory. The first step in this process lies in a growing devotion to tradition and submission to its expression of transcendent authority. To the degree that we are successful in doing this, we will be successful in radically undermining the dominant liberal paradigm of modern thought. Insofar as we are able to begin living our lives according to traditions that pre-date liberalism, we will be able to begin avoiding the violence of standardization within the logic of liberalism. To do so is to become better aligned with the normative ordering of the world for submission to that which comes to us from beyond ourselves is to foster more democratic ways of life.

We began with a quote from Wittgenstein: "we have got on to slippery ice where there is no friction and so in a certain sense the conditions are ideal, but also, just because of that, we are unable to walk. We want to walk: so we need friction. Back to the rough ground!" For the sake of peace, order, and good government, let us return to the rough ground and learn to walk again.

Bibliography

Ackerman, Bruce. *Social Justice in the Liberal State*. New Haven: Yale University Press, 1980.

Arendt, Hannah. *The Human Condition*. Chicago: Chicago University Press, 1958.

– *On Revolution*. London: Penguin, 1965.

– *On Violence*. New York: Harcourt, 1970.

Aristotle. *The Metaphysics*. London: Penguin, 1998.

– *On the Heavens*. Translated by W.K.C. Guthrie. Cambridge: Harvard University Press, 1953.

– *Physics*. Translated by Philip Wicksteed and Francis Cornford. Cambridge: Harvard University Press, 1957.

Axelrod, Paul. *The Promise of Schooling: Education in Canada, 1800–1914*. Toronto: University of Toronto Press, 1997.

Bacon, Francis. *The Advancement of Learning*. Edited by William Wright. Oxford: Clarendon Press, 1885.

Baker, G. Blaine. "'So Elegant a Web': Providential Order and the Rule of Secular Law in Early Nineteenth-century Upper Canada." *University of Toronto Law Journal* 38 (1988).

Balkin, Jack. "Respect-Worthy: Frank Michelman and the Legitimate Constitution." *Tulsa Law Review* 39 (2004).

Barabási, Albert-László. *Linked: The New Science of Networks*. Cambridge: Perseus, 2002.

Barnard, Frederick. *Herder on Nationality, Humanity, and History*. Montreal: McGill-Queen's University Press, 2003.

Barry, Brian. *Justice as Impartiality*. Oxford: Clarendon Press, 1995.

– *Theories of Justice*. Los Angeles: University of California Press, 1989.

Baumeister, Andrea. *Liberalism and the "Politics of Difference."* Edinburgh: Edinburgh University Press, 2000.

Belloc, Hilaire. *The Servile State*. London: Constable and Co., 1927.

Berdyaev, Nicholas. *The End of Our Time.* Translated by Donald Attwater. London: Sheed & Ward, 1933.

Bernstein, Richard. *Beyond Objectivism and Relativism: Science, Hermeneutics, and Praxis.* Philadelphia: University of Pennsylvania Press, 1983.

– "Fred Dallmayr's Critique of Habermas." *Political Theory* 16 (1988).

Bertness, Mark, and Ragan Callaway. "Positive Interactions in Communities." *Trends in Ecology & Evolution* 9, no. 5 (1994).

Blankenburg, Erhard. "The Poverty of Evolutionism: A Critique of Teubner's Case for 'Reflexive Law.'" *Law & Society Review* 18 (1984).

Blond, Phillip. "Emmanuel Levinas: God and Phenomenology." In *Post-Secular Philosophy: Between Philosophy and Theology*, edited by Phillip Blond. London: Routledge, 1998.

– "Introduction: Theology Before Philosophy." In *Post-Secular Philosophy: Between Philosophy and Theology*, edited by Philip Blond. London: Routledge, 1998.

– *Red Tory: How the Left and Right Have Broken Britain and How We Can Fix It.* London: Faber & Faber, 2010.

– "Rise of the Red Tories." *Prospect.* 28 February, 2009. http://www.prospect-magazine.co.uk/2009/02/riseoftheredtories. Accessed 6 February 2016.

Bobbitt, Philip. *The Shield of Achilles: War, Peace, and the Course of History.* New York: Knopf, 2002.

Bourdieu, Pierre. *Outline of a Theory of Practice.* Translated by Richard Nice. Cambridge: Cambridge University Press, 1977.

Boyle, Robert. "New Experiments Physico-Mechanical, Touching the Spring of the Air." In *The Works*, edited by Thomas Birch. Vol. I. Hildesheim: Georg Olms Verlagsbuchhandlung, 1965.

Braithwaite, John. *Restorative Justice and Responsive Regulation.* Oxford: Oxford University Press, 2002.

Bruni, Luigino, and Stefano Zamagni. *Civil Economy: Efficiency, Equity, Public Happiness.* Berne: Peter Lang, 2007.

Burke, Edmund. *Reflections on the Revolution in France.* London: J.M. Dent & Sons, 1910.

Butler, Judith. *Gender Trouble: Feminism and the Subversion of Identity.* New York: Routledge, 1999.

Cardinal, Harold. *The Unjust Society: The Tragedy of Canada's Indians.* Edmonton: M.G. Hurtig, 1969.

Castells, Manuel. *The Power of Identity, Vol. II of The Information Age: Economy, Society and Culture.* Oxford: Blackwell, 1997.

– *The Rise of the Network Society, Vol. I of The Information Age: Economy, Society and Culture.* Oxford: Blackwell, 1996.

Cavanaugh, William. "Killing for the Telephone Company: Why the Nation-State Is Not the Keeper of the Common Good." *Modern Theology* 20, no. 2 (2004).

Chandler, Michael, and Christopher Lalonde, "Cultural Continuity as a Hedge against Suicide in Canada's First Nations." In *Healing Traditions: The Mental Health of Aboriginal Peoples in Canada*, edited by L. Kirmayer and G. Valaskakis. Vancouver: University of British Columbia Press, 2008.

Chateaubriand, François-René. *An Historical, Political, and Moral Essay on Revolutions, Ancient and Modern*. London: Cox & Baylis, 1815.

Couthard, Glen. "Subjects of Empire: Indigenous Peoples and the 'Politics of Recognition' in Canada." *Contemporary Political Theory* 6 (2007).

Crowder, George. "Chantal Mouffe's Agonistic Democracy." Paper presented to the Australasian Political Studies Association conference, University of Newcastle, 25–27 September 2006.

Deleuze, Gilles. *Foucault*. Translated by Seán Hand. London: Continuum, 1999.

– *Negotiations: 1972–1990*. Translated by Martin Joughin. New York: Columbia University Press, 1990.

– *Nietzsche and Philosophy*. Translated by Hugh Tomlinson. London: The Athlone Press, 1992.

– "Postscript on the Societies of Control." *October* 59 (Winter 1992).

Deleuze, Gilles, and Félix Guattari. *A Thousand Plateaus*. Translated by Brian Massumi. Minneapolis: University of Minnesota Press, 1987.

Delgamuukw v. British Columbia, [1997] 3 SCR 1010.

Descartes, René. *Principles of Philosophy*. Translated by Valentine Miller and Reese Miller Dordrecht: Kluwer, 1991.

Devigne, Robert. *Recasting Conservatism: Oakeshott, Strauss, and the Response to Postmodernism*. New Haven: Yale University Press, 1994.

Dorf, Michael. "Legal Indeterminacy and Institutional Design." *New York University Law Review* 78 (2003).

Dorf, Michael, and Charles Sabel. "A Constitution of Democratic Experimentalism." *Columbia Law Review* 98 (1998).

Dryzek, John. *Deliberative Democracy and Beyond: Liberals, Critics, Contestations*. Oxford: Oxford University Press, 2000.

Durham, Frank, and Robert Purrington. *Frame of the Universe: A History of Physical Cosmology*. New York: Columbia University Press, 1983.

Dworkin, Ronald. *Sovereign Virtue: The Theory and Practice of Equality*. Cambridge: Harvard University Press, 2000.

– *Taking Rights Seriously*. Cambridge: Harvard University Press, 1978.

Ehrlich, Eugen. *Fundamental Principles of the Sociology of Law*. Translated by Walter Moll. New York: Arno Press, 1975.

Ellul, Jacques. *The Technological Society*. Translated by John Wilkinson. New York: Vintage Books, 1964.

– *The Theological Foundation of Law*. Translated by Marguerite Wieser. New York: The Seabury Press, 1969.

Fanon, Frantz. *The Wretched of the Earth.* Translated by Constance Farrington. New York: Grove Press, 1963.

Feiling, Keith. *Toryism: A Political Dialogue.* London: G. Bell & Sons, 1913.

Ford, Cristie. "In Search of the Qualitative Clear Majority: Democratic Experimentalism and the Quebec Secession Reference." *Alberta Law Review* 39 (2001–02).

Foucault, Michel. "Afterword: The Subject and Power." In *Michel Foucault: Beyond Structuralism and Hermeneutics,* edited by H.L. Dreyfus. Chicago: University of Chicago Press, 1983.

– *Discipline and Punish: The Birth of the Prison.* Translated by Alan Sheridan. New York: Vintage Books, 1995.

– "The Subject and Power." *Critical Inquiry* 8 (Summer 1982).

Fraser, Nancy, and A. Honneth. *Redistribution or Recognition? A Political-Philosophical Exchange.* London: Verso, 2003.

Gadamer, Hans-Georg. "The Historicity of Understanding." In *The Hermeneutics Reader: Texts of the German Tradition from the Enlightenment to the Present,* edited by Kurt Mueller-Vollmer. Oxford: Basil Blackwell, 1986.

Galloway, Alexander. *Protocol: How Control Exists After Decentralization.* Cambridge: MIT Press, 2004.

Galloway, Alexander, and Eugene Thacker. *The Exploit: A Theory of Networks.* Minneapolis: University of Minnesota Press, 2007.

Gandhi, M.K. *Non-Violent Resistance.* New York: Schocken Books, 1961.

Gatto, John. *Dumbing Us Down: The Hidden Curriculum of Compulsory Schooling.* Gabriola Island: New Society Publishers, 2005.

Gellner, Ernest. *Nations and Nationalism.* Ithaca: Cornell University Press, 1983.

Gerstenberg, Oliver, and Charles Sabel. "Directly-Deliberative Polyarchy: An Institutional Ideal for Europe?" In *Good Governance in Europe's Integrated Market,* edited by Christian Joerges and Renaud Dehousse. Oxford: Oxford University Press, 2002.

Gibbard, Allan. "Constructing Justice." *Philosophy and Public Affairs* 20 (1991).

– *Wise Choices, Apt Feelings: A Theory of Normative Judgment.* Oxford: Oxford University Press, 1990.

Gibson-Graham, J.K. *A Postcapitalist Politics.* Minneapolis: University of Minnesota Press, 2006.

Giddens, Anthony. *The Nation-State and Violence.* Berkeley: University of California Press, 1987.

– "Reason without Revolution?" In *Habermas and Modernity,* edited by Richard Bernstein. Cambridge: Polity Press, 1985.

Grant, George. *English-Speaking Justice.* Toronto: Anansi Press, 1974.

– *Philosophy in the Mass Age.* Edited by William Christian. Toronto: University of Toronto, 1995.

– *Technology and Empire.* Concord: House of Anansi Press, 1969.

Gudeman, Stephen. *Economy's Tension: The Dialectics of Community and Market.* Oxford: Berghahn Books, 2008.

– "Necessity or Contingency: Mutuality and Market." In *Market and Society: The Great Transformation Today,* edited by Chris Hann and Keith Hart. Cambridge: Cambridge University Press, 2009.

Habermas, Jürgen. *Autonomy and Solidarity: Interviews,* edited by Peter Dews. London: Verso, 1986.

– *Between Facts and Norms: Contributions to a Discourse Theory of Law and Democracy.* Translated by William Rehg. Cambridge: MIT Press, 1996.

– *Knowledge and Human Interests.* Translated by Jeremy Shapiro. Boston: Beacon Press, 1971.

– *Postmetaphysical Thinking: Philosophical Essays.* Translated by William Hohengarten. Cambridge: MIT Press, 1992.

– "Questions and Counterquestions." In *Habermas and Modernity,* edited by Richard Bernstein. Cambridge: Polity Press, 1985.

– *The Theory of Communicative Action: Lifeworld and System.* Translated by Thomas McCarthy. Boston: Beacon Press, 1987.

– *The Theory of Communicative Action: Reason and the Rationalization of Society.* Translated by Thomas McCarthy. Boston: Beacon Press, 1981.

– "Wahrheitstheorien." In *Wirklichkeit und Reflexion: Festschrift fur Walter Schulz,* edited by Helmut Fahrenbach. Pfullingen: Neske, 1973.

– "What Is Universal Pragmatics?" In *On the Pragmatics of Communication,* edited by Maeve Cooke. Cambridge: MIT Press, 1998.

Hall, Eric. *Internet Core Protocol: The Definitive Guide.* Sebastopol: O'Reilly, 2000.

Hardt, Michael, and Antonio Negri. *Empire.* Cambridge: Harvard University Press, 2000.

Harman, Graham. "Heidegger on Objects and Things." In *Making Things Public: Atmospheres of Democracy,* edited by Bruno Latour and Peter Weibel. Cambridge: MIT Press, 2005.

– *Tool-Being: Heidegger and the Metaphysics of Objects.* Chicago: Open Court, 2002.

Hart, H.L.A. *The Concept of Law.* Oxford: Clarendon Press, 1961.

Hassan, Robert. *Empires of Speed: Time and the Acceleration of Politics and Society.* Leiden: Brill, 2009.

Hegel, Georg Wilhelm Friedrich. *The Phenomenology of Spirit.* Oxford: Oxford University Press, 1977.

– *Philosophy of Right.* Translated by S.W. Dyde. New York: Cosimo, 2008.

Heidegger, Martin. *Die Frage nach dem Ding.* Frankfurt: Vittorio Klostermann, 1984.

– "Phenomenology and Fundamental Ontology: The Disclosure of Meaning." In *The Hermeneutics Reader: Texts of the German Tradition from the Enlightenment to the Present,* edited by Kurt Mueller-Vollmer. Oxford: Basil Blackwell, 1986.

– "The Thing." In *Poetry, Language, Thought*, translated by Albert Hofstadter. New York: Harper Colophon, 1975.

Held, Virginia. *The Ethics of Care: Personal, Political, and Global.* Oxford: Oxford University Press, 2006.

Heyman, James, and Dan Ariely. "Effort for Payment." *Psychological Science* 15, no. 11 (2004).

Hirsch, Fred. *The Social Limits to Growth.* Cambridge: Harvard University Press, 1976.

Hobbes, Thomas. "De Corpore (Concerning Body)." In *The English Works*, Vol. I, translated by W. Molesworth. London: Scientia Aalen, 1839.

Hollis, Martin. *Trust within Reason.* Cambridge: Cambridge University Press, 1998.

How, Alan. *Critical Theory.* New York: Palgrave, 2003.

Hulswit, Menno. *From Cause to Causation: A Peircean Perspective.* Dordrecht: Kluwer, 2002.

Hume, David. *Enquiry Concerning Human Understanding.* Edited by Eric Steinberg. Indianapolis: Hackett, 1977.

Illich, Ivan. *Deschooling Society.* London: Marion Boyars, 1999.

Janik, Allan. "Wittgenstein's Critical Hermeneutics: From Physics to Aesthetics." In *The Legacy of Wittgenstein: Pragmatism or Deconstruction*, edited by Ludwig Nagl and Chantal Mouffe. Frankfurt: Peter Lang, 2001.

Kant, Immanuel. *Critique of Pure Reason.* Translated by J.M.D. Meiklejohn. London: Henry G. Bohn, 1855.

– *The Doctrine of Virtue.* Translated by M.J. Gregor. Philadelphia: University of Pennsylvania Press, 1971.

– *Foundations of the Metaphysic of Morals.* Translated by Lewis White Beck. New York: Macmillan, 1959.

– *To Perpetual Peace: A Philosophical Sketch.* Translated by Ted Humphrey. Indianapolis: Hackett, 2003.

Karkkainen, Bradley. "Collaborative Ecosystem Governance: Scale, Complexity, and Dynamism." *Virginia Environmental Law Journal* 21 (2002–03).

Kilbourn, William. *The Firebrand: William Lyon Mackenzie and the Rebellion in Upper Canada.* Toronto: Dundurn Press, 2008.

Kirk, Russell. *The Conservative Mind: From Burke to Eliot.* Chicago: Regnery Books, 1987.

Kymlicka, Will. "Liberalism and Communitarianism." *Canadian Journal of Philosophy* 18 (1988).

– "Liberalism and the Politicization of Ethnicity." *Canadian Journal of Law and Jurisprudence* 4 (1991).

Laden, Anthony. *Reasonably Radical: Deliberative Liberalism and the Politics of Identity.* Ithaca: Cornell University Press, 2001.

Lakatos, Imre. "Lakatos to Feyerabend." In *For and Against Method: Including Lakatos's Lectures on Scientific Method and the Lakatos-Feyerabend Correspondence*, edited by Matteo Motterlini. Chicago: University of Chicago Press, 1999.

Lasch, Christopher. *The Revolt of the Elites and the Betrayal of Democracy*. New York: W.W. Norton & Company, 1995.

– *The True and Only Heaven: Progress and Its Critics*. New York: Norton, 1991.

Latour, Bruno. "An Attempt at a Compositionist Manifesto." *New Literary History* 41 (2010).

– "From Realpolitik to Dingpolitik or How to Make Things Public." In *Making Things Public: Atmospheres of Democracy*, edited by Bruno Latour and Peter Weibel. Cambridge: MIT Press, 2005.

– "Networks, Societies, Spheres: Reflections of an Actor-Network Theorist." Keynote speech for the International Seminar on Network Theory: Network Multidimensionality in the Digital Age, Annenberg School for Communication and Journalism Los Angeles, 19 February 2010. http://www.bruno-latour.fr/sites/default/files/121-CASTELLS-GB.pdf. Accessed 6 February 2016.

– *Pandora's Hope: Essays on the Reality of Science Studies*. Cambridge: Harvard University Press, 1999.

– *Reassembling the Social: An Introduction to Actor-Network Theory*. Oxford: Oxford University Press, 2005.

Bruno Latour, Pablo Jensen, Tommaso Venturini, Sébastian Grauwin, and Dominique Boullier. "The Whole is Always Smaller Than Its Parts: A Digital Test of Gabriel Tarde's Monads." *The British Journal of Sociology* 63 (2012).

Levinas, Emmanuel. *Totality and Infinity: An Essay on Exteriority*. Translated by Alphonso Lingis. Pittsburgh: Duquesne University Press, 1969.

Liebman, James, and Charles Sabel. "A Public Laboratory Dewey Barely Imagined: The Emerging Model of School Governance and Legal Reform." *NYU Review of Law & Social Change* 28 (2003–04).

Lobel, Orly. "The Renew Deal: The Fall of Regulation and the Rise of Governance in Contemporary Legal Thought." *Minnesota Law Review* 89 (2004).

Locke, John. *Essay Concerning Human Understanding*. London: T. Tegg and Son, 1836.

Loughlin, Martin. *The Idea of Public Law*. Oxford: Oxford University Press, 2004.

Luhmann, Niklas. *Political Theory in the Welfare State*. Translated by John Bednarz, Jr. Berlin: Walter de Gruyter, 1981.

Lukes, Steven. *Power: A Radical View*. New York: Palgrave, 2005.

Lyotard, Jean-François. *The Postmodern Condition: A Report on Knowledge*. Translated by Geoff Bennington and Brian Massumi. Minneapolis: University of Minnesota Press, 1984.

MacIntyre, Alasdair. *After Virtue: A Study in Moral Theory*. London: Duckworth, 1981.

– *Dependent Rational Animals: Why Human Beings Need the Virtues.* Chicago: Open Court, 1999.

Mackenzie, William. *The History of the Destruction of the Colonial Advocate Press by Officers of the Provincial Government of Upper Canada and Law Students to the Attorney & Solicitor General.* York: Colonial Advocate, 1827. http://ia600707. us.archive.org/19/items/cihm_92892/cihm_92892.pdf. Accessed 8 February 2016.

Macpherson, C.B. *The Real World of Democracy.* Toronto: Canadian Broadcasting Corporation, 1965.

Mack, Johnny. "Hoquotist: Reorienting through Storied Practice." In *Storied Communities: Narratives of Contact and Arrival in Constituting Political Community,* edited by Hester Lessard, Rebecca Johnson, and Jeremy Webber. Vancouver: UBC Press, 2011.

Magnusson, Warren. *The Search for Political Space: Globalization, Social Movements, and the Urban Political Experience.* Toronto: University of Toronto Press, 1996.

Magnusson, Warren, and Rob Walker. "De-centring the State: Political Theory and Canadian Political Economy." *Studies in Political Economy* 26 (1988).

McCarthy, Thomas. *The Critical Theory of Jürgen Habermas.* Cambridge: MIT Press, 1978.

– "The Politics of the Ineffable: Derrida's Deconstruction." In *Hermeneutics and Critical Theory in Ethics and Politics,* edited by Michael Kelly. Cambridge: MIT Press, 1991.

– "Translator's Introduction." In *Communication and the Evolution of Society,* translated by Thomas McCarthy. Boston: Beacon Press, 1979.

McFarlane, Peter. *Brotherhood to Nationhood: George Manuel and the Making of the Modern Indian Movement.* Toronto: Between the Lines, 1993.

M'Gonigle, Michael. "Green Legal Theory: A New Approach to the Concept of Environmental Law." *Ökologisches Wirtschaften* 4, no. 34 (2008).

Misak, Cheryl. *Truth, Politics, Morality: Pragmatism and Deliberation.* London: Routledge, 2000.

Motterlini, Matteo. "Reconstructing Lakatos: A Reassessment of Lakatos' Epistemological Project in the Light of the Lakatos Archive." *Studies in History and Philosophy of Science* 33 (2002).

Mouffe, Chantal. *Deconstruction and Democracy.* London: Routledge, 1996.

– "Deconstruction, Pragmatism and the Politics of Democracy." In *Deconstruction and Pragmatism,* edited by Chantal Mouffe. London: Routledge, 1996.

– "Deliberative Democracy or Agonistic Pluralism." *Political Science Series* 72 (2000).

– *The Democratic Paradox.* London: Verso, 2000.

– *On the Political.* London: Routledge, 2005.

Newman, Saul. *Power and Politics in Poststructuralist Thought.* London: Routledge, 2005.

Newton, Isaac. *The Mathematical Principles of Natural Philosophy*. Translated by A. Motte London: Dawson, 1729.

Oakeshott, Michael. "On Being Conservative." *Rationalism in Politics and Other Essays* London: Methuen & Co., 1962.

Paley, William. *The Principles of Moral and Political Philosophy, Vol. IV of Collected Works.* London: C. and J. Rivington, 1825.

Peperzak, Adriaan. *To The Other: An Introduction to the Philosophy of Emmanuel Levinas.* West Lafayette: Purdue University Press, 1993.

Perelman, Michael. *The Invention of Capitalism: Classical Political Economy and the Secret History of Primitive Accumulation.* Durham: Duke University Press, 2000.

Pettit, Philip. "Keeping Republican Freedom Simple: On a Difference with Quentin Skinner." *Political Theory* 30, no. 3 (2002).

– *Republicanism: A Theory of Freedom and Government.* Oxford: Oxford University Press, 1997.

Philpott, Daniel. *Revolutions in Sovereignty.* Princeton: Princeton University Press, 2001.

Plumwood, Val. *Feminism and the Mastery of Nature.* London: Routledge, 1993.

Polanyi, Karl. *The Great Transformation.* Boston: Beacon Press, 1944.

Popper, Karl. *A World of Propensities.* Bristol: Thoemmes Antiquarian Books, 1990.

Putnam, Robert. *Bowling Alone: The Collapse and Revival of American Community.* New York: Simon & Schuster, 2000.

Quinton, Anthony. *The Politics of Imperfection: The Religious and Secular Traditions of Conservative Thought in England from Hooker to Oakeshott.* Boston: Faber & Faber, 1978.

Rancière, Jacques. *Disagreement: Politics and Philosophy.* Translated by Julie Rose. Minneapolis: University of Minnesota Press, 1999.

Rawls, John. *A Theory of Justice.* Cambridge: Belknap Press, 1971.

– *Political Liberalism.* New York: Columbia University Press, 1993.

Reference Re Secession of Quebec, [1998] 2 SCR 217.

Restakis, John. *Humanizing the Economy: Co-operatives in the Age of Capital.* Gabriola Island: New Society Publishers, 2010.

Rheinstein, Max. *Max Weber on Law in Economy and Society.* Cambridge: Harvard University Press, 1954.

Robbins, Lionel. *A History of Economic Thought: The LSE Lectures.* Edited by Steven Medema and Warren Samuels. Princeton: Princeton University Press, 1998.

Robin, Richard. *Annotated Catalogue of the Papers of Charles S. Peirce.* Amherst: University of Massachusetts Press, 1967.

Rosa, Hartmut. "Social Acceleration: Ethical and Political Consequences of a Desynchronized High-speed Society." In *High-Speed Society: Social Acceleration,*

Power, and Modernity, edited by Hartmut Rosa and William Scheuerman. University Park: Pennsylvania State University Press, 2009.

Rosen, Stanley. *Hermeneutics as Politics*. New York: Oxford University Press, 1987.

Rousseau, Jean-Jacques. *Discourse on Political Economy and The Social Contract*. Translated by Christopher Betts. Oxford: Oxford University Press, 1994.

Russell, Bertrand. "Introduction to Principia Mathematica." In *The Basic Writings of Bertrand Russell, 1903–1959*, edited by Robert Egner and Lester Denonn. London: Routledge, 1992.

– "Vagueness." *The Australasian Journal of Psychology and Philosophy* 1 (1923).

Sabel, Charles. "A Quiet Revolution of Democratic Governance: towards Democratic Experimentalism." In OECD Secretariat. "Governance in the Twenty-first Century." Paris: Organisation for Economic Co-operation and Development, 2001.

Sabel, Charles, and Jonathan Zeitlin. "Learning from Difference: The New Architecture of Experimentalist Governance in the EU." *European Law Journal* 14 (2008).

Sabel, Charles, and Michael Dorf. "Drug Treatment Courts and Emergent Experimentalist Government." *Vanderbilt Law Review* 53 (2000).

Sandel, Michael. *Liberalism and the Limits of Justice*. Cambridge: Cambridge University Press, 1982.

– *What Money Can't Buy: The Moral Limits of Markets*. New York: Farrar, Straus and Giroux, 2012.

Schacht, Richard. "Hegel on Freedom." In *Hegel: A Collection of Critical Essays*, edited by Alasdair MacIntyre. New York: Doubleday, 1972.

Scheuerman, William. "Between Radicalism and Resignation." In *Discourse and Democracy: Essays on Habermas's* Between Facts and Norms, edited by René von Schomberg and Kenneth Baynes. Albany: State University of New York Press, 2002.

– "Democratic Experimentalism or Capitalist Synchronization?: Critical Reflections on Directly-Deliberative Polyarchy." *Canadian Journal of Law & Jurisprudence* 17 (2004).

– *Liberal Democracy and the Social Acceleration of Time*. Baltimore: The Johns Hopkins University Press, 2004.

Schmitt, Carl. *The Concept of the Political*. Translated by George Schwab. Chicago: University of Chicago Press, 1996.

– *The Crisis of Parliamentary Democracy*. Translated by Ellen Kennedy. Cambridge: MIT Press, 1985.

– *Dictatorship*. Somerset: Wiley, 2013.

– *Political Theology: Four Chapters on the Concept of Sovereignty*. Chicago: University of Chicago Press, 2006.

Schneider, Eric, and Dorion Sagan. *Into the Cool: Energy Flow, Thermodynamics, and Life*. Chicago: University of Chicago Press, 2005.

Schumacher, E.F. *Good Work*. New York: Harper & Row, 1979.
– *Small Is Beautiful: A Study of Economics as if People Mattered*. London: Vintage Books, 2011.
Sen, Amartya. *Identity and Violence: The Illusion of Destiny*. London: Penguin, 2006.
– *Inequality Reexamined*. Cambridge: Harvard University Press, 1992.
Shapin, Steven, and Simon Schaffer. *Leviathan and the Air-Pump: Hobbes, Boyle, and the Experimental Life*. Princeton: Princeton University Press, 1985.
Sharp, Gene. *Waging Nonviolent Struggle: 20th Century Practice and 21st Century Potential*. Boston: Porter Sargent, 2005.
Shaw, Karena. *Indigeneity and Political Theory: Sovereignty and the Limits of the Political*. London: Routledge, 2008.
Shirky, Clay. *Here Comes Everybody: The Power of Organizing without Organizations*. New York: Penguin Books, 2008.
Shiva, Vandana. "Biodiversity, Biotechnology and Profits." In *Biodiversity: Social and Ecological Perspectives*, edited by Vandana Shiva. London: Zed Books, 1991.
– *Earth Democracy: Justice, Sustainability, and Peace*. Cambridge: South End Press, 2005.
Sidney, Algernon. *Discourses Concerning Government*. Vol. II. Edinburgh: G. Hamilton and J. Balfour, 1750.
Skinner, Quentin. *Liberty before Liberalism*. Cambridge: Cambridge University Press, 1997.
– "A Third Concept of Liberty." *Proceedings of the British Academy* 117 (2002).
Smith, Adam. *An Inquiry into the Nature and Causes of the Wealth of Nations*, Vol. I. Edinburgh: William Creech, 1806.
– *The Theory of Moral Sentiments*. London: A. Millar, 1761.
Spaeder, Joseph. "Co-management in a Landscape of Resistance: The Political Ecology of Wildlife Management in Western Alaska." *Anthropologica* 47, no. 2 (2005).
Spaeder, Joseph, and Harvey Feit. "Co-management and Indigenous Communities: Barriers and Bridges to Decentralized Resource Management: Introduction." *Anthropologica* 47, no. 2 (2005).
"Statement of the Government of Canada on Indian Policy, 1969." Indian and Northern Affairs Canada. http://www.aadnc-aandc.gc.ca/eng/1100100010189/1100100010191. Accessed 8 February 2016.
Stephens, Megan. "Lessons From the Front Lines in Canada's Restorative Justice Experiment: The Experience of Sentencing Judges." *Queen's Law Journal* 33 (2007).
Stirner, Max. *The Ego and Its Own*. Edited by David Leopold. Cambridge: Cambridge University Press, 1985.
Stout, Jeffrey. *Democracy and Tradition*. Princeton: Princeton University Press, 2004.

– *The Flight from Authority: Religion, Morality, and the Quest for Autonomy.* London: University of Notre Dame Press, 1981.

Taylor, Charles. *Hegel.* Cambridge: Cambridge University Press, 1975.

– *Hegel and Modern Society.* Cambridge: Cambridge University Press, 1979.

– *The Malaise of Modernity.* Toronto: House of Anansi Press, 1991.

– *Philosophical Arguments.* Cambridge: Harvard University Press, 1995.

– *Philosophy and the Human Sciences: Philosophical Papers.* Vol. 2. Cambridge: Cambridge University Press, 1985.

– *Radical Tories: The Conservative Tradition in Canada.* Toronto: House of Anansi Press, 1982.

– *A Secular Age.* Cambridge: Belknap Press, 2007.

– "Shared and Divergent Values." In *Options for a New Canada*, edited by Ronald Watts and D. Brown. Toronto: University of Toronto Press, 1991.

– *Sources of the Self: The Making of the Modern Identity.* Cambridge: Harvard University Press, 1989.

Teuber, Andreas. "Kant's Respect for Persons." *Political Theory* 11 (1983).

Teubner, Gunther. "Societal Constitutionalism: Alternatives to State-Centred Constitutional Theory." *Yale Law School* (2003–04). http://papers.ssrn.com/sol3/papers.cfm?abstract_id=876941#PaperDownload. Accessed 8 February 2016.

– "Substantive and Reflexive Elements in Modern Law." 17 *Law and Society Review* (1983).

Thomas, Craig. "Habitat Conservation Planning." In *Deepening Democracy: Institutional Innovations in Empowered Participatory Governance*, edited by Archon Fung and Erik Olin Wright. London: Verso, 2003.

Toffler, Alvin. *Future Shock.* New York: Bantam, 1970.

Tully, James. *Public Philosophy in a New Key: Democracy and Civic Freedom.* Vol. I. Cambridge: Cambridge University Press, 2008.

– *Public Philosophy in a New Key: Imperialism and Civic Freedom.* Vol. II. Cambridge: Cambridge University Press, 2008.

– *Strange Multiplicity: Constitutionalism in an Age of Diversity.* Cambridge: Cambridge University Press, 1995.

– "Wittgenstein and Political Philosophy: Understanding Practices of Critical Reflection." *Political Theory* 17 (1989).

Ulanowicz, Robert. *Ecology, the Ascendent Perspective.* New York: Columbia University Press, 1997.

– "Perspectives: Oecologia ex machina?" *Ecomod* 11, no. 2 (1993).

– "The Propensities of Evolving Systems." In *Evolution, Order and Complexity*, edited by Elias Khalil and Kenneth Boulding. London: Routledge, 1996.

Volf, Miroslav. *Exclusion and Embrace: A Theological Exploration of Identity, Otherness, and Reconciliation.* Nashville: Abingdon Press, 1996.

Warnke, Georgia. "Social Identity as Interpretation." In *Gadamer's Century: Essays in Honor of Hans-Georg Gadamer*, edited by Jeff Malpas, Ulrich Arnswald, and Jens Kertscher. Cambridge: MIT Press, 2002.

Webber, Jeremy. "The Hobbesian Premise." Draft Paper. 22 October, 2007.

– "A Nationalism that is Neither Chauvinistic nor Closed." Lecture delivered to the Trudeau Foundation in Quebec City, 24 March 2011.

– "Naturalism and Agency in the Living Law." In *Living Law: Reconsidering Eugen Ehrlich*, edited by Marc Hertogh. Oxford: Hart Publishing, 2009.

– *Reimaging Canada: Language, Culture, Community and the Canadian Constitution.* Montreal: McGill-Queen's University Press, 1993.

Weber, Max. *Economy and Society: An Outline of Interpretive Sociology*, edited by Guenther Roth and Claus Wittich. New York: Bedminster Press, 1968.

– *The Protestant Ethic and the Spirit of Capitalism*, translated by Talcott Parsons. New York: Charles Scribner's Sons, 1958.

Weil, Simone. *Formative Writings: 1929–1941*. Edited and translated by Dorothy McFarland and Wilhelmina van Ness. Amherst: University of Massachusetts Press, 1987.

Wittgenstein, Ludwig. *On Certainty*. Translated by Denis Paul and G.E.M. Anscombe. Edited by G.E.M. Anscombe and G.H. von Wright. Oxford: Blackwell, 1969.

– *Philosophical Investigations*. Translated by G.E.M. Anscombe. Oxford: Blackwell Publishing, 1953.

– *Tractatus Logico-Philosophicus*. Translated by David Pears and Brian McGuinness. London: Routledge, 1974.

Wolfram, Stephen. *A New Kind of Science*. Champaign: Wolfram Media, 2002.

Wolterstorff, Nicholas, and Robert Audi. *Religion in the Public Square: The Place of Religious Convictions in Political Debate*. London: Rowman & Littlefield, 1997.

Young, Iris Marion. *Justice and the Politics of Difference*. Princeton: Princeton University Press, 1990.

Žižek, Slavoj. "Holding the Place." In *Contingency, Hegemony, Universality: Contemporary Dialogues on the Left*, edited by Judith Butler, Ernesto Laclau, and Slavoj Žižek. London: Verso, 2000.

– *Violence: Six Sideways Reflections*. London: Profile Books, 2008.

Index